Evolution in Mind

HENRY PLOTKIN

Evolution in Mind

AN INTRODUCTION TO
EVOLUTIONARY PSYCHOLOGY

HARVARD UNIVERSITY PRESS
CAMBRIDGE, MASSACHUSETTS
1998

In memory of my brother, Ron, who introduced me to many things, including evolution

Library of Congress Catalog Number 97-074915

Contents

Preface   vii

1   Just What Kind of Science Is Psychology?   1

2   Plato's Question   36

3   The Revolution in Our Neighbour's House   73

4   The Structure of the Mind   121

5   Prediction and Mind-reading: The Evolution of Causal Understanding   177

6   Culture: One of the Last Great Frontiers of Science   222

7   Promises of a Marriage Made in Heaven?   261

Index   273

Preface

A science of mind is an extraordinary idea because the ability we have to do science is dependent upon the properties of our minds. This reflective quality is unique to psychology and the neurosciences. It is also the case that psychology is significant science because virtually every issue of public policy requires an understanding of human behaviour. From the problem of aggression, through how best to teach our children, and on to diet, food choice and drug use, to mention just a very few, all are issues in psychology. Recognition of the importance of psychology has been accompanied by its increasing popularity as an academic subject in many countries. The number of general introductory texts in the subject has increased accordingly, yet there is a particular kind of uniformity to these books. A little history tells a story and explains that uniformity.

Psychology's origins as a serious science, which is how the subject is taught in the great majority of universities, and increasingly at school level as well, is usually traced to the work of Helmholtz and Wundt amongst others, who were physiologists by training and practice, during the 1860s and 1870s in Germany. This coincides with the period immediately after the publication of Charles Darwin's *The Origin of Species* and all that then followed. Every scientist then as now knew about evolutionary theory, of course, and some psychologists took it very seriously. Yet evolutionary theory was never integrated into the science of psychology, which remains the case to this day. Psychology has always seen itself as the same kind of science as the physiology from whence it had come. The methodology and language of scientific psychology are dominated by controlled experimentation, and the explanatory framework emphasizes proximate (immediate) causes with a strong flavour of neuroscience reduction. These are the characteristics of physiology, and there is nothing wrong with any of it. But for introductory works, virtually every text that I have ever looked at lacks balance. Evolutionary biology and evolutionary theory are either paid lip-service with just a few pages out of many hundreds, or are dismissed with downright hostility, evolutionary explanations of psychological phenomena being rejected as 'pop' biology.

A few years ago, I surveyed *Psychological Review* and *Psychological Bulletin*, two of the most important review and theory journals of academic psychology. I was looking for evidence that the revolution in the study of animal behaviour which occurred over the period of 1964 to 1980, centring on Selfish Gene Theory, behavioural ecology and Game Theory, was influencing psychology. I could find none. Such theory has not penetrated through to the work of the makers of opinion in academic psychology; it is hardly surprising, then, that it has had so little impact on the writers of textbooks. Yet evolutionary theory is at the heart of modern biology, and this bias in the kind of science that psychology is has distorted the general understanding that students and public alike have of the subject. It deprives people of a feel for what should be a properly rounded understanding of the human mind, which is as much a product of evolution as are our hands or our eyes; and it denies easy access to a deeply interesting approach to human science.

This book is an attempt to remedy this situation in some small way. I have written it for undergraduate students in psychology, and also for the non-student public who like to keep themselves informed. I have tried to make it an easy-to-read book and so have avoided the academic style of citations. At the end of each chapter is a short list of suggested readings which can be followed up by those who find an issue especially interesting. I have also tried to be fair in attributing important work to individuals and can only hope that I will not offend scholars not mentioned. It seemed to me that attempting to be encyclopaedic in a book of this kind, and so trying to look at every aspect of psychology through evolutionary eyes, would be a mistake. Instead I have chosen to pick my way through a restricted number of topics. Others may have chosen different areas. None the less, all make the same point, which is that evolutionary theory has important and interesting things to say about matters of the mind.

Chapter 1 is concerned with the kind of science evolutionary biology is and how this may have affected its reception by psychologists. Chapter 2 gets to what I believe to be the nub of the matter of evolutionary theory's place in psychology. Chapter 3 deals with important additions to evolutionary thinking that occurred in the 1960s. Chapters 4 and 5 concern fundamental issues of the structure of the mind and causal understanding respectively. That most extraordinary of human attributes, culture, is considered in Chapter 6. And the final chapter points to some other psychological issues that also lend themselves to evolutionary thinking.

I thank Robert Bolick who put me in mind to write this book, and Ravindra Mirchandani, lately of Penguin UK, who encouraged me in the project. Stefan McGrath, also of Penguin UK, was especially helpful in completing the final stages of the work. I have been reading evolutionary psychology, evolutionary theory and related matters for several decades. I am grateful to all those biologists, psychologists and philosophers of science, only a few of whom are mentioned in the following pages, whose writings have taught me so much. I am specifically indebted to Robin Dunbar, Celia Heyes and Kevin Laland who read and commented on parts of the book. As always, though, none of the faults in the pages that follow can be attributed to them.

London
1997

I

Just What Kind of Science Is Psychology?

The theory of evolution is the central theorem of biology. It tells us about origins, and also something about why living things have the structures and functions that they have. One of the great evolutionists of this century, Theodosius Dobzhansky, once remarked that nothing in biology makes sense except in the light of evolution. This is a very strong claim, but is it so? In the first part of this chapter I want to examine Dobzhansky's assertion to see what truth there is in it. What we will find is that he would have been entirely correct if the dictum read, 'Nothing in biology makes *complete* sense except in the light of evolution.' Well, if the theory of evolution is indeed the central theorem of biology, just how central is it to psychology? And if it isn't, why isn't it? These questions will be answered in the second part of this chapter where we will consider whether the dictum, in its modified form, does apply to psychology. In so doing, we will form a view of the kind of science psychology was, the kind that it is now, and just how important evolutionary theory is, and should be, to psychology.

Some readers, however, will question whether we are going down the right road at all. 'Dobzhansky's assertion', they will argue, 'might or might not be relevant to genetics or anatomy, for instance. But psychology isn't biology, or at least not much of it, and certainly not the important bits. The rest, and much the greater part including those important bits, is a different kind of science. It's social science, or human science if you prefer.'

Well, social science some of psychology certainly is. But the proportion and the degree of importance that should be ascribed to it are irrelevant because the argument advanced here is that social science *is* a branch of biology, even if a special branch. Social science is not a conceptually separate exercise from other forms of science, nor is biology a single, monolithic subject. Biology is that cluster of the natural sciences that deals with life, and has many component parts or areas, one of which, the social sciences, is concerned with just those aspects of human psychology that make us unique and different from all other creatures. That, however, does not remove the social sciences from the realm of biology.

It is worth expanding the argument just a little, because this entire book stands or falls with it. Human beings are animals. Singular in certain respects we may be, but we are a part of the animal kingdom, and, like all other living creatures, we are one of the many end-products of 3,800 million years of life on Earth. We are members of just one of perhaps as many as ten million or more extant species. There is, of course, something unique to every species and *Homo sapiens* is no exception. However, what we have in common with other creatures is much greater than what makes us uniquely different. Like our closer animal relatives, when pricked we bleed; like many, many living things, we respire; and like all living things, we expire. This is the first and primary perspective that we must have on ourselves, and it is the perspective of biology. We are members of a small branch of the tiny order of primates, which in turn is part of a not very large mammalian class of vertebrates, which is, it is true, much the larger part of the phylum called the Chordata. But the chordates are just one of more than twenty-five phyla that make up the animal kingdom; and the inevitability of expiring is something we share with all other forms of life, which includes plants, fungi and single-celled life forms. We share our deepest characteristics with all of them, especially the animals. And we share almost all our characteristics with a small number of our closest animal relatives. We are different from chimpanzees in only 2 per cent of our genes. That 2 per cent, to be sure, is not trivial in its consequences. It is what makes us special and what makes us human. This is the second perspective, and the subject area of the social sciences. However, our uniqueness can only be understood, indeed can only be recognized, in the wider context of our biology.

How does this argument about the relationship between biology and the social sciences unfold when considered in the specific context of psychology itself? Psychology is a subject area of very wide scope, and is variously defined as the science of mind or, less diffusely, the science of mental processes and the way in which these processes drive our behaviour. Whether psychology is itself a unitary science goes back to its very beginnings as a science in the 1870s, and remains an arguable issue to this day. Certainly the breadth of psychology's subject matter is considerable. It ranges from sensory processing and perception, through motor control, learning memory and reasoning, signalling and language, and on to complex social interactions, emotions and attachments – and, of course, pathologies of all of these which may be as circumscribed as the inability to remember the names of fruits and vegetables (referred to technically as a category-specific anomic aphasia), or much more diffuse states of disorder such as schizophrenia, or the generalized memory loss that accompanies various forms of dementia.

Now, many of the phenomena that psychologists study are not identifiable as solely human attributes, hence cannot be defined as social science in any strict sense. The processes that control skilled movements, including the contribution of rapidly changing sensory input, are common to many species of animal. Less obvious examples are learning and memory, which are properties of many animals. Most other members of the phylum Chordata are able to learn and remember what they have learned in a manner not too dissimilar from humans, and animals such as some forms of insect that are only remotely related to ourselves also have these abilities. There is some evidence that even certain single-celled creatures have simple forms of learning.

Another example of shared psychological ability, and perhaps shared processes, is transitive inference whereby knowing that (a) is greater than (b) and that (b) is greater than (c) leads to the deduction that (a) is greater than (c). It has been demonstrated that monkeys, and even pigeons, are capable of such 'reasoning'.

Attachment is another instance of psychological processes which might be common to a number of species. John Bowlby, the English psychiatrist who fostered the notion of a biologically driven bond formed between human infants and their caretakers, which is a formative experience in the development of the normal ability to enter into close affectional relationships with others, was much stimulated in his thinking by the findings of ethologists, biologists who study the behaviour of animals under natural conditions. Ethologists had described bonding in a variety of mammals and birds; Bowlby considered such bonding to be an integral part of human emotional development.

In all these examples one must be cautious and not assume too easily that the psychological processes underlying seemingly similar if not identical behaviours are indeed identical. These are dangerous conceptual waters, but I have no doubt that in many of the cases where behaviour, and the circumstances that seem to be the sources of the behaviour, are the same across species, and the species are relatively closely related, there is also some commonality in the processes underlying those behaviours. If I am correct in this, then many areas of psychology study phenomena that are not uniquely human, hence could not be considered to be solely the province of the social sciences. Human affiliative behaviour may well be identical to that of other mammals. This should not, though, be taken to apply to all psychological processes or structures; it does not mean that, say, human memory is the same in all respects as marmoset memory or the memory of birds and bees. This is clearly not the case. My memory of my Aunt Sarah, that I can conjure up at will and extend and imaginatively transform in any number of ways, has no equivalent in other species of animal. But certain features of the processes that are responsible for my memory are undoubtedly similar, for instance, to those that lead marmosets to behave in a special manner towards animals with whom they have been reared.

Other psychological attributes of humans are, however, clearly unique to us. As I will argue in Chapter 4, there is no good evidence of language in any other animal. Culture, the subject of Chapter 6, is also the outcome of processes that only humans have. These are phenomena that are driven by psychological processes which fall squarely into the human or social sciences. Yet even these aspects of psychology can have revealing light shed upon them by considering them within a 'biological' perspective. Language in children is the outcome of a complex process of development, and development is a distinctive and important area of biological study. Language is dependent upon a sensitivity to temporal order, and this is not a feature peculiar only to language. And there is strong evidence to support the view that language is partly dependent upon innate structures in the brain. Thus even a psychological attribute as distinctively human as language needs to be understood within a wider biological perspective.

So, even within the specific confines of psychology, it can be seen that there is little, if anything, in psychology that can be fully understood as social science and social science alone. Psychology, and specifically human psychology, is no different in this most general sense, then, from any other form of science that takes in human beings. Having made the point that what goes for human anatomy or human genetics also goes for the psychology of humans, we can now look in a bit more detail at Dobzhansky's dictum, because if his claim is true for anatomy and genetics, why then it must also apply to psychology. We will do this in two stages. First, because the claim is about evolution, we will consider the nature of evolutionary theory and how it differs from most other sciences. Having nailed down that difference, we will then be in a position to examine just what 'the light of evolution' is, and whether the illumination it casts is indeed essential in biology.

The causal nature of evolutionary theory

Science aims to explain the world and the universe, including ourselves as a part of the world and the way in which it impinges upon our senses and becomes interpreted as the phenomena of human experience. However complex the interaction between 'what is out there' and our own processes of knowing, science assumes that there is indeed a world out there which can be at least partially known. The way science works is a two-stage process of flip-flopping between theory – a statement which says that the world is like this and that – and testing the theory by as accurate observation as possible – this is the empirical side of science. Of course, the theory can range from highly formalized and abstract notation to rather simple and ordinary linguistic accounts; and the observations may be merely descriptive, or closely measured exercises, or cleverly controlled experiments, or combinations of these. And the linkage between what is being explained, the nature of the explanation and how the explanation is tested, is often extraordinarily complex and indirect. One of the triumphs of modern science has been the increasing understanding that our explanations often hinge critically upon entities that we cannot directly detect or observe with our ordinary senses, even if the consequences of these entities are plainly experienced. No one has ever seen an atom unaided or touched a gene, yet no scientist now doubts the existence of either or questions their absolutely central role in the physical world and in the transmission of characters from parents to offspring. You don't get much more indirect than coming to understand, and being able to manipulate, parts of the world whose existence has absolutely no place in our daily lives.

But what does it really mean for scientists to say that something is understood? In essence, and conventionally, it means that they know what *causes* the phenomenon of interest, that is, what are the necessary generative conditions that give rise to the phenomenon; and it also means that those causes can be conceptually bound together in some integrated way to supply a causal explanation of the regularities of the world, these being the so-called general principles or general laws that science aims to list. Causal explanation cast in the framework of general laws allows prediction and, in some circumstances, control of the phenomenon. This trinity of causes–laws–prediction defines understanding for a scientist.

Now, until the theory of evolution established itself as a significant part of science in the nineteenth century, causes in scientific explanations were, and largely still are, held to be the causes of now-and-forever. The resurgence of science in post-Renaissance Europe was largely what we would now call physics and chemistry. Newton's conception of universal gravitation and his deduction 'that the forces which keep the planets in their orbs must be reciprocally as the squares of their distance from the centres about which they revolve' was meant to explain the structure of the solar system at any time, not just at the period in the seventeenth century when Newton enunciated his inverse square law of gravity. This meant that gravitational forces could be manipulated and experimented upon, and the outcomes predicted, because the inverse square law that Newton deduced on

Monday would still be operating in exactly the same way on Tuesday and Wednesday. Two centuries later, Mendeleev, building on Dalton's notion of atomic weight, ordered the elements into the Periodic Table. In so doing he correctly predicted the existence of additional elements, and even their properties, not then discovered. He was able to do this because he understood that atoms are not indivisible, but have an internal structural complexity which causes elements to have the properties upon which the Periodic Table was ordered, and in 1897 the first constituent part of atoms was discovered, thus confirming Mendeleev's insight. These astonishing intellectual feats were built upon the fact that the gold sought after by the alchemists of the Middle Ages had the same properties centuries later when chemists came to understand why pure metals like gold have the properties that were known for millennia. Causes–laws–predictions were thought of as explaining something *now* because the same causes operate at all times.

We now know from theoretical physics and cosmology that scientists like Newton and Mendeleev were only partially correct in their theories. The physics of Newton and the chemistry of Mendeleev did not provide universally true explanations. After the Big Bang, the cataclysmic event that marks the beginnings of the universe, the universe underwent massive change in a very short time. Newton's laws of physics and Mendeleev's Periodic Table would not have held then. Perhaps only the deep laws of quantum physics have ever been constant and unchanging, or at any rate constant and unchanging within a second, or at most tens of seconds, after the origins of the universe. Within one million years, and certainly by one billion years of the Big Bang (still just one-eighteenth or so of the history of the universe), the elements as we now know them had been formed. When the solar system came into existence the elements (hydrogen, potassium, sodium, etc.) were the same as they were when Mendeleev began his work four and a half billion years later. So, to indulge in a thought experiment, had Mendeleev been a working chemist at the time the Earth was formed, the constancy of physico-chemical cause was by then sufficient for him to have constructed the Periodic Table *then* just as he was able to do in the last century, in the *here and now*. It is only, however, through twentieth-century science that we have come to understand that Mendeleev's assumptions and inferences are not universally true. The universe, we now know, has a history in which truly universal, truly general, causal explanation requires that not only the laws of physics and chemistry but also historically antecedent events and conditions be taken into account. This applies especially to the early history of the universe when change was rapid and radical. But in principle, this two-part explanation of now-and-forever cause embodied in physico-chemical laws plus historical antecedence always applies. It so happens that the last quarter of the universe's history, which encompasses the origins of the solar system, has been marked by much slower change – so slow, that scientists mistook it for total constancy. They thought, and reasonably so for their time, that the causal explanations they gave did not have to have an historical component and would always be the same. That this is not universally true does not, of course, detract from Mendeleev's or Newton's genius. The assumption of constancy of cause in the science of the seventeenth, eighteenth and nineteenth centuries was good enough to generate remarkable scientific insights. And it was an assumption that came to lie at the heart of the thinking of all scientists.

Evolutionary theory, however, was different from post-Renaissance physics and chemistry, and this difference was so great that until quite recently, some scientists and philosophers of science seriously questioned the status of evolutionary biology. (I shall consider here, for obvious reasons, only the case of evolutionary biology, but evolutionary science is not the only science to depart from the accepted notion of science dealing just with now-and-forever causes. I have already mentioned cosmology, but that came later. It was no coincidence that evolutionists like Darwin and Huxley were so influenced by geologists because nineteenth-century geologists preceded the evolutionists in realizing that some phenomena cannot be wholly understood with now-and-forever causes. Parts of psychology similarly depart from chemistry and physics. As already mentioned, if contemporary attachment theory is correct, then the extent to which adults can enter into satisfying and close relations with others now, today, is caused, at least in part, by the relationship that they had as infants, yesteryear, with their primary care-givers. The departure from now-and-forever causation may not be as great in terms of time as that of geology or evolutionary biology, but the principle is exactly the same.) In order to understand this difference between conventional scientific explanation and evolutionary explanation, a very brief résumé of evolutionary theory must be given.

There are many excellent, quite widely available accounts of evolutionary theory. A brief guide to some of these is given at the end of this chapter. Readers unfamiliar with evolutionary theory, particularly students using this book as a supporting source to some more general introductory psychology text, are urged to acquaint themselves with evolutionary theory, for without doing so the value of this book to them will be much reduced. What follows in the next few paragraphs is only the barest outline and no substitute for reading a fuller account.

Evolutionary theory did not begin with Darwin, but contemporary evolutionary theory is derived from Darwin, and so that is where we will begin. Evolutionary theory considers that species are not fixed and immutable in form and number. The great majority of species that ever existed are now extinct. Species that became extinct in more recent times, comparatively speaking, are more similar in form to existing species than are species that became extinct in less recent times. That species become transformed in time, often over very, very long periods of time, was recognized by Darwin, and by others before him, and it was upon this understanding that Darwin built his central conception, which is that ultimately all living things are related because all of life is a single tree-like structure that is descended from a common origin.

A famous example of common descent is the finches of the Galapagos Islands, which were collected and studied by Darwin during the *Beagle* voyage. Scattered across this group of Pacific Ocean islands some hundreds of kilometres off the coast of northern South America are more than a dozen different species of finch. Darwin judged them to be closely related, which we now know through detailed chemical as well as other measures is correct, and he thought that they must have as their common ancestor a small group of South American mainland finches. Darwin's finches are just a very small branch, a twiglet really, of the giant tree of life.

Of course, an even more famous case of common ancestry is that shared by ourselves, *Homo sapiens*, with the other great apes. Humans, chimpanzees, gorillas and orang-utans share a common ancestral species from which we, modern humans and the human and human-like species leading to modern humans, finally diverged somewhere between five and seven million years ago. Depending upon which molecular measure is used, we are probably more closely related to chimps (the favourite at present as our closest living relative) and gorillas, and common ancestry with chimps is now put closer to five million years. It is generally thought that our ancestry with orangs is a little more distant.

Common ancestry, however, is not just for birds and apes. Common ancestry is a universal for all forms of life on Earth. We share a common ancestry with Darwin's finches, though you would have to go a long way back in time to find it. Modern birds evolved from a reptilian lineage called the diapsids whilst mammals originated from a separate reptilian lineage, the synapsids. These two lineages diverged from some common stem-reptile ancestry early in the evolution of reptiles, about 340 million years ago. Common ancestry of our phylum, the chordates, with other multicellular phyla such as molluscs (snails, for instance) or arthropods (an enormous group of animals which includes insects) goes back to around 550 million years ago. And so, in principle, all living things form a vast branching tree that reaches back through three and a half billion years.

Such vast sweeps of time and such seeming lack of commonality between, say, green algae and dolphins, troubles normal imagination. It is easier to think about, and to study, restricted groups of animals that arose more recently. So, consider again the Galapagos finches. They arose from one or two closely related mainland species of finch. Yet now they constitute at least thirteen different species, each slightly different from one another, notably with regard to the form of their beaks and feeding behaviour. Why is this? How did it occur? Darwin's great discovery, perhaps invention would be a better word, was the explanation for the evolution of thirteen species where before there had been only one or two. This explanation he called natural selection.

Natural selection is not some single and simple notion. It encompasses a group of processes embodied in a very complex set of mechanisms. In brief, it deals with how it is that creatures of every sort (though from here on I will only be talking about sexually reproducing animals like humans) do not all survive equally well and do not all produce equal numbers of offspring. In an important sense, natural selection is centred upon the differences between animals, upon variation and diversity of every kind. Except for identical twins, all sexually reproducing animals, including members of the same species, are different from one another in innumerable ways. Some die before reaching sexual maturity, and those that do reach the age of reproductive maturity will vary in the numbers of offspring that they have, and in the numbers of offspring that themselves survive and reproduce. Biologists refer to this as differences in fitness. Fitness is the result of the sum of features, which differ from one animal to another, that increase or decrease the likelihood of survival and reproduction. These features are known as adaptations. If these features, these adaptations, can be passed on to offspring, then those animals with relatively good suites of adaptations, who hence survive better than those animals of the same species who do not have such good adaptations, and who therefore go on to reproduce more successfully, will pass these adaptations on to their offspring. Adaptations, whilst they are features of animals, bear functional relationships to aspects of the environment of that animal. Thus the frequency and form of adaptations in a population will change in time because the world is changing all the time. Darwin argued that such small and gradual changes across time will accumulate and eventually so alter the structural and behavioural characteristics of the individuals making up that population that the result is the emergence of a different, a new, species.

Think again of the Galapagos finches. Because the Galapagos Islands contain few other species of non-marine birds, these finches were able to exploit niches that on the South American mainland are occupied by different species of land bird. They could do this because the range in variations of their bodily features included traits that allowed them to fit into these novel niches. The result was that in time different populations of finches, isolated from one another on different islands in the Galapagos group, adopted diets and associated feeding behaviours different from the ancestral mainland birds, and different from other finch populations on other islands. In time, as these differences accumulated, the birds confined to their own islands had diverged sufficiently from one another to become separate, though closely related, species.

This was Darwin's explanation. We now know that the selection of adaptive traits over time is not the only process that drives evolution. Speciation is a complex matter, often multiply caused, including factors such as mutation (the random alteration of traits), drift (change brought about by concerted chance events), the linkage between traits, and the degree of isolation of the breeding populations. We also now understand that all these events revolve around the system of inheritance (genetics) of individual animals and the populations to which they belong – the genes, and the ways in which they combine at conception and develop under different conditions to result in individuals, are the essential matrix upon which evolutionary events are played out. Darwin emphasized selection and adaptation. Very little was known about biological inheritance in the nineteenth century. The addition of these other factors to Darwin's theory of evolution based on selection is now often referred to as neo-Darwinism.

Despite the importance of genetics to contemporary evolutionary theory, the concepts of adaptation and fitness remain important to that theory, and are especially important to an examination of evolutionary theory when applied to psychology. For that reason they warrant a few additional words. Adaptations are found across the whole range of structural and behavioural characteristics of animals. For example, protective coloration in many species is an adaptation that enhances the chances of survival in a dangerous world. Another is the swiftness of predators like cheetahs, an adaptation for capturing prey in relatively open grassland. Flinching and ducking in humans are an adaptive response to something looming in the visual field. Thus adaptations are special and important features of animals, but a word of warning is in order. Not all features of animals are adaptations. There are a number of well-understood causes for the existence of some features, and these are causes not directly related to survival and reproduction. And even when, as in the case of coloration, one can be certain that what one is dealing with is an adaptive feature that contributes significantly to fitness, that does not mean that the adaptation is the perfect device for the function that it serves. Most adaptations, for a number of reasons, are not nearly perfect – indeed some are quite a long way from perfection, and a competent engineer would have designed something much more suitable. For this reason, many evolutionists think it reasonable to consider adaptations as rather muddled, 'make-do' traits that none the less do contribute to fitness – evolution, it is argued, is more correctly depicted as a tinkerer rather than a perfecter. It should also be remembered that adaptations are always the products of complicated sequences of development and often, in the case of behavioural adaptations, have to be learned. The caricature of behavioural adaptations as being innate, utterly fixed at birth instincts, is quite wrong.

Now, why does all this make evolution a different kind of science from, say, chemistry of the last century? Let us stick with Darwin's finches and compare the explanation for the shapes of the beaks of these birds with an explanation of a commonplace occurrence in chemistry. When the two elements sodium and chlorine are mixed together they form a compound, ordinary table salt, that has very different properties from those of its two constituent elements. Now, the causal explanation that a chemist gives for this is in terms of the internal structures of the atoms of sodium and chlorine. These structures, to all intents and purposes, are always the same in time and space. Mix sodium and chlorine together a million years ago or a million years hence, do it here on Earth or on a planet belonging to some distant galaxy, and the result, and the explanation of that result, is the same. Such now-and-forever causal explanation for the beaks of Darwin's finches is not, however, adequate. This is because living creatures may be altered by the forces of evolution at a sufficiently high rate that the required explanation varies with what is being explained. A background of causal constancy cannot always be assumed. In other words, now-and-forever causal explanations are not necessarily enough. Historical antecedence must become a part of the explanation in biology. The shape of the beaks of the finches that first colonized the Galapagos hundreds of thousands of years ago was different from the shapes of beaks described by Darwin. To be sure, part of the explanation, which concerns the *processes* by which evolution occurs (the presence of variation and the selective conservation of only some variants and their propagation via genetic transmission), would be the same whenever (and wherever) one is explaining a trait like beak shape. These are the now-and-forever causes of the process of evolution – why evolution of any kind ever occurs. But another part of the explanation of any specific feature or trait of any organism, historical antecedence, will always differ because what you are explaining now, a beak shape for instance, is the way it is because of selection forces, mutations, drift or whatever, acting sometime in the past on a beak of a different shape.

The logical positivists, a twentieth-century school of philosophy of science, believed, amongst other things, in the 'covering law' model of explanation. This is a deductive exercise or argument in which the event or entity being explained is subsumed under a universal law that serves as a premise in the explanation. Put simply, the covering law, which is assumed to be truly general, is applied to any specific instance in the sense of 'Let's see how the general law applies in this or that case.' For example, Newton's law of universal gravitation is the covering law, which is then used, in combination with the specific features of the coast of Brittany, to explain the very large tidal movements in the west of France. There are no 'laws of tidal movements in France' as such; the law is of universal gravitation which is then cashed out into specific explanations. Now, it might seem possible to identify the invariant processes of evolution, the now-and-forever causes, as the covering law, and the causes of antecedence with the specific cases to which the covering law should be applied. That, however, would be an error. Construing historical antecedence merely as a concatenation of events and entities in time is to miss the point that 'where one is coming from' is a *cause* (not an instance) of 'where you are now'. The covering-law model of explanation, which may work in physics or chemistry, just does not fit the case of explanations in evolutionary biology.

So, in the words of the American evolutionist S. J. Gould, Darwin taught us that history matters, and causal explanations depend not only on a complex and very dynamic set of causes that constitute selection acting now and forever, but also on the history of selection and other causal events that are stretched out over time and constitute a set of causes unique to any one of millions of species. Antecedence becomes cause.

In so far as historically antecedent causes are necessary for an explanation of some phenomena in biology, that kind of biology is seemingly different from chemistry or physics. It is only *seemingly* different because cosmology teaches us that the entire universe has a history of change, hence everything about us, including table salt, requires history for a total explanation. However, when the changes are either so slow, or so far in the past, it is reasonable to leave historical causation out of one's account of something. But the evolution of life on Earth has occurred on a very different time scale from the development of the universe. Evolutionary change is often – not always but often – something tucked away not too far in the past of many living creatures – or, indeed, is happening right now. In such cases, causes of historical antecedence may become a necessary, indeed a central, part of scientific explanation.

Dobzhansky's dictum revisited

The importance of historical antecedence to evolutionary explanations marks off evolutionary biology as different from other areas of biology, as well, of course, as different from sciences like chemistry. But it is worth repeating that the difference is really one of scale and of just how complete one wants one's explanation of anything to be. Classical chemistry assumes constancy, or near constancy, of cause over such long periods that the very early history of the universe can be ignored. But, of course, the gradual evolution of the elements could be woven into an explanation in chemistry if one wanted to be that detailed. For the most part, this is simply not necessary, however. And there are many areas of biology where history is not necessary either.

Consider the example of the remarkable abilities of birds of some species to cache food at sites widely scattered through their habitat. The birds are able to remember where they have cached the food, and also which stores they have visited and from which the food has been removed. The proximate, now-and-forever causal explanation of this ability is in terms of the operation of spatial memory and the anatomy and physiology of nerve nets in specific areas of the brains of individual birds. However, like humans, different birds of the same species do not all have an identical degree of excellence of memory. Variation, as in virtually every macromorphological and behavioural trait across every group of organisms, is the rule. Some birds cache food in more places, and can better remember the sites of storage and which have already been depleted of their caches, than can other birds of the same species. Thus they use less energy in recovering the food than do birds with slightly less good memory. And birds with better memory will have larger energy resources available to them in the winter months, hence will be better able to withstand the rigours of bad weather. Being in better shape, they may produce more viable offspring, perhaps by breeding earlier in the year or more often in a breeding season. They might also be somewhat better able to rear the chicks they have. Let us assume that spatial memory is heritable, that is, that the memory abilities of parents and offspring are correlated. This has not, to my knowledge, yet been demonstrated in food-hoarding bird species, but it is not a preposterous assumption because other forms of learning have been shown to be heritable in mammals. So, if spatial memory in these birds is indeed heritable, then the young of birds with good memory will, on average, have slightly better memory than the young of those with less good memory. Gradually the spatial learning ability of the bird populations will improve across generations.

What we see here, when fitness and selection are at work, is that the causal explanation of a trait like memory becomes much more complex. It is not just nerve nets and spatial memory that must be invoked to explain the abilities of these animals to find the food that they have stored, but a complex set of interactions occurring both inside each bird and between the birds and their environment whereby memory has fitness and reproductive consequences, and, provided that the trait is partly genetically caused (even if partly means only a very little, a part cause is a part cause), the causal interactions ripple outwards to take in lineages of parents and offspring. So, when natural selection enters into a causal explanation, that explanation is a great deal more complex than when it is not there because the proximate causes have not disappeared. Instead they have been supplemented by a large number of other causes that involve other organ systems and an extensive chain of animal–environment interactions over time.

It is not only a more extensive causal story that must be told. It is also more complete.

Now, this is not an artificial and self-serving argument. It is not being claimed that Mendeleev was justified in assuming constancy of physico-chemical cause but biologists never are. Biologists certainly may, and usually do, do just that. Spatial memory in birds, or humans, may quite legitimately be seen as a problem 'just' in memory and hippocampal function (the hippocampus is a part of the vertebrate forebrain that has been implicated in spatial learning). But it is possible to put an evolutionary spin on a trait like memory and the brain structures that support memory, and it is not outrageous to do so. Our species, *Homo sapiens*, especially in its most recent form, is no more than tens of thousands, perhaps a couple of hundred thousand years old at most. In geological time this is very little time at all. Furthermore, the evolution of our species, and especially the increase in brain size, which had to have had implications for human psychology, has been quite rapid. We are a recent product of vigorous evolutionary change, some of it, as we will see, leading to the appearance of a phenomenon, culture, whose biological significance rivals the evolution of sexual reproduction over 500 million years ago. So not only is it not outrageous to take an evolutionary view of ourselves, but it is important that we do so.

Furthermore, if one is dealing with a heritable trait which is present in a population with a high degree of variation and which is being strongly selected for, then an evolutionary explanation is no longer an optional extra but a necessity. Contrary to a widely held view that evolution is always a slow and gradual event, it can, in fact, lead to rapid change. Many instances are well documented including, interestingly enough, the finches of the Galapagos Islands. Darwin's finches have now been shown to undergo significant morphological change over just a few generations when conditions of extreme selection pressure, driven by major climate changes, occur. Calculations suggest that speciation may result in as little as hundreds of years under such conditions. In every case of such relatively rapid rates of change in some trait or group of traits because of strong selection, then the complexity of explanation of that trait becomes even greater because the selection events are now stretched over time. Evolution, according to the old slogan, is descent with modification. Descent refers to the transmission of the trait in question from parents to offspring and to the offspring of the offspring, and so on down the generations; and modification refers to the changes in that trait as it develops during the lifetimes of the individual animals. Furthermore, considered in this way, historical antecedents now enter into the causal explanation of a phenomenon in two ways, not just one.

Evolution, of course, is the first way in which changes in time intrude into biological explanation. The second way in which history demands to be taken into account, as already indicated, is through individual development, which also always imposes a burden of historical explanation. It is the same problem as evolutionary explanation but on a smaller and more rapidly changing scale. Both evolution and individual development, technically referred to as ontogeny, are concerned with transformations in time. If a human adult trait, for example our capacity for entering into emotional relationships with other people, is indeed crucially forged by events in infancy and early childhood, and if attachment in humans has evolved from similar bonding devices in ancestral primates, then the causal explanation of my or your ties of affection to others not only rests on now-and-forever proximate causes that are focused in our limbic systems (a part of the brain that is involved in emotional behaviour) *now*, but also on events smeared across time, both individual lifetime (the experiences you and I had as infants and children) and the time over which the trait has evolved in our ancestors (perhaps because affectional bonds are important in reproducing and rearing our offspring). This is complex causation writ large.

But to emphasize the point, let me repeat it. Selection and historical antecedence as causes will only *have* to be brought into account in biology under special circumstances – including, of course, the circumstance in which one deliberately chooses to do so. However, even when history need not be invoked, if the phenomenon one is studying has been directly, or even indirectly, affected by the processes of evolution, then a truly complete causal account would have to invoke both proximate causes as well as historical cause, be it individual or species history. It has been argued at times that history either is not science at all, or is poor science. This is surely nonsense. The universe has a history; so too does life on Earth; and so too do all individual organisms. It may be the case, and often is, that invoking historical antecedence as cause is difficult science, and that those, like chemists or physiologists, who do not have to take in the sweep of time with its changing conditions are fortunate indeed to have to deal only with relatively easily approached now-and-forever causes. And it is certainly the case that proximate causal explanations alone can do a good job in many circumstances. But adding a historical dimension can only add to the power of any explanation by making it more complete. So, you see, Dobzhansky was almost correct. He should have said that 'Nothing in biology makes *complete* sense except in the light of evolution.'

The kind of science psychology is

Until the centre of gravity of world science shifted to the United States during the first two or three decades of the twentieth century, post-Renaissance science had been largely a European matter, and increasingly a Northern European one. The possibility of a science of mind goes back at least to the eighteenth century and the work of the Scottish philosopher David Hume, and still earlier to the English philosopher John Locke. Both belonged to the philosophical school known as British Empiricism which was closely identified with the rise of modern science. What marked out the British Empiricists was their belief that innate knowledge does not exist, and that the mind can be partitioned into elementary units, perhaps feelings or thoughts or ideas, whose origins lie in sensations. These elements, it was supposed, become aggregated according to certain principles. Define the elements and study their form and function, measure them in some way, and, most importantly, understand how they aggregate or group to form higher-order mental states, and you have a science of mind. Hume in particular was influenced by Newtonian mechanics, and he advocated a kind of mental mechanics analogous to physical mechanics. The elements, and the principles by which they become organized into groups, were the forerunners of twentieth-century associationism. Hume was the first advocate of a scientific psychology, even if he did not practise as a scientist. To do that, one needs a methodology, some means of testing your ideas by experiments. Although there were a number of sources for such a methodology, two in particular were important.

The first concerned what came to be known as the personal equation, introduced thus to all psychology students by the great historian of experimental psychology, Edwin G. Boring: 'At Greenwich in 1796 Maskelyne, as every psychologist knows, dismissed Kinnebrook, his assistant, because Kinnebrook observed the times of stellar transits almost a second later than he did.' Maskelyne was then Astronomer Royal and he clearly considered Kinnebrook's 'error' to be serious for, in Boring's words, 'upon such observations depended the calibration of the clock, and upon the clock depended all other observations of place and time'. What Maskelyne and his assistant (and other astronomers) were doing was making a judgement from the ticking of a clock about how long it took for a star to cross a set distance in the field of a telescope. Rather than being a simple task which, it must have been judged before this incident, would take virtually no time at all and for that reason show no or negligible differences between individuals, it is, in fact, quite a complex judgement and there is something about the mental 'work' involved in making the judgement which takes time. Had anyone bothered to think upon the matter it might have been obvious that all mental work must take some finite period of time, but the Greenwich incident was the first recording of such mental work time in what seemed a simple task.

Over twenty years later Bessel, a German astronomer with a special interest in measurement and errors of measurement, came across a brief description of the events at Greenwich. It was Bessel who systematically investigated the magnitude of the individual differences that arise when judgements are being made, and who conceived of the notion of a personal equation which might be used to correct the time judgements of individuals making astronomical observations. Subsequently, the work on the personal equation was expanded both empirically and theoretically. It was realized that the time that it takes to make a judgement depends not only on the complexity of the required mental operations, but also upon the prior state of the person making the judgement, for example what they were paying attention to; and physiologists began to ponder what the time was being taken up with, especially as in the earlier part of the nineteenth century the nervous impulse was thought to be an event conducted from one part of the nervous system to another almost instantaneously. When the great physiologist Helmholtz was able to measure the rate of nerve conduction and show that it was really a rather slow phenomenon (in the order of tens of metres per second, at most around 120 metres per second), the time taken up by thought became more explicable.

The timing of thought became known as mental chronometry. It developed as an important part of the experimental and observational armoury of the first experimental psychology laboratory to be set up by Wundt. In this century, transmuted into the study of reaction time, it became so standard a psychological procedure as to be a regular part of undergraduate laboratory work. Eclipsed for a period by the behaviourist era in the twentieth century and the concentration on learning, especially animal learning, the timing of mental processes re-emerged in the 1950s and 1960s and became once again a powerful experimental tool for cognitive scientists. But the point had been made 130 years before by Bessel. The workings of the mind take finite, sometimes quite long, periods of time. Here was something that could be measured; and the metric, time, was something that made a science of mind not only a possibility, but a science in some way comparable with, and capable of being related to, other sciences.

The second line of experimental methodology that formed the basis for a science of psychology was begun by a German physicist and philosopher by the name of Fechner, and culminated in what we now know as psychophysics. This combination of physicist and philosopher was important. As the latter, Fechner was consumed with an interest in mental life. As the former, he understood that a science of mental life required methods of measurement. According to Boring, Fechner's great insight came to him whilst in bed of a morning in 1850: 'the relative increase of bodily energy' was to be related to 'the increase of the corresponding mental intensity'. Fechner knew of the prior work of another German physiologist, Weber, who had discovered that the smallest perceptible difference between two sensations was related to the ratio between the stimulus energies leading to the sensations. That is, if for a stimulus of magnitude 100 one has to have an increase of 1 per cent to 101 to notice the difference, for a stimulus of magnitude 300 a change will only be detected if it is increased to at least 303 magnitude. Fechner made many observations based upon his general insight that the only way to measure sensation is to compare it with other sensations. He generalized Weber's law, asserting that the just noticeable differences between any pairs of stimuli are perceptually equal, and expressed this in a mathematical form (which states that the perceived magnitude of a stimulus is proportional to the logarithm of its physical intensity). Fechner showed us not only how to measure sensations, but how to formulate the findings mathematically.

The lessons to be learned from the work both of Fechner and in the study of the personal equation were clear: there is a methodology that can be exploited by which the workings of the mind can be probed, and probed in such a way that quantifiable data can be obtained of a sufficient degree of orderliness and with sufficient consistency that general laws of mental function might be drawn. In short, a science of mind was, by the middle of the nineteenth century, becoming possible, and the man who realized this in actual laboratory, experimental practice was Wundt, who founded the first laboratory of experimental psychology in Leipzig in 1879. Wundt had originally studied for a degree in medicine, and then trained further for research in physiology, the life of a research physiologist being his goal. In doing so he came under the direct influence of Johannes Muller and von Helmholtz. Helmholtz was one of the great scientists of the nineteenth century, being at once a mathematician, a physicist and a physiologist. Muller was the doyen of German physiology. Wundt's own influence on the subsequent development of the science of psychology was enormous.

Across the Atlantic Ocean, in both the old and new universities of the United States, psychology was beginning to blossom, and at a rate that was soon to outstrip the developments in Europe. North American philosophers and physiologists were not far behind their European colleagues in seeing what an extraordinary and exciting science experimental psychology could be. When this burgeoning of a scientific psychology did occur in America, however, it was initially largely under the guidance of people who had been trained in varying degrees by Wundt and his disciples, or who had travelled in Europe and had had extensive contact with the European physiological psychologists.

This thumbnail sketch of the origins of scientific psychology makes a simple point. Psychology as science was, to borrow the style by which the parentage of a horse is described, out of philosophy sired by physiology. Physiology is one of the branches of biology that operates entirely on the basis of explanation by proximate, now-and-forever causes. It is one of the archetypal laboratory sciences carried out by people clad in white coats. Psychology, at least in its origins, was modelled upon physiology in terms of being a laboratory science that seeks explanations of a particular kind. The beginnings of psychology as science coincide with the years in which Darwin and his colleagues were developing the theory of evolution. The publication of *The Origin of Species* in 1859 preceded by just one year the appearance of Fechner's *Elemente der Psychophysik*. The buzz of excitement, scandal and debate surrounding Darwin's theory, and its explicit extension to humans in the 1871 book, *The Descent of Man*, coincided roughly in time with the publication in 1873 of Wundt's *Physiologische Psychologie*, described by Boring as 'the most important book in the history of modern psychology', and the period running up to the founding of that first experimental laboratory in Leipzig. Wundt and the other European physiologists of that time knew, of course, of Darwin's theory and referred to it in their writings. (Wundt eventually rejected evolutionary theory when the Lamarckian version that he favoured fell into disrepute.) But there was no synthesis, no meeting of minds, no essential conceptual interleaving between these two approaches to biology. So, while the beginning of those two new sciences coincided in time, as sciences they were very different in their conception. Psychology broke no new ground in terms of the adherence to the trinity of causes–laws–predictions and a commitment to explanation only in terms of now-and-forever causes, being modelled on existing science. Evolution, though, was indeed different because of its insistence on the importance of historical cause. It was this difference which was partly responsible for the mixed reception it received from established sciences like physiology; and it may well have been this difference that led the early science of psychology to have so little to do with evolutionary theory.

There is one exception to the story of the early years of psychological science and its response to the theory of evolution, and that is William James. James was an American scholar, widely travelled, extremely well informed and amazingly clever. At a time when a scientific knowledge was sufficiently limited that one mind could encompass large parts of all of biology, James had just such a mind. He seemed to know everything, and though he was never an experimental psychologist in spirit, his thinking was not far behind that of the physiologists in Europe; and had he been an experimenter, the centre of psychological science might have been established in the United States even earlier than was the case. What marked James out as different from all other psychologists of the nineteenth century, and perhaps as different from all others from any period of the subject including the present, was his extraordinary capacity to see each side of the psychological coin. He knew as much as anybody about the physiology of his day; he understood the philosophical issues better than most; he had a deep understanding of the fundamental issues of the new science of psychology, and as a result he made truly creative contributions to the subject; and he realized from the outset that evolutionary theory was important to the new science.

James's contributions to psychology are too great, and too interesting, for me to be able to do more than just mark him out for further attention by the reader. But I will indicate in the briefest manner possible why James's response to evolutionary theory was one of wholehearted welcome rather than of merely distant interest. James was initially an admirer of Herbert Spencer, the English philosopher who was also a convert to Lamarckian evolutionary theory years before the publication of Darwin's first book in 1859. Now, what marks out Lamarckian evolutionary theory as different from Darwinian theory is its sense of 'passivity' of the organism in the face of a 'dominating' environment whose effects instruct the organism to take this form or adopt that behaviour. The world, as it were, stamps its impressions upon a passively receiving organism. This is quite different from the Darwinian theory of selection where the organism is made up of traits, each one of which varies from similar traits in other organisms of the same species. Selection acts to preserve only some variants and the source of variation in traits *is independent of selection.* The decoupling of variation from selection is *the* central feature of Darwinian evolution, which is frequently, and rather misleadingly, referred to as rendering evolution 'blind' – an altogether meaningless and tendentious phrase. In any event, we do now know quite a lot about the origins of the variations in terms of genetics and the complex of interactions that constitutes development, but in the last century the sources of variation were unknown. They seemed to be 'spontaneous', to arise from within the organism (as indeed they do), and as such they gave a sense of power or control to the organism which is not to be understood as subservient to overwhelming and irresistible circumstances.

I phrase the differences between Lamarckian and Darwinian theory in this form because a historian of science, Robert Richards, makes a powerful and persuasive case that William James's conversion from Spencer's Lamarckianism to Darwinism was the result of deep-seated needs in the personality of the young James, who came close to, or actually descended into, madness. Appalled by the image of passivity and determinism that Spencer's psychology presented, James was emotionally and intellectually rescued by a theory that gave scope for indeterminacy and choice. James discovered, independently of T. H. Huxley who had played with similar ideas, that it was possible to apply Darwin's theory to the workings of the mind, or at least part of the mind. If the mind is shaped not by a passive reception of the impressions of the world, but by the spontaneous, autogenous generation of ideas (variation); and if the ideas that are retained and sharpened up are those that provide the best ways of dealing with the world (selection); if that is how one thinks the mind works, which is what James offered, then you have a theory of psychology that saves one from the passivity and determination of Spencer's psychology and history. It certainly saved William James, according to Richards.

Well, whatever the reasons, James embraced Darwinism in a way that no other of the new experimental or scientific psychologists did. (There were, of course, many naturalists, whose preferred form of observation concerned how animals behave, who were strong proponents of Darwin's theory. I am thinking here of the likes of George Romanes and Conwy Lloyd Morgan. I will take up this point in Chapter 3, and simply assert here that naturalistic studies of animal behaviour have never been a part of scientific psychology.) It was not only James's evolutionary epistemology (which is how the notion that evolution is something that happens inside of the mind as well as in the 'outside' world is referred to), but also his belief in the importance of using the concept of adaptation in explaining the existence of certain features of mind, like consciousness, that led him to embrace evolutionary theory in his voluminous writings on psychology. James simply could not accept that so pervasive a property of mind as consciousness did not have adaptive function, and it was this kind of thinking, more than his evolutionary epistemology, that was his legacy to twentieth-century psychology. It was what historians of psychology like Thomas Leahey and Edwin Boring refer to as functionalism, or the functionalist school of thought in psychology.

Functionalism started off by asking what something – attention, consciousness or whatever – is for, and for a time came to stand in direct opposition to the school of thought often referred to as structuralism (not to be confused with the more recent structuralism of anthropologists and literary criticism), which in the psychology of Wundt and his followers, notably the American Titchner, meant seeking to know what the contents of mind are. Of course, structuralist and functionalist approaches are not antithetical enterprises at all. Being complementary to one another, not only could they co-exist, but functionalism was a natural and necessary form of enquiry to follow from structuralism, as Titchner eventually and famously came to admit. Functionalism quickly came to dominate American psychological science, and by then (and indeed for all time since then), it is the United States that becomes the dominating centre of this science. However, and this is an important however, functionalism as a school of thought in psychology soon lost the strong evolutionary connections that had been forged by William James.

We are now, in our all too brief history, at the turn of the century, and one reason why evolutionary theory may have begun to lose its hold on psychology was that by then Darwinism had become a much reduced force among biologists at large. After Darwin's death in 1882, evolutionary theory seemed to run into the sands. Scepticism about the strength of natural selection abounded, and the application to humans, who so pride themselves on their rational capacities, of a theory in which chance events play such a central role, was always going to run into strong opposition. The rise of another new science, genetics, in the early part of this century dealt a further serious blow to Darwinian ideas. Leading geneticists like William Bateson and de Vries were open opponents of the notion that natural selection was a causal force in the evolution of species. They proposed that macro-mutations, sudden large-scale changes in genetic constitution, were the major force in the transformation of species in time, with natural selection having no place in their thinking. It was only in the period from 1918 to 1932 that the Darwinian notion of natural selection was conceptually married to genetics, especially population genetics, and the modern theory of neo-Darwinism was born. But that was a long way in the future. At the turn of the century and into its first decade, Darwinism seemed to be dying, psychology was changing fast, and part of that change was a turning away from the few evolutionary ideas it had ever had.

Functionalism soon became transmuted from a search for what something is for, what its purpose is, which makes easy connections with the evolutionary concept of adaptation, to how that something works. (These alternative interpretations of meaning for the words function and functionalism continue to confuse discussion in psychology to this day.) It was just at this time that physiologists were making great advances in describing and understanding the reflex arc, that most basic of functional (see how easy it is to use that word in connection with how something works?) units of the nervous system. Under the strong influence of the philosopher John Dewey, the attention of scientific psychology began to focus upon the minimalist reflex arc and the simple behaviours that are generated by it. Reflex action is behaviour with minimal conscious content. Indeed, it is but a small step from there to the sidelining of mind as the principal phenomenon to be explained by psychology, and it was not long before psychology duly took that route. The birth of behaviourism, the school of thought that placed the prediction and control of observable behaviour, with 'explanation in physico-chemical terms' (now-and-forever causes in the terminology of this book) as the central aim of scientific psychology, is usually put at 1913 with the publication of John Watson's 'Psychology as the behaviorist views it' in the journal *Psychological*

Review, then and now the most influential journal devoted to psychological theory. The rise of behaviourism destroyed the place of evolutionary thinking in psychology for almost half a century.

Before expanding a little on behaviourism, two other streams in the history of psychology must be mentioned. The first concerns thinking about instincts as a part of human psychology. I will have much more to say about this in a number of places in later chapters. For now it should simply be noted that Darwin's theory gave scientific legitimacy to the idea that human behaviour is to some extent determined by inbuilt or innate instincts. Indeed Francis Galton, Darwin's cousin, vigorously pursued the idea that intelligence should be similarly understood as a trait that is inherited and present at birth in a relatively fixed form and quantity. Galton was at the centre of the rise of the eugenics movement, which was devoted to the study of ways of improving the human species, especially by means of selective breeding. Eugenics was highly controversial. As the twentieth century advanced it also became ideologically as loaded an issue as any in all of science. And, as genetic understanding grew, it became clear that the goals of the eugenics movement simply could not be achieved by selective breeding, however odious or desirable the overall objectives of the movement were considered to be. Thus, though eugenics did have a significant following for a time (and some surprising adherents to the cause), it was eventually thoroughly discredited, both scientifically and politically (see Chapter 2 for more on eugenics).

Eugenics' 'sister' enterprise, instinct theory, did no better. It had long been believed that behaviour of animals was entirely, or almost entirely, governed by inborn instincts (see Chapter 2 again). Darwin's theory, however, told of continuity between species. Humans, in this respect, are no different from other animals. So, it was concluded, some of our behaviours must be driven by instincts. The hunt for human instincts around the turn of the century and during its first and second decades marks a low point in the human sciences. Without empirical or theoretical justification of any kind, thousands of human instincts were invented, many of them extraordinarily trivial and silly. Worse still, some writers attributed putative characteristics of whole nations to instincts. Again, ideology and, in this case chauvinism, intruded into the application of a concept derived from evolutionary theory to human psychology. This early phase of ascribing human action to instincts cannot be called either science or psychology of any description. Although William James himself had come, after a time and with some qualms, to champion the idea of the existence of at least some human instincts, even his great reputation could not save so weak a conceptual edifice. The net effect of the work of the eugenicists and instinct theorists during this sorry episode in the human sciences was not only to discredit the idea of instincts, but by association, seriously to weaken the influence of evolutionary ideas within psychology.

Behaviourism was not a direct reaction to instinct theory. Watson had been brought up as an 'animal' psychologist and so was entirely familiar with the notion of instincts. His eventual rejection of instincts as having a place in psychological explanation was based upon a wider rejection of any explanation of behaviour rooted in unobservable causes. Instincts took their place alongside mental states such as consciousness as unobservable causes, and cast into the darkness of unscientific explanation. After all, historical causes are, at least at first glance, unobservable causes. Psychology was defined as 'the science of behaviour', and explanation was to be confined to 'stimulus and response ... habit formation ... habit integration'. The latter are especially important pointers to the behaviourist enterprise. Central to behaviourism was the study of learning. This was based on the experiments of the Russian physiologist I. P. Pavlov on conditioning in dogs, and that of the American experimentalist E. L. Thorndike, a student of James, on trial-and-error learning in cats. Pavlov and Thorndike laid the foundations for one of the most fruitful areas of psychological study. The understanding of animal learning is one of psychology's success stories, running as a consistent threat of progressive understanding from associative learning in a wide range of animals, including many forms of invertebrates, to quite complex cognitive abilities in non-human primates. In recent times the study of animal learning has somewhat fallen out of favour. However, during a long period extending from the 1920s for over thirty years, animal learning was the *sanctum sanctorum* of academic psychology; it stood as psychology's main claim to being an empirical science. What is important to this brief history is the extent to which much of this work was embedded in a commitment to understanding animal learning in terms of now-and-forever causes. Pavlov himself viewed his work on conditioning as an extension to the understanding of cerebral physiology. Thorndike was passionate in his pursuit of psychological science by means of the understanding of proximate causes teased apart by rigorous experimental procedure. Later generations of learning theorists like C. L. Hull and even B. F. Skinner (who would have objected to the label of theorist, at least for a part of his long life in psychology) would make occasional reference to evolution, but pursued their work entirely within the framework of now-and-forever causation.

Watson fused the study of animal and human psychology with the tools of Pavlov and Thorndike. It was a powerful combination which swept aside the fragile and seemingly insubstantial notion of instinct. Whilst behaviourism preceded the rise of cultural determinism in anthropology by a decade or so, it was eventually substantially reinforced intellectually by a rampant cultural anthropology. The overall effect was to purge psychology, and indeed all human science, of evolutionary thinking.

Psychology, as we have seen, began as science in the form of physiological psychology. Like animal learning, physiological psychology also runs as a steady and successful stream through the history of psychology. Indeed, much of physiological psychology was pursued in tight methodological and theoretical alliance with learning theory because the subjects of the physiological psychologists, non-human animals, were best understood psychologically by way of that aspect of their psychology which was best understood, namely their learning. Twentieth-century physiological psychologists, like their nineteenth-century forebears, were in all important respects physiologists. As one of the mainstays of psychology's development as a science, the influence of their thinking and their methodology on the rest of the subject should not be underestimated.

The message of this rapid survey should by now be quite clear. Evolutionary ideas, apart from exceptions of the like of William James, had little impact on the emerging science of psychology and by around 1920 had virtually no presence in it. This remained the case until the 1960s. Then things began to change, if only a little.

There were two main reasons, one general and one specific. The former was the widespread rise in interest in matters evolutionary. The centennial year of the publication of *The Origin of Species*, 1959, was marked by various conferences, and subsequently the publications of their proceedings, devoted to neo-Darwinism. Then, in the 1960s several popular and widely read accounts of humans as products of evolution appeared. *The Naked Ape* by Desmond Morris is notable in this story because Morris was an ethologist and he gave his work a behavioural and psychological significance that were generally lacking in previous popular works on human evolution. Another ethologist, Konrad Lorenz, also published an accessible book, *On Aggression*, that had a considerable impact within psychology itself (see Chapter 3). Indeed, the rise to prominence of ethology under the stewardship of Lorenz and Nico Tinbergen had had quite significant effects within psychology. Ethology aggressively propounded the importance of understanding the behaviour of all animals, including humans, from an evolutionary perspective. Relationships with psychologists were abrasive, which in itself attracted attention. Then in 1973, Lorenz, Tinbergen and von Frisch, the latter being the discoverer of how honey bees signal where a food source is to other bees, were awarded a Nobel Prize, the first time that one had been awarded to scientists for their studies of behaviour and behaviour's causes. That it was ethologists rather than psychologists who received it was widely discussed. It further raised the profile of evolutionary theory, which was the central and essential conception behind ethology; this contrasted starkly with psychology where the proximate causation of physiology was the central conception. There was also the zeitgeist of the 1960s. Green issues of every kind were becoming important, and ecology and evolution marked out areas of increasing public and political interest. The rise of sociobiology in the 1970s had an even greater effect than ethology. In Chapters 2 and 3 the ideas behind ethology and sociobiology will be considered in some detail. For this chapter's purpose the point is that while they certainly did not convert psychologists into evolutionists, these movements did make psychologists think seriously about evolution in a way that had not happened this century.

The specific reason for the return of some small amount of evolutionary thinking in psychology was a deep shift, a systemic change, in psychology that surfaced in the 1950s and then blossomed in the 1960s. This was the rise of cognitivism. Cognitivism is less easily defined than behaviourism. It is a broad school which aims to understand those processes and structures of mind by which humans come to know, understand and adjust to their world. Cognitivism itself can be divided into sub-schools, and there are clear elements of both functionalism and structuralism in contemporary cognitive psychology. Cognitivism has roots in previous eras of psychology, notably the Gestalt psychologists and other Europeans such as Jean Piaget, who had never accepted that behaviourism was the way to pursue a scientific programme in psychology. Indeed, nascent signs of cognitive thinking appear in the writings of learning theorists in the 1940s who simply did not accept the absurd strictures of behaviourism. So while it is the case that cognitivism did not spring fully formed into the world following upon a few seminal publications by G. Miller (in 1956) and D. Broadbent (in 1957) on information processing, memory and attention, by Newell, Shaw and Simon (published in 1958) who viewed human problem-solving from the point of view of a general-purpose computational device, or by Noam Chomsky's (1959) devastating criticism of Skinner's behaviourist account of language (see Chapter 4), their close grouping in time does mark them out as seminal events with collective seismic consequences. By the mid-1960s cognitivism had become the major approach of scientific psychology and behaviourism was dead. Now, thirty years on, cognitivism remains the dominating force in the subject.

What is important in cognitivism, and what marks it off so clearly from behaviourism, is the acceptance that there are hidden causes of behaviour. For example, Chomsky argued (see Chapter 4) that the rapidity and uniformity of language learning by children acquiring any language in a linguistically degraded environment can only be accounted for by the existence of mental and neurological structures that are the source of the rule-governed behaviour of language use. Miller, similarly, argued that certain features of human memory can only be explained by the presence of a limited form of information-processing device which is present in all human beings. In both cases, whether it be a language acquisition device that imposes certain rules on language or a short-term memory store of limited capacity, these are structures of the mind that in non-trivial ways cause our behaviour to be what it is.

Now, as mentioned earlier in this chapter, one of the remarkable features of most, or perhaps all, sciences is that they rely heavily upon causal explanations that invoke causal elements that are not a part of normal life and everyday experience. Not only is there no scientist who denies the existence of atoms, but we now invoke the constituent structures of atoms to give us causal explanations for why sodium and chlorine combine in the way that they do to yield ordinary table salt. What behaviourism did was forbid causal explanations if they did not lie within the limits of ordinary everyday experience. Scientifically this was an extraordinarily bankrupting stance. Cognitivism rescued psychology from this cripplingly narrow vision. It liberated psychologists conceptually and allowed causal powers to be relocated in the mind and brain, only a very small part of whose workings are visible. No one had ever seen or touched a language acquisition device. But being allowed to contemplate the existence of such things enabled psychology to mature into a science that is in important ways now comparable with physics or genetics.

Well, the thesis expounded here is that cognitivism did a little bit more than that, even if unintentionally. If short-term memory store could be invoked as a cause even if nobody has ever been able to see or touch the human short-term store, then other kinds of hidden events or entities could also be invoked as having causal powers. Provided that there was enough empirical and analytical force behind the claim, it then became possible to invoke historical cause too, another class of not-directly observable causes, as an explanation in psychology. For example, in the 1960s, and increasingly in the 1970s and 1980s, evidence began to appear from studies of animal learning that in many species the consequences of learning, and in some cases perhaps the very processes as well, were different from one another in different species. These differences tied in well with larger life-history patterns, and it became possible, and indeed imperative, to explain these effects in terms of evolutionary theory. That this should have happened in the study of animal learning, the former heartland of behaviourism, was extraordinary. The application of evolutionary theory to human psychology was not far behind.

This is not to say that evolutionary explanation has now become commonplace in psychology. Quite the opposite. It remains a comparative rarity (see Chapters 2 and 3), though there is now a small but quite vigorous movement called evolutionary psychology, of which this book is one expression and that of Steven Pinker of the MIT, listed at the end of this chapter, is another. But what has appeared in recent years is an increasing tolerance of evolutionary ideas in psychology, a willingness to listen, even if not yet open acceptance.

What, then, can be said about the nature of 'the light of evolution', and just what kind of illumination does it cast over psychology? The long answer is to be found in the following chapters. The short answer is that we are looking at antecedence as cause which gives rise to constraint on processes and structures operating in the ecological theatre of today. There is also the light of disciplined comparison with other species in the place of the *laissez-aller* of comparative psychology – evolutionary theory certainly has cast a particularly strong critical light, that comes from an established body of theory, on the rather lax kinds of comparison that psychologists are wont to make. Finally, evolutionary theory has spawned mini-theories and more restricted laws and rules, and some of these (for example, Hamilton's Rule, which is discussed in Chapter 3) may have some kind of application to understanding human action.

Perhaps this is pitching the language too high. The fact is that we modern humans are a relatively recently evolved sub-species within a genus and family that has shown vigorous evolutionary change in the last two to three million years. Much of this change, especially since the appearance of *Homo sapiens*, has been centred upon our brains and our behaviour. Evolutionary thinking cannot help but be interesting to many students of human science. An exercise that seeks to look at psychology from an evolutionary perspective may not change the minds of many scientists working in psychology now. But it might be of more than passing interest to the students of today's scientists, and it is they who will determine the future of the subject in the next century.

Just how should one proceed in a book like this? There are two possibilities, and I am going to avail myself of both. The one is a 'bits-and-pieces' approach that looks at how evolutionary theory might help in explaining isolated, discrete phenomena like learning, language, or even rather global functions such as consciousness. The second is to use evolutionary theory as an instrument of synthesis by which genetics, development, culture and psychology are bound together in a single explanatory framework. We will begin in the next chapter with the latter and consider a problem that has plagued thinking about human behaviour and human science for millennia.

Suggested Readings

Boring, E. G. (1957, 2nd edition) *A History of Experimental Psychology*. New York, Appleton-Century-Crofts. (The classic, if somewhat whiggish, account of the early history of psychology as a science.)

Gould, S. J. (1986) 'Evolution and the triumph of homology, or why history matters.' *American Scientist*, vol. 74, 60–69. (On Darwin as historical methodologist.)

Grant, P. R. (1991) 'Natural selection and Darwin's finches.' *Scientific American*, vol. 266, 60–65. (Describes work of the last few decades on the species that so intrigued Darwin.)

Leahey, T. H. (1987, 2nd edition) *A History of Psychology*. Englewood Cliffs, NJ, Prentice-Hall. (A more modern, externalist, approach to psychology's history.)

Pinker, S. (1997) *How the Mind Works*. London, Allen Lane. (A wide-ranging and very peppy review of evolutionary psychology.)

Richards, R. J. (1987) *Darwin and the Emergence of Evolutionary Theories of Mind and Behaviour*. Chicago, Chicago University Press. (The best history ever written of the interplay of evolutionary and psychological thinking.)

Ridley, M. (1985) *The Problems of Evolution*. Oxford, Oxford University Press. (A brief and readable account of contemporary evolutionary theory.)

Ridley, M. (1993) *Evolution*. Oxford, Blackwell. (A much wider, deeper and more detailed review of neo-Darwinism than his 1985 book.)

2

Plato's Question

In the *Meno*, Plato begins the dialogue as follows: 'Can you tell me, Socrates, – can virtue be taught, or is it rather to be acquired by practice? Or is it neither to be practised nor learned, but something that comes to men by nature or in some other way?' Plato is asking about the causes of human disposition and behaviour, and casting it within the archetypal form of the nature–nurture question. Almost 2,000 years after Plato had written his dialogues, Shakespeare, in *The Tempest*, has Prospero describing Caliban as 'a devil, a born devil, on whose nature Nurture can never stick' (Act IV, Scene i). For Shakespeare nature seems to be the cause of greater force, at least in the case of poor Caliban. More to the point, for both Plato and Shakespeare, nature and nurture seem to be separable causes of behaviour. Is this the case or not? And if not, just how do nature and nurture relate to one another? These are some of the defining problems of the human sciences, especially psychology. Whether it be in the explanation of linguistic competence, the reasons for differences in intelligence between people, or the causes of schizophrenia (to name but a few of many possible examples), the issue is always cast in terms of nature and nurture. 'Tell me, Psychologist, is autism a consequence of a child experiencing emotionally cold and rejecting parents, or is it something that comes to them by nature, perhaps is present even at birth, or could it be some combination of experience and innate endowment?', to paraphrase Plato's question with regard to a condition which, when first described in the 1940s, was considered to be caused by nurture. Now, our views as to the causes of autism are different (see Chapter 5) and complex. Well, replace autism with virtually every human skill, person-

36

ality trait or social response, and the question remains the same.

The way in which the problem is solved is the conceptual resolution to one of the great puzzles of late-twentieth-century science, viz. the relationship between the social and the biological sciences. Put another way, when we understand the relationship between the social and biological sciences then we will have solved, in general form, the nature–nurture problem.

In this chapter I will consider first the way in which the problem developed following the appearance of Darwinian evolutionary theory. Then I will briefly review some of the modern solutions that have been offered. Finally I will argue that the nature–nurture problem is *the* crucible within which psychology's relationship to evolutionary theory must be forged. This is not because there is a simple mapping, hence separation, of nature on to historical cause and nurture on to now-and-forever proximate causes. There isn't such a mapping. Both nature and nurture are to be explained by both sets of causes. What is important to understand, so important as to constitute a sort of conceptual epiphany for those who have not yet come to this understanding, is that nurture has itself evolved. Nurture can only be fully understood in the light of historical cause. Nurture has nature.

Darwin, instincts and intelligence

The *Oxford English Dictionary*'s definition of nature as 'the inherent and innate disposition of character of a person (or animal)' is traced to first English usage around 1300. Nurture, defined as 'breeding, upbringing, training, education', dates from as early as 1330, and is most frequently associated with notions of experience and learning. Of course, the ideas captured by the words, and the matter of their relationship to one another, are almost as old as recorded human thought, as we see from Plato's question. Plato himself and other rationalist and intuitionist philosophers, who counted Descartes and Kant among their numbers, subscribed to the notion of innate ideas and functions. They were on the side of nature. The more recent empiricist tradition in philosophy, whose *tabula rasa* view of the human mind was a vote for the supremacy of nurture, includes Bacon, Hobbes, Locke, Hume and Berkeley. So too was Montesquieu's rather odd theory of the climatic determination of social behaviour. Between these two polarized approaches were the likes of the sensationlists who held that intelligence is a form of imaginative association of internalized representations of the external world which is widespread among animals, and which precedes the appearance of blind instinct in a species. All this, however, was philosophy, and until the middle of the nineteenth century no scientific vehicle was available from which the different positions could be more clearly articulated and empirically tested. The theory that provided that scientific basis for the analysis of nature and nurture was Darwin's (1859) *The Origin of Species*.

For Darwin, as for many writers before him, nature in behavioural or psychological terms meant instincts. He devoted an entire chapter to instincts in *The Origin of Species*, but confined his discussion to non-humans. Only in attempting to clarify his meaning did he consider the case of man: 'If Mozart, instead of playing the pianoforte at three years old with wonderfully little practice, had played a tune with no practice at all, he might truly be said to have done so instinctively.' Darwin's meaning is quite clear. Instincts are actions that are inborn, carried out without necessary prior practice or experience, and often in very young animals. Hence, he assumed, they are inherited, 'as important as corporeal structures for the welfare of each species', and the result of natural selection leading to 'the slow and gradual accumulation of numerous slight, yet profitable variations'. So while instincts are not identical in all members of a species, demonstrating variation in much the same way that ears or noses do, instinctive acts will be mostly very similar in different individuals of the same species.

It was twelve years later that Darwin first wrote at length on the issue of man's inherent nature and how it might, or might not, be affected by experience and training, in *The Descent of Man*. There are innumerable places in this work where nature and nurture are jointly discussed. No one of these makes any clearer point than any other. The following typifies Darwin's view:

The fewness and the comparative simplicity of the instincts in the higher animals are remarkable in contrast with those of the lower animals. Cuvier maintained that instinct and intelligence stand in an inverse ratio to each other; and some have thought that the intellectual faculties of the higher animals have been gradually developed from their instincts. But Pouchet . . . has shewn that no such inverse ratio really exists. Those insects which possess the most wonderful instincts are certainly the most intelligent. In the vertebrate series, the least intelligent members, mainly fishes and amphibians, do not possess complex instincts; and amongst mammals the animal most remarkable for its instincts, namely the beaver, is highly intelligent.

Yet just one paragraph later:

Although . . . a high degree of intelligence is certainly compatible with complex instincts, and although actions, at first learnt voluntarily can soon through habit be performed with the quickness and certainty of a reflex action, yet it is not improbable that there is a certain amount of interference between the development of free intelligence and of instinct – which latter implies some inherited modification of the brain.

(The Modern Library edition, pp. 446–7)

Darwin's use of the word 'intelligence' to stand for all the forces and sources of nurture, including experiencing, training, learning and creatively inventing, is one that will be followed here. The difficulties that such generic use leads to will be considered below. Before that, there are three points worth noting about these passages. First, there is much uncharacteristic confusion here from someone who normally wrote with great clarity. It is not clear whether Darwin supports Cuvier or Pouchet, both important nineteenth-century biologists. This is partly because in Darwin's day there was nothing that anyone could count or measure that would have resolved the issue. Words were just being used in an intuitive and common-sense way, which for that time was quite usual. Second, Darwin hints at two entirely opposite possibilities: that either intelligent behaviour somehow precedes its incorporation into the instinctive repertoire of some animals, or instincts take evolutionary precedence over intelligence, and somehow give rise to intelligence. This is an old argument that first appeared long before Darwin's work and still finds occasional expression today.

Third, such links in the evolution of one or other notwithstanding, Darwin clearly distinguishes between intelligence and instinct. Like Plato and Shakespeare, he considered them quite separate sources of behaviour, in humans as well as non-human animals. There is nothing that I know of in Darwin's writings to suggest that, apart from some speculation on evolutionary precedence, he thought of them as being in any way related, especially in terms of their acting in concert and simultaneously to cause behaviour. Thus, although one of the triumphs of Darwin's theory was to present a convincing argument that humans descended from other animals, what this in turn did was to support the nature–nurture dichotomy: some human behaviour, like most of the behaviour of other animals, is instinctive, that is, derived from nature; the rest is the consequence of individual intelligence, which serves nurture. The mix of 'how much nature' and 'how much nurture' varies from species to species. But the dichotomy between instinct and reason, as Frank Beach later pointed out, was never challenged by Darwinian theory. This is a sufficiently noteworthy point for me to have given it a special name, the doctrine of separate determination, in previous writings.

Of course, very little was understood about the transmission of phenotypic characters of any sort from parents to offspring. (The phenotype is the physical expression of the information in the genes as it becomes embodied during development – you and me, in short.) But the concept of instinct, thousands of years old, suited Darwin's purposes admirably in that it furnished him with the behavioural equivalent of morphological features of the phenotype. Instincts did, or did not, increase the likelihood of their possessor surviving and reproducing; behavioural variants that did increase the fitness of animals would thence be passed on to offspring, whose chances of survival and reproduction were thus enhanced, and the frequency of these variants increased whereas those that did not contribute to survival and reproduction were reduced in frequency in a population. The assumption was that, whatever the means of transmission between generations, instincts were like any other trait in that once present in a phenotype, they could not be easily changed.

The ease with which nature could be equated with instincts is to be contrasted with the difficulties raised by equating nurture with intelligence. Indeed, in general terms, intelligence has always posed more problems than has instinct. Most of the conceptual difficulties arise because intelligence is a faculty that drives behavioural change within the lifetime of an individual. Whether or not the products of intelligence, the changed behaviours, are passed on to offspring was part of a wider Lamarckian issue and one that generated not a little difference of opinion in the nineteenth century. Darwin's own position on the inheritance of acquired characters was not constant. Furthermore, whether intelligence as a trait could be passed on to offspring was not something on which Darwin seemed wholly committed, though his theory clearly required it to be so. Darwin's cousin Galton, on the other hand, was sceptical of the notion of the inheritance of acquired characters, but fiercely committed to the idea that intelligence is a characteristic that is inherited. And Galton came to occupy a central, and highly influential, position in the nature–nurture controversy as it unfolded through the latter part of the nineteenth century and on into this one.

Here, then, is room for much confusion on the issue of intelligence, whereas the notion of instinct seemed to be quite clear. Furthermore, the difference in the relative clarity and confusion surrounding these words, and the schools of thought that crystallized around each, became the greater when the followers of Galton, the eugenicists, adopted the position that, in effect, intelligence was to be viewed as an instinct in so far as it is relatively unchanged by the environmental conditions of the individual and passed on to offspring. It was the opponents of the eugenicists who had to unpick the trait from its consequences; worse, when it later became clear that intelligence is not immune to the conditions of the environment, it became necessary to disentangle that attribute, intelligence, that changes with environmental conditions, from the effects of that attribute, behavioural changes, that are an adaptive response to changing environmental conditions. The difficulties presented by this have bedevilled thinking about intelligence up to the present time.

Something else should be noted. The belief in nurture was initially a belief in the supremacy of the environment in determining behaviour over internal factors mediated by some form of inherited brain structure. If nature plays no part at all, then the environment acts via a *tabula rasa.* The latter, of course, is indubitably an internal structure, but it has very limited causal power. It merely changes in response to experiences and serves to adjust future behaviour. A *tabula rasa*, though, does not initiate anything. It is entirely without creativity. As was noted in Chapter 1, this is what so distressed William James about Spencer's psychology. Any subsequent shift from the notion of a *tabula rasa* to a more creative and autonomous intelligence or reason is a shift from external to internal control of behaviour, though one remaining in the realm of nurture, but this seemed to pass unnoticed in the heated debate of the controversy that extended to about 1930. At the time it was not important, since any kind of intelligence merely represented the internal factor necessary for nurture to have its effect. But the dichotomy did change from one in which behavioural determination is either wholly internal (nature) or external (nurture), to one in which the determination of behaviour is due either to some kind of inheritance from an ancestor (nature), or to the effects of the environment acting upon another set of internal factors comprising the mental faculties of intelligence and reasoning (nurture). Later, when intelligence came to be seen as an active process and not merely a passive recipient of external conditions, then the shift did assume importance because it became a source of even greater confusion. Add to that the notion that intelligence itself is an inherited attribute and the jangle of confusion becomes considerable. That, however, is jumping ahead of the story.

The first round in the great nature–nurture debate

For all these reasons, it was the scientific formulation of instincts rather than intelligence that was the immediate beneficiary of Darwin's writings. Instincts were easy to conceptualize and fit to a theory which demanded structural variation, and which had a simple conception of inheritance and precious little to say about development. The quotations from Darwin in the previous section show a clear recognition of the importance of intelligence in certain species, but Darwin himself provided no real basis for placing intelligence within an evolutionary context. By that I mean that while it is clear that Darwin believed that intelligence had evolved in any species whose members are intelligent, he gave no substantive analysis as to how and why it had done so. Galton's formulation of intelligence as just another instinct was ingenious and conceptually neat. But he too failed to confront the crucial questions that are raised by the assertion that intelligence has evolved: precisely what advantages does intelligence bestow upon its possessor that instincts do not? What role does intelligence itself play in evolution?

There was, though, one indirect benefit of Darwin's theory for the study of intelligence. This derived from his convincing arguments for the evolution of humans from other animals. If this is correct, which it undoubtedly is, then it is likely that humans possess features in common with our animal ancestors. And our currently living animal relatives might show certain attributes that are similar to, perhaps identical with, human traits, or identifiable as precursors to those traits. Thus began the search for instincts in man and intelligence in animals. The latter, astonishingly, was a relatively novel idea and the beginnings of a new science. Part of the significance of the work of Thorndike, who systematically studied trial-and-error learning in cats, and Pavlov, the discoverer of classical conditioning in dogs at the turn of this century, as mentioned in the previous chapter, was that they were the first laboratory-based, controlled demonstrations of intelligence in non-humans. They supplanted the anecdotal methods of the sensationalists of the eighteenth century and of Romanes and Morgan in the nineteenth, and laid the foundations for the science of animal intelligence (better known for a time as animal learning theory) which has flourished ever since, coming for a period to have an extraordinarily privileged status within experimental psychology.

The study of instincts in humans, as mentioned in the previous chapter, has had a much less successful history. Largely it has been a story of backing the wrong scientific horses, a lack of intellectual discernment and a general sense of excess. There was, though, a time when the supporters of nature did seem to be triumphing over those of nurture. Even as experimentalists were laying the foundations for the systematic study of intelligence, learning and reasoning in both man and other animals, the eugenics movement, which peddled an extreme form of naive nativism, was cresting a wave of scientific and lay popularity. In part this was fuelled by the discoveries of the new science of genetics, which, ironically given what was to come, in its early years gave the followers of Galton a sense of scientific credibility. In part it was the result of a thriving belief in instincts, albeit in a very limited number of areas of psychology, which arose when Darwinism made it respectable to think seriously of human behaviour in instinctivist terms.

The first decade of this century saw the flowering of this movement in psychology, which included the likes of Sigmund Freud and W. McDougall, who were serious and accomplished scientists. Freud's was a significant and complex theory of human development which anticipated the move towards some kind of interactionism by decades. Freud postulated that humans are born with certain fundamental instincts that are the foundation-stones of the human mind, but experiences during development then have a powerful effect in shaping those instincts, hence in determining the structure and functioning of the adult mind. Equally, McDougall well understood that one should never think that merely giving something a name constitutes an explanation of the thing named. Others, however, did not. Despite the lack of conceptual power and content in the practice of explaining human actions, and even national attributes and historical events, by giving them names such as 'fear', 'self-abasement' or the 'need to dominate inferiors', hundreds of authors of books and articles proposed literally thousands of human instincts in the first two decades of this century. It was an extraordinarily ill-disciplined and undiscerning phase in psychology's history.

Such descriptive nonsense could not long pass as science. It was bound to succumb to a stronger idea, and almost any idea was stronger than early-twentieth-century instinct psychology. It is a measure of the conceptual weakness of instinctivism that it was behaviourism that wielded the axe. As we have seen, Watson had little time for explanations based upon unobservables, and though instincts are observable behaviours their causal origins most certainly are not. In 1919 Knight Dunlap published a famous paper entitled 'Are there any instincts?' Social psychologists either began to develop frankly anti-hereditarian biases in their writings, or to argue persuasively for a more realistic and balanced social psychology based on proper biological thinking. Behaviourism very quickly conquered the experimental arena, and by 1930 the concept of instincts had almost disappeared from experimental psychology.

The demise of the eugenics movement as a whole was not far behind. There were at least four reasons for this. The first, as just mentioned, was the development of an unremitting hostility to the idea of instincts in wide reaches of psychology. Second, the hereditarian bias of the American mental testing movement came under fierce attack from intellectuals at large, who were steadily turning away from a narrow 'biologism' with its sinister ideological undertones. Third, the cultural determinists led by Franz Boas and Alfred Kroeber, and supported by the findings of Margaret Mead in Samoa (of which more in Chapter 6), had gained the ascendancy among American anthropologists in the arguments about the proper explanation of cultures and cultural differences between groups of people. Fourth, and much the most important reason, was that by 1930 science at large no longer supported the claims of the eugenicists. Genetics, which in the early years of the century was taken as supporting so strongly the claims and aims of a movement that believed in the preponderance of nature over nurture, was beginning to understand that, even if that were true, selective breeding would not eliminate 'the feeble-minded, the criminal and the morally degenerate'. Quite apart from Bernard Shaw's quip to a beautiful actress that the problem with eugenics was that their child might end up with her brains and his looks, other 'technical truths' began to emerge. Some related to the expression of genes in the phenotype seldom being invariable. Embryology specifically, but developmental sciences in general, including developmental psychology, were firm in their support of these findings. It was also becoming increasingly clear that 'feeble-mindedness', with a few exceptions, and 'criminality', with no exceptions, are not caused by single genes. And even if they were, because recessive genes may not find expression in their carriers, calculations showed that selective breeding, no matter how stringently practised, would not succeed in eradicating such unfortunates for thousands of years. It had become clear that, whatever the morality of the eugenics movement, and the rise of fascism in the 1930s taught us a great deal about that, its aims could never be realized by simple selective breeding.

The decline of the eugenics movement meant even less support for nature in the human sciences. Thus, after decades of dispute, some of it bitter and often politically and ideologically driven, the nurture–nature argument seemed to come to an end – at least temporarily. There had been no widely accepted resolution to the problem of how man's social and biological attributes are to be related to one another. With cultural determinism triumphant in anthropology, and behaviourism holding powerful sway in experimental psychology, the social sciences seemed to have become strongly anti-hereditarian in bias. The argument had not been resolved by either decisive findings or powerful argument. This first round of the debate was settled not because environmentalist views were strong but because the instinctivists were so weak. As a result, for the next twenty to thirty years, nature simply became unfashionable in the social sciences.

The deceptive calm of a non-solution to the problem

For more than twenty years after 1930 the nature–nurture debate rested in a kind of limbo. Scientists were either busy with other things, or considered the problem solved, or declared it to be a non-problem. Evolutionary biology was absorbed in the construction of the new synthesis, the fusion of genetics and Natural Selection Theory, and the social sciences had entered into an abiological era where members of different schools of thought were not so much hostile to biological ideas as concentrating upon the solution to their problems without feeling the need to have recourse to biology. Anthropology typifies the social sciences of the time. For the cultural or social anthropologists the field of anthropology embraced the likes of ethnography, cultural processes and dynamics, linguistics, comparative sociology and various specializations such as the study of technology, political organization, religion and art. This was the very stuff of the social sciences. Biology, as represented by physical anthropology, was peripheral. Summing up this era in the early 1950s, Kroeber, who had inherited the mantle of leadership in cultural or social anthropology from Boas, wrote that 'the central field of anthropology is culture. I do not mean in any way to belittle physical anthropology. Culture presupposes

human organisms, and their interrelation constitutes a basic problem
. . . I mean merely that our most distinctive field, the one around
which we can best organize our data, is culture.' Kroeber also spoke
of culture as 'an emergent level', which at that time was, and largely
still is, a code for saying that it could only be understood in its own
terms and not by reduction to lower-level mechanisms, processes or
concepts.

None the less, anthropology was divided into two, a division formed
by, and underlying the failure to resolve, the nature–nurture problem.
In Europe anthropology meant physical anthropology. The implications of so fundamental a schism within a subject could not be ignored,
even if for some time the acrimony and antipathy of the nature–
nurture debate had died down. Thus Kroeber wrote:

I submit that man as a set of social phenomena, including his culture in all
its aspects – along with values – not only is *in* nature, but is *wholly part* of
nature. It is evidently going to be somebody's business to deal scientifically
with these human phenomena; to work at more than aesthetic comprehension
of them. Such a comprehension would be intellectual, aiming at an intelligible
concord with reality, resting on both specific evidence and on a broad coherent
theory.

Indeed it was going to be somebody's business, but obviously the
cultural anthropologists of that day did not see it as theirs. In the
penultimate chapter of this book we will return to this theme and see
who did make it their business.

The situation in psychology was no more clear or encouraging. The
puritanism of Watson's behaviourism was short-lived and gave way in
the mid-1930s to large-scale behavioural theories, essentially learning
theories, which had no qualms about having explanatory recourse to
hypothetical internal events such as inhibitory potentials in the case
of C. L. Hull or E. C. Tolman's cognitive maps, and which cheerfully
acknowledged certain 'innate' determinants of behaviour. In 1943,
for example, Hull famously (to some infamously because it was
thought to be a serious case of premature formalism and pseudo-
quantification, though it was a hugely influential work) published a
book which contained a formal set of postulates to account for learning
in all animals that do learn, including humans. Postulate 3 stated that

'organisms at birth possess receptor–effector connections' which are non-arbitrary and important in satisfying need states. This is a statement about predisposition, and can only be interpreted as inherited predisposition. Moving further forward in time, even Skinner acknowledged 'an innate capacity to be reinforced by damage to others traceable to phylogenic contingencies', which is a very contorted way of saying that some animals are innately aggressive. Thus, while psychology at this time continued to be centred on nurture, these were theories that acknowledged some degree of genetically determined constraint on learning. None the less, these 'grand' theories were largely theories of learning, and references to neurological, genetical and developmental events were invariably exercises in lip-service without any explanatory force. No attempt was made to say how learning was to be understood in the light of genetics and development. If only by default, then, the doctrine of separate determination still held sway in these learning theories.

At this point, having used the word 'innate' quite often in this chapter, a word which some, not to their credit, consider to be a sin, I had better say what is meant by it. Innate usually means present at birth (or hatching), hence inborn; more correctly, it also connotes part-cause in the information contained in genes. It does not mean that innate behaviour is only caused by genes, and it does not mean that such behaviour cannot subsequently be altered during development or by experience. It does mean that were the DNA base pairs that code for the central nervous system randomized at conception, then these behaviours would not occur. (DNA stands for deoxyribonucleic acid, which is the complex chemical structure from which genes are built.) So, unless otherwise stated, that is what is meant by innate in this book. Present, actually or potentially, at birth and part-caused by genetic information.

The Gestalt theorists of this period, whose work was concentrated upon perception and how it is that we make sense of our sensory experiences, came much closer to a real rapprochement between so-called nature and nurture than did the learning theorists. Perceptual theories were cast in terms of perceptual primitives (nature) modified by experience (nurture). Kurt Lewin's concept of 'psychological ecology', and the basic theoretical stance in terms of fields and field forces, where a field is 'the totality of coexisting facts which are conceived of as mutually interdependent', were theoretical stances which recognized the importance of both intrinsic and extrinsic factors in the determination of perception and how perception guides behaviour. They also showed a clear understanding that the form of the interaction between them is of great importance. But here too, at bottom, these forces were dichotomized into two sets, those internal to the organism and those outside of it. Thus both nature and nurture were recognized and given due and equal weighting within a single approach. But they were still kept separate.

Social psychology also developed a form of interactionism in the 1920s, which remains essentially unaltered in the present time. Social psychologists seem to have developed a deeper historical understanding of the nature–nurture problem than most other kinds of psychologists, and they were also keenly aware of the importance of writing a theory of social behaviour that is rooted in acceptable biological thought. Like the Gestaltists, a form of developmental interactionism became central to their view. For example, in a social psychology text published in 1942, LaPiere and Farnsworth wrote:

it has become apparent that these two variables (nature and nurture) are not independent, but are interdependent: thus the effect of a given biological heritage will depend upon the given social environment, and the effect of the latter will depend upon the former. In the study of the origins of behavior we are not, therefore, dealing with two separate causes that together produce an effect, but rather with 'causes' each of which affects the other. This interactional view of heredity and environment is one aspect of the shift . . . from one-way cause-and-effect analysis to interactional analysis.

This passage displays a fine appreciation of the problem; so fine, indeed, that the notion of different categories of cause is explicitly rejected. This is a conceptually very important step. But in not having any theoretical scheme to replace the rejected notion of separate causation, the inevitable result of such interactionist accounts was to resort by default to the dichotomy of causes.

Coinciding with the emergence of this form of interactionism was the development by R. A. Fisher, the great evolutionist and one of the founders of the modern synthesis, of the statistical method known as the analysis of variance. In the analysis of variance the relative contributions of different factors to the overall variation of a measure can be calculated, and factors may interact. The statistical analogy was quickly adopted by the social psychologists. For instance, Murphy and others wrote in 1937:

There is never, in fact, a separation of heredity and environment; but there is always a problem in regard to the statistical weight to be assigned to variations in stock as compared with variations in environment with respect to measured outcome in the behavior of all the individuals in an experimental group.

Further:

Statistical separation of the hereditary from the environmental is not the issue; the issue is of statistical separation of variability of one type and variability of the other type. The concrete social individual is literally and absolutely indivisible, and the nature–nurture problem, as applied to an individual, is without any meaning whatever.

These are as nice a statement of accounting for and apportioning variance using the statistical methods of the time as one can get: but, of course, assigning a percentage of variance accountable to factor X and another percentage figure to factor Y does not tell one anything of the nature of the relationship between X and Y. Furthermore, asserting a literal and absolute indivisibility of the traits of an integrated, intact individual says nothing about the causal determinants of those traits.

I have quoted here at length because what was being said was that such approaches had solved the nature–nurture problem, which is to be conceived as if it were a problem that can be resolved into a two-way analysis of variance. But the statistical analogy is incomplete and unsatisfactory because, whatever the interaction, a two-factor analysis of variance presupposes a dichotomy, in effect. The distinction between nature and nurture as causes is not denied; and the nature of the interaction is not given. So the statistical analogy is wholly unenlightening with regard to the nature–nurture problem. It does not begin to tell us how to relate social man to biological man.

In contemporary social psychology, nature and nurture have given way to external versus internal variables (situationalism versus trait theory, for example). The change of words, though, has not altered the nature of the problem: the essence of the causal dichotomy and possibility of interactionism as a solution remains the same now as forty years ago.

During the middle and late 1950s the grand theories of Hull, Tolman and others collapsed. This period witnessed the emergence of a radical, if thinly populated, neobehaviourism under Skinner, and the vigorous development of cognitivism as the mainstream conception for much of psychology to fill the vacuum left by the demise of the grand theories. None of these important developments in psychology affected the nature–nurture problem, the battle around which had re-ignited but was being fought by others. Cognitivism had made it respectable again to have recourse to hidden, unobservable causes in psychological theory. These hidden causes were, and are, widely assumed to be identifiable, in principle if not in fact, with brain structures and functions. But the early cognitivists, with the obvious exception of the likes of Chomsky, whose notion of language deep-structures as innate brain structures was a form of nativism, eschewed the arguments as to developmental origins. They deemed this to be barren theoretical ground.

This potted, all-too-simple and descriptive history makes a single point: whether nature and nurture, alone or one preponderantly, gives rise to certain behaviours, psychological processes or psychological dispositions, it was and remains widely held that nature and nurture represent two separate causal sources in such determination. This is the doctrine of separate determination, not of a phenotypic attribute (behavioural or otherwise), but of the *causes* of that attribute. It has remained largely intact from Darwin's day down to the present. It is only largely intact – not wholly so – because a breach of the doctrine was established by Lorenz in 1965 in a book, *The Evolution and Modification of Behaviour*, that deserved to be more widely read and discussed than was the case. It would take a skilled historian to explain properly why Lorenz's writings on this matter have had so little effect. I will mostly confine myself in the following to an account of that part of his work that had a bearing on the nature–nurture problem.

Round two: a partial solution unrecognized

The very idea of instincts might have been virtually outlawed in psychology, but another behavioural discipline, ethology, would have nothing to do with such conceptual sanctions. Ethology as a science has its origins in the activities of nineteenth-century naturalists and biologists. Von Pernau was an important early practitioner of ethology. He studied the behaviour of birds and was especially interested in behaviour that seemed not to be the result of experience with conspecifics. The English naturalist Spalding had similar interests. He deprived chicks of certain sensory experiences and observed the effects upon their behaviour. He also raised swallows in cages so small that they could not flap their wings, and yet he noted that when released they 'flew excellently' – one may doubt the claim, but that is beside the point, which is what such experiments were trying to get at. These observations were forerunners of what later came to be called the 'deprivation experiment', the general logic of which is to deprive an individual animal of normal developmental experiences and then to see how such deprivation affects behaviour. If not at all, or even very little, then the conclusion is that experience is not an important causal factor in the development of the behaviour in question, the causes being primarily internal and innate. Von Pernau and Spalding typified, at this very early stage, the preoccupation of ethology with so-called 'innate' behaviours, and their study in birds.

Darwin's view that a significant proportion of behaviour has both functional (survival) value and particular phylogenetic distributions because of the relatedness of species was seminal in the development of ethology. Later important contributors included Whitman, Craig, Heinroth and Von Uexkull. But it was Konrad Lorenz, a disciple of Heinroth's, who in the 1930s laid the foundations for ethology as an established area within biology. After the Second World War Lorenz and others, notably Tinbergen, began seriously to challenge comparative psychology as the proper study of animal behaviour – indeed to some extent, to challenge psychology at large.

The gestation period for ethology therefore was about 100 years, the birth occurring in the 1930s. Less than half a century ago it was a very young science and going through a brash and abrasive phase in its development. Tinbergen's *The Study of Instinct*, the first book to be published under the label of ethology, but of course by no means the first book on animal behaviour, defined ethology as the 'objective study of behaviour'. Thorpe, just a few years later, wrote that 'the ethologist is looking at his problems from the point of view of one primarily interested in the animal kingdom as a whole, and not as adjunct to the study of human psychology or social relations. So I consider that ethology means the scientific study of animal behaviour', and he went on to suggest that experimental psychology should be subsumed under the more inclusive banner of ethology. Similar claims about the lack of objectivity, irrelevance or secondary status of established areas of science in the light of a new and supposedly more powerful science were to be made for sociobiology (see next section and next chapter) by E. O. Wilson twenty years later, and the results in both cases were the same. The relationship between the new science, ethology, and the older science, psychology, especially experimental and comparative psychology, was, to say the least, strained.

The arguments between ethology and psychology in the 1950s and 1960s were, in effect, the next round in the nature–nurture debate. It had not been properly settled thirty years before and so it was only a matter of time before the controversy would surface again, with ethology presenting the arguments for nature and psychology defending nurture on this occasion. The principal differences between these two approaches to the study and understanding of behaviour all stemmed from fundamental differences in the way these two disciplines perceived themselves and their subject matter. Psychology in this century, though fond of generalizing its findings to a mythical beast called 'the organism', was, and properly remains, a human-oriented discipline, and as discussed in the previous chapter, was, and still is, wedded to a different kind of causal thinking than that of evolutionary biologists.

Ethology presents a stark contrast. Its early development was dominated by European biologists. The founders of classical ethology, including Lorenz and Tinbergen, were Darwinians through and through. All classical ethology's core concepts were based on the notion that behaviour is adaptive. If behaviour is adaptive, then it must be the product of evolution. It must also be a set of heritable phenotypic traits, that is to say, differences in behaviour must be at least partly caused by genetic differences between individuals and species, and such differences could be genetically transmitted from parents to offspring. This adherence to neo-Darwinian theory as the central theorem of all biology, including behavioural biology, meant that classical ethology was committed to the view that adaptive behaviour is to be seen as an 'inherent and innate disposition of a character', that is, as being instinctive. Being children of their time and employing the methodology of their time, the classical ethologists considered behaviour to be a set of phenotypic characters that can be investigated and understood within a strict and conceptually meaningful comparative framework, viz. homology, where similarity of two phenotypic attributes (a') and (a''), in two species Y and Z, is the result of some species X, ancestral to both Y and Z, having had a phenotypic attribute (a) from which (a') and (a'') are both derived. The comparative method centred about the concept of homology was a widespread research tool among evolutionary biologists in the earlier part of this century. Thus Lorenz wrote:

Comparative anatomy and systematics, using a broad basis of induction gained by observation and description, brought order into the multiplicity of living species and prepared the way for the recognition of the common origin of all living creatures. Once this basic evolutionary fact was established, it was an unavoidable conclusion that a historical explanation is needed for practically every detail of structure and function observed in living creatures. Such historical explanation is indeed also a *causal* one: if we ask why a man has auditory organs at the sides of his head, with auditory canals connecting them with the pharynx, one of the causal explanations of this state of affairs is that all this is so, because man is descended from water-breathing vertebrates which had a gill-opening in that part of their anatomy. Thus research into the phyletic history of an organ or function becomes an indispensable part of its scientific study.

As a full-blooded evolutionist, Lorenz clearly understood the significance of historical antecedence as cause, and he saw his mission as being the application of this approach to behavioural science. In his view comparative study, which when properly undertaken is a method of establishing historical cause, takes priority over the understanding of the 'survival value' of behaviour, which he placed second in importance in ethology's aims. In his Nobel Prize address Lorenz declared that his 'most important contribution in science' had been the use of the comparative method in tracing the evolution of behaviour.

It is little wonder that ethology would see itself at odds with a man-oriented, learning-centred (nurture) and instinct-rejecting (nature) psychology. Interestingly, when the nature–nurture (this time round usually couched in terms of an opposition of instincts and learning) argument erupted again in the early 1950s, battle was joined for the psychologists not by archetypal anti-biological social-scientist ideologues, but by people who, though nominally physiological (such as the great Donald Hebb) and comparative (for example Schneirla and Lehrman) psychologists, were biologists themselves and hence able to argue their case with assurance and competence.

I am not concerned to trace the claims and counterclaims, the arguments and counterarguments, with any semblance of completeness or even fairness, since what I am aiming at is the centrepiece of Lorenz's rebuttal of the arguments of the proponents of nurture. Suffice it to say, then, that Lorenz's opponents attacked ethology in general, and Lorenz specifically, on four main points. The first was a form of interactionism. Instincts cannot be innate. There always has to be an external or experiential set of variables that co-determine species-typical behaviour patterns. In short, the information contained in the genes can never find expression in a vacuum. The environment of development is as essential as genes. Second, and closely related to the first point, the innate–learning dichotomy of the ethologists left out of the equation of behavioural determination a crucial factor or set of factors, viz. individual development (technically referred to as ontogeny). Many behavioural phenomena were pointed to which clearly were partly due to experiential variables, and which equally clearly could not be accounted for by learning, at least not learning as psychologists understood the word. One example of this is the way in which certain forms of social deprivation in some species of monkey early in development, and long before sexual maturity, altered and impaired adult sexual behaviour. Another popular example is the way in which temperature during certain stages in the development of insects affects the ability of adults to fly. Learning cannot be invoked to explain a temperature effect induced at a larval stage to explain impaired flying at later stages in the life cycle. The third criticism called into question the status of the deprivation experiment, both in terms of its logic and the nature of its findings. Finally, certain crucial assumptions of classical ethology were contradicted by careful empirical work. A good example of this was the American behavioural biologist Hailman's work showing that Tinbergen's earlier studies of the behaviour of gull chicks had reached incorrect conclusions.

It is worth noting that what was at stake was not the existence of instincts, but rather how they are to be investigated and understood. It is unwise, wrote T. C. Schneirla, to

attempt to distinguish what is 'innate' from what is 'acquired', or to estimate the proportionate effects of these or to judge what kinds of effects they might produce separately. There exist no separate entities of this sort, for conditions at any stage are the complex product of trace effects from previous stages entering into interactions with prevalent extrinsic–intrinsic conditions, them-selves composite acquisitions . . . The 'instinct' problem is one of development . . . 'instinct' is not a real and demonstrated agency in the causation of behavior, but a word for the problem of species-typical behavior . . .

And 'Consequently, "instinct" study must examine the ontogeny of behavior in each type of organism.'

It is striking how similar the arguments are to those presented by the social psychologists in the 1930s. In many ways, little in the attempt to explain how to resolve the nature–nurture problem had changed from that previous era. Perhaps the only real difference lay in the clarity of expression. Epigenesis is the notion that individual development is not a simple and inevitable unfolding of some inner potential, but is instead a highly variable process resulting from a cascade of immensely complex interactions between genetic information, the developing features of the individual, and the environment in which development is occurring. Schneirla was a true epigeneticist and he insisted on the recognition of individual development as a process of great intricacy and importance. Lorenz, on the other hand, was a true evolutionist, and very much one of his time. He was raised intellectually in the evolutionary tradition of the supremacy of the Weismann maxim that insisted on the division of biology into phylogeny (the appearance of species across time, often immense reaches of time) and ontogeny (the appearance of individual features of organisms within very short periods of time). So what separated Lorenz from his critics in the 1950s and 1960s was this fundamental schism in theoretical biology between evolution and development that is still with us, and which has yet to be resolved.

Now, three of the criticisms made by the psychologists of the ethologists were either wholly or partly correct. Individual development had indeed been largely neglected in the early work of the classical ethologists. In a highly influential paper published in 1963, Tinbergen added ontogeny to Julian Huxley's 'three major problems of biology' (these being proximate physiological causes, survival value causes, and phylogenetic or evolutonary causes). This was a frank admission by one of the leaders of ethology of the central role of developmental studies, and of development, to behavioural biology. Even Lorenz made a grudging acknowledgement of the omission with his comment that 'Among these [innate] functions there may be some that require ontogenetically acquired information for their full development. Even the function of retinal elements requires "practice" . . .'

Difficulties with the deprivation experiments, especially the extent to which subsequent empirical studies produced findings different from those of earlier reports, are to be seen in the general context of the problems of all empirical behavioural work. Problems of replication are widespread in behavioural studies and were much more severe fifty years ago when data were gained and saved using paper-and-pencil methods. Small, and often unnoticed, alterations in innumerable variables may lead to different findings, and it is likely that disputes about the accuracy of empirical studies will continue for as long as psychological science exists. The deprivation experiment itself received a long and hard look from Lorenz in his 1965 monograph. He, and subsequently others as well, have pointed to some curious logical features of the experiment, which can only tell one what is *not* essential for normal development. It says something about the power of science as an opportunistic process that, whatever its flaws, the deprivation experiment has played a central and essential role in work on bird-song, which has been arguably the most successful area of behavioural biology of recent times.

However, it was on what Lorenz, with obvious intention to insult, called the 'first behaviouristic argument' that he dug in his conceptual heels and groped towards a different kind of solution from anything that either side had offered before. The quintessential difference between early Lorenz and his critics may be expressed as follows. Take any behaviour and it will comprise a series of constituent elements. For Lorenz, each element was 'pure' in its provenance, that is, either internal (genetic) or external (ontogenetic or learned). The behaviour as a whole would be a mix of both kinds of element, hence the behaviour itself could not be claimed as either 'innate' or 'not innate'. But each individual element could, in principle, be so classified. For Lorenz's critics too the total behaviour was mixed, but for different reasons. Each element has its origins in some interaction of internal and external causes. No element is ever pure in its provenance. As is so often the case in science, the difference separating the two sides to the argument appears to the outsider to be minute and inconsequential, since both accept that any behavioural act is an inextricable mix of internal and external determinants. The difference turns on whether that mix applies to individual elements in the behaviour or to the behaviour as some entire unit. What is quite clear is that prior to 1965, both sides were seeing the problem through those old 'dichotomizing' eyes, with internal variables on the one hand and external variables on the other – the difference lay with where the mix was occurring. This incessant and pernicious dichotomizing is what Lorenz in 1965 moved against: 'I think that I can show that this assumption (of dichotomy and of "insensibly graduated mixtures between the two") is not only bad strategy for research but completely unfounded and in all probability false.'

The way to do this was to move to an entirely different kind of image and conceptualization which did not hang on a dichotomy of internal and external determining factors (the doctrine of separate determination), but was also one which did not deny the obvious existence and importance of identifiable external and internal factors. Lorenz tried to do this by focussing upon a unifying notion that he termed adaptive modification. His great insight was to point to a characteristic of learning which he claimed, with justice, to be its most crucial feature and which had always been overlooked or ignored by learning theorists: 'The amazing and never-to-be-forgotten fact is that learning does, in the majority of cases, increase the survival value of the behavior mechanisms which it modifies. The rare instances in which this survival function miscarries serve to illustrate rather than to negate this – but this fact itself demands an explanation.' In a later section he wrote: 'I came to realize rather late in life that "learning" was a concept illegitimately used by us as a dump for unanalyzed residue and that, no better than our criticized critics, none of us had ever bothered to ask why learning produced adaptation of behavior.'

Lorenz buttressed his claims about the adapted nature of learning and what this must mean by arguing that random change introduced into a complex system is unlikely to have a beneficial effect: mostly it will be either deleterious or without effect, as in the case of genetic mutations.

The more complicated an adapted process, the less chance there is that a random change will improve its adaptedness. There are no life processes more complicated than those which take place in the central nervous system and control behavior. Random change must, with an overpowering probability, result in their disintegration.

There is a connection here with a more general argument, made in the past by the likes of R. Ashby, that as a system becomes more complicated, the chances that random connection in that system will lead to stability become vanishingly small. Therefore, if learning is usually beneficial in outcome, it can only be because learning somehow is the result of, and induces, CNS changes that fit, and are fit, within the complex state of that CNS.

How can this be? If learning is adapted, then what exactly does this mean for our understanding of learning? These are the great questions that Lorenz posed. He was only able to give a partial answer, but its importance matched the greatness of the questions. Learning is adaptive in outcome, he suggested, because learning is an innately based capacity or process; it is adaptive because innate (that is, genetic) information somehow ensures that only certain constrained and restricted events or acts or relationships are learned. He called these innate bases 'innate school-marms' or, in a later publication 'innate teaching mechanisms'.

In this way, Lorenz brought his thinking on learned behaviour into line with that on unlearned behaviour. If behavioural characteristics are adaptive, then the source of the information underlying such adaptedness ultimately lies in the natural selection of genes. This applies as much to learned behaviour as to unlearned behaviour. In the words used earlier in this chapter, if the DNA base pairs that code for the central nervous system were randomized at conception, then neither learned nor unlearned coherent behaviours would occur. If learned behaviour is adaptive, as it most often is, it is because learning is itself built upon innate, gene-based information. In the old sense of the word innate, learning as a set of processes and mechanisms *is* innate. Thus the causal dichotomy is destroyed. Internal and external factors are crucial for both learned and unlearned behaviour. The image that is conjured up is of the oneness of learned and unlearned behaviours in terms of the contributions of both internal and external factors. Whatever distinction is to be drawn between learned and unlearned behaviours, and of course such distinctions can and must be specified, it cannot be in terms of nature and nurture conceived of as a crude causal dichotomy based on internal and external factors because learned behaviour, like all behaviour, is a product of both. Lorenz understood, as no one had before, that nurture has nature; that nurture is evolved and has historical antecedence as cause.

It will seem extraordinary to the reader of the 1990s that conceptual inertia in science can be such as to perpetuate debate about, and such late acceptance of, the notion that both intrinsic and extrinsic factors are essential for the formation of all phenotypic attributes, including learning and intelligence and species-typical behaviour patterns. Furthermore, this acceptance seemed to leave no clear way of understanding, beyond ordinary common sense, how learned and unlearned behaviour both differed from one another and how their relationship to each other was to be understood. Lorenz provided no clear model, and so it is worth repeating and summarizing the position that emerged from the 1965 monograph. Since all phenotypic attributes require both internal and external factors (causes) for their formation, differences between these sets of factors themselves cannot form the basis for any significant distinctions to be drawn between any phenotypic attributes. This applies to learned and unlearned behaviours as much as any other phenotypic attributes. Hence learned and unlearned behaviours cannot be distinguished on the basis of their formation by internal and external factors. This means that the differences, and the relationship, between unlearned and learned behaviours remained unspecified, through Lorenz did invoke CNS storage (memory) and the properties resulting from such storage as the basis for the differences between learned and unlearned behaviour.

By no means did Lorenz present a complete solution to the nature–nurture problem. But he had taken it a significant step further. Why was this not generally recognized? Why is Lorenz still portrayed as propagating an unreconstructed nature–nurture distinction? There are several possible reasons which I outline for completeness and without any attempt at a detailed analysis.

The first is that ethology and psychology in the middle and late 1960s were both in a state of profound change, and both entering into a phase of mutual reconciliation. There was the cognitive revolution in psychology and the accompanying demise of Skinner's behaviourism and other non-biological or abiological approaches to behaviour. There was much bridge-building work going on and Lorenz seemed to be a person who was not good at building bridges. Also important was the steady rise in the empirical content of ethology, especially in the United States, with its orientation increasingly guided by Tinbergen's 'four problems' or questions that should be asked about behaviour. Tinbergen was the great healer and did much to bring the two subjects closer together and to render rather irrelevant the old divisions that were closely identified with Lorenz. Yet another, and closely related, reason is that ethology never achieved the status of the comparative science at which Lorenz had aimed. Mostly this was because ethology was soon to become behavioural ecology with the core conceptual issues shifting away from homology towards inclusive fitness, Optimality Theory and Game Theory, more of which in the next chapter. The comparative method had not been shown to be the wrong way to do things. People merely came to feel that there were other, more interesting, things to be doing. The comparative method had simply become unfashionable, and with it its most ardent and prominent advocate had become unfashionable too.

So, whatever his achievements, no one seemed to be listening. Lorenz's great insight was either not understood or simply ignored as irrelevant. Round two of the debate saw no resolution to the nature–nurture problem. Without any recognition of conceptual ground having been gained, it was only a matter of time before the argument would break out again. It duly did so with the publication in 1975 of a book written by the American entomologist E. O. Wilson entitled *Sociobiology: The New Synthesis*.

Round three: the curious case of sociobiology

Since the whole of the next chapter is devoted to sociobiology, little space will be given to it here. This is appropriate in the context of the nature–nurture problem because, while the sociobiology controversy which followed the publication of Wilson's book owed quite a lot to the lack of resolution of the nature–nurture issue, sociobiology itself, and the reactions to it, contributed nothing to the matter. Sociobiology is a school of thought which is centred on the idea that because the perpetuation of genetic material is the driving force of evolution, many of the properties of animals – indeed, the properties of all living things – including their social behaviour, must be understood in that light.

The claims were vividly asserted. Wilson, for instance, wrote that 'the organism does not live for itself. Its primary function is not even to reproduce other organisms; it reproduces genes, and it serves as their temporary carrier.' The English biologist Richard Dawkins made the point even more strongly, saying that genes 'created us, body and mind; and their preservation is the ultimate rationale for our existence'. Well now, these are deeply interesting claims, and others like them will be found in Chapter 3, as well as an examination of whether they could be true. However, they do not reflect upon how sociobiologists think about development and learning. By and large, they had little to say on these topics, and when they did it usually was nothing new or interesting.

A good historian of science will have a field day relating the lack of resolution of the nature–nurture problem in general, and Lorenz's perceived role in the argument specifically, to the hysterical reaction accorded to sociobiology by some of its fiercest critics. However, as we will see, the sociobiologists were not making a land grab on the territory of the psychologists and anthropologists; they were not trying to resuscitate turn-of-the-century instinct psychology; and they were not trying to explain everything by genetic reductionism. Whatever it was they were saying, it simply didn't impinge upon Plato's question.

Where are we now?

The nature–nurture problem has not gone away. In early 1995 the popular media in Britain carried stories about genes for criminality, stimulated by a scientific meeting held in London on the genetics of criminal behaviour. Around the same time, a convicted murderer in the United States appealed against his impending execution on the grounds that his behaviour was not in his 'control', but caused, unstoppably, by his genes. This is an interesting transmutation and extension of the nature–nurture problem into a variant of the mind–body problem. Almost every sensational case of murder and brutality stimulates discussion in the mass media about whether the bad and the mad are so by nature or driven to it by circumstance. One no more expects journalists and talking heads to be able to give an up-to-date technical account of contemporary thinking about the nature–nurture issue than that they should be able to explain the geophysics of earthquakes. However, one might expect a similar level of folk wisdom. No journalist now writes of natural disasters as if they are caused by evil spirits or are God's punishment on wrongdoers. Yet journalists, politicians and pundits, indeed almost everyone, still subscribe to the doctrine of separate determination – the notion that nature and nurture are separable causes. She is mad because of her genes. He is bad because of his experiences.

Nor is this woeful state of affairs confined to psychological 'outsiders'. The technical literature of psychology often carries eloquent laments from the likes of Susan Oyama and Timothy Johnston, both

American developmentalists, on the perpetuation of dichotomous thinking by psychologists about psychological issues in psychological journals. Why does this continue to be the case? One likely reason is that people think more easily when contrasting pairs of opposites. A second is that the solutions on offer are both complex and far from simple to cash out into practical or empirical form. There are, in fact, two possible ways of resolving the matter, both being extensions of positions already described. The first will be referred to as the developmental solution; the second is the nested hierarchy view. Several voluminous accounts of both will be found in the reference section to this chapter.

The developmental solution was most powerfully proffered in the 1950s and 1960s, principally and most elegantly by Schneirla and Lehrman. Contemporary exponents, like the developmental psychologists Oyama, Johnston and Thelen, are now integrating this approach with the thinking of other sciences of complex systems, using, for example, non-linear dynamical systems theory; others, like Elman and his collaborators (see the end-of-chapter reading list), are marrying developmental concepts to neural network modelling. While there is no simple way of describing complex theories of complex systems, the bare bones of their thinking are not difficult to understand. What the developmentalists have done is provide an image of a coalescence of causes around a highly complex and dynamic developmental process. The interactionist programme is often rejected because interaction is a word that contains an implicit separateness of the causes that are entering into the interaction. The approach proceeds 'by refusing to partition the phenotype between genetic and environmental determinants', in Johnston's words. Oyama prefers to talk about co-action or co-determination, though the prefix itself implies separate causes to this writer. However, the conceptual package is stronger than the individual words. It is intensely holistic in approach and rejects what it sees as the rest of the world's fixation on genes. 'The developmental system', writes Oyama, 'includes . . . not just genes, but whatever else in the living or non-living environment contributes to or supports development.' The great strength of the approach is that it synthesizes in a powerful way the external world and the organism, which has real advantages for theorists who consider that evolutionary theory is too gene-centred. C. H. Waddington, the British evolutionist and developmentalist, used to stress that individual development is an indivisible complex of the organism *in* its world, and this complex is as species-typical as individual traits or whole organisms. If anything, Oyama's vision is even stronger. 'Traits do not pass from one organism to another, but must be constructed in ontogeny.' In rejecting the conceptual dependence most biologists have on genes, she points out that inheritance must apply to 'whatever it takes to make a trait', and that includes much more than genetic information – indeed, Oyama challenges the very notion of genetic information as having biological meaning. Genes only convey information in so far as they are embedded within self-organizing developmental systems. Furthermore, 'whatever it takes to make a trait' will always include the conditions of the world within which development occurs. A bird or a wasp (or a human) that constructs a nest which provides a relatively stable early environment for its young is bequeathing to those offspring a particular kind of world. Inheritance is more than genes.

The neural network approach of Elman and his colleagues is one of the most significant contributions to the nature–nurture debate of the last thirty or forty years. Everyone with an interest in this matter, which means everyone with an interest in any aspect of human science, should read this recent book because it provides an intense examination of the concept of innateness; and because it offers a resolution of the nature–nurture problem within a developmental perspective that does not wholly discard the concept of innateness but instead redefines it. Perhaps the most interesting feature of this approach is that it argues for the existence of general-purpose learning machinery, known as a connectionist neural network architecture, as the basis for all human cognition (in Chapter 4 we will consider the problem of general versus specific learning mechanisms in somewhat greater detail). However, even Elman and colleagues, and others who have written about connectionism like the philosopher–neuroscientist Andy Clark, accept that such general-purpose networks can be biased to operate in certain preferred or predisposed ways. Clark's nice phrase of 'minimal nativism' expresses the way in which such neural network structures can be constrained. There is no reason why Lorenz's innate teaching mechanisms should not be biases operating within generalist neural networks, and the possible existence of generalist networks in no way argues against the existence of constraints on the operation of these networks. But where, oh where, are these constraints or biases coming from? There is only one possible place, because while inheritance may be more than genes, it also includes genes.

The general problem with most developmental approaches is that they do not make real the importance of historical cause rooted in a history of selection. It does not give sufficient prominence to the central notion of the second possible way of resolving the nature–nurture problem, which is that historical cause always leads, via genes, to constraint on processes and structures operating in the ecological theatre of here and now. This is the view which Lorenz had been working towards, but which was largely overshadowed by the attention paid to his distinction in the 1965 monograph of sources of information in the construction of behaviour, which was taken to be a hardening of his position as the great dichotomizer of causes. As already made clear, this was an error of interpretation. Lorenz was moving towards a particular kind of causal synthesis, different from that of the developmentalists, but equally effective in destroying the dichotomizing of causes. The most user-friendly name one can give to this approach is evolutionary Kantianism, though it is often also known as a type of evolutionary epistemology. What follows is the briefest of résumés of a theoretical stance described in some length in *Darwin Machines and the Nature of Knowledge* (see end-of-chapter reading list).

Immanuel Kant, the great eighteenth-century philosopher, thought that our knowledge of the world, imperfect and fallible as it is, is made possible by certain *a priori* intuitions and categories concerning, amongst other things, space, time, quantity and relations. These *a prioris*, according to Kant, are innate. They are not acquired by learning – doubtless Kant would have been happy to accept the contemporary developmentalist view about the significance of developmental experience in the construction of any trait within a developmental environment. That, however, is not the point. For Kant there is an innate basis for human knowledge; we come into this world with certain structures inside our head which make knowledge possible.

Well, that is precisely what the neo-Kantian Lorenz was arguing for. Learning, he asserted, is almost always adaptive in outcome because learners come into this world with the equivalents of Kant's *a prioris*, that is, with innate structures that determine the adaptive outcome of learning. These structures are not there by chance. They are a consequence of past selection pressures and processes for neural structures that will learn what the individuals of the species concerned must learn, and learn most effectively. Often the most important element in effective learning is the capacity to filter out the irrelevant – to focus learning upon limited features of the world. Lorenz, as we have seen, called these learning-enabling structures innate schoolmarms or innate teaching mechanisms.

Part of the strength of his argument lies in the accumulating evidence, almost all of it arrived at quite independently of Lorenz by behavioural scientists who would not have identified themselves as followers of classical ethology, that learning is indeed constrained in a manner that is congruent with general life-history strategies (life-style, to be less technical), such that learning does increase the fitness of the learner. Chapter 4 will review some of the evidence, human and non-human, about the limitations of learners to know their worlds. All we need to understand for now is that no learner of any species is a generalist. Whether it be the human capacity for language learning, the ability of song-birds to learn to sing the song of their own species but not that of others heard during the sensitive period when song develops, or the expertise of polygamous male voles in spatial learning which is absent in the males of monogamous vole species who are relatively sedentary in their habits, all point to the general principle that learning is constrained.

Well, what is the source of such constraint? It is not good enough to point only to species-specific developmental patterns. That is only half an answer. The other half of the answer must be that learning constraints are caused by the history of past selection events which now exert their influence through a genetic shaping of those structures of the brain that subserve learning and memory. It is no coincidence that current best estimates are that more than half of the genetic information in humans is directed towards the construction of the central nervous system. There must be a reason for this. Understanding exactly how the information contained in our genes is translated into the structures of our brains is going to be one of the great growth areas of twenty-first-century science.

The kind of image that others have tried to develop from Lorenz's basic position is best described as a nested hierarchy, a sort of Russian doll of things within things, but relating to control rather than structural containment. Through eons of selection events, each species of learner, in the same way that it has parts of its genome partly directing the construction of limbs or kidneys, has other parts of its genome that, under species-typical developmental conditions, will direct the structuring of brain regions concerned with learning and other forms of intelligence, such that the operation of these structures is tuned to the formation of only certain forms of intelligently adapted behaviours. This is a three-level hierarchy – if you prefer, we are talking of three Russian dolls. The third or innermost level is the actual operation of those psychological processes and mechanisms that are generating the adaptive behaviours. From that level all that one can see is the second level. This is the level of development, in which the cascade of epigenesis results in the structures within which resides the potential for learning, memory and other forms of intelligence such as reasoning and problem solving. Hidden behind that second level is the larger and wholly enclosing first level of control, which is the long historical process of evolution, of variation and selective retention of constrained forms of intelligence, and of their endless forging by way of individual development.

So imagine, if you will, that you are some kind of intelligently adapted behaviour looking at its own causal landscape. What is surrounding you is the neural machinery which is your most immediate, proximal cause. Beyond the neural machine are the epigenetic processes by which the machine was constructed. These are what 'told' the machine how to do its job. And then behind the epigenetic processes you can just glimpse, none too clearly, a history of evolutionary processes and events that stretch all the way to the horizon and beyond; it is these that 'prompted' the developmental processes that led to the formation of the neural machinery that produced you. Intelligence, then, is doubly nested. First, within the processes of development, and second, within the processes of evolution. Nature and nurture are inextricably enfolded within one another because nurture has nature, and yet nature must be nurtured and nurture is a part-cause of nature.

Imprinting is a form of learning that occurs early in the lives of many species of bird and mammal. It determines which animal these young creatures follow about in the world, and which they will later choose as mates. A bird that imprints (nurture) has its choice of mate in the future, and hence its impact on the genetic constitution of its breeding population (nature), part-caused by that nurture. The human case may be far, far more complicated, but the differences between ourselves and imprinting birds are ones of quantity. The same deep biological principles apply to us as well. If someone is 'bad', it is because they have acquired what we judge to be inadequate or destructive social behaviours. The acquisition was not random or uncaused. It is a consequence of the workings of certain forms of intelligence operating in a particular environment. The intelligence itself is a product of development, and 'badness' is a consequence of specific kinds of developmental event. It is a commonplace that children who suffer violence and abuse from their parents will wreak violent and abusive 'solutions' upon their own children. A 1995 report on violent young people in the United Kingdom showed that over 90 per cent of such young offenders had themselves been physically, emotionally or sexually abused. So there is actually a doubled effect working here. Intelligence is distorted, and the consequence of that distortion is magnified by a distorted acquisition within a poor environment. In other words, the result is poor learning of bad things. But no intelligence, *and its capacity for distortion*, springs fully formed just from development. History has put in place intelligences susceptible to the damaging effects of deleterious environments.

While most forms of 'badness' need to be explained in terms of all three levels of our control hierachy, some forms of 'madness' might only need two levels. It is likely that conditions such as autism and schizophrenia require only development and the deadly genes or gene combinations that result in the development of these illnesses. It is very unlikely that children learn to be autistic. But the conceptual scheme works whether or not individual intelligence is operating. So, for the human case, nature and nurture are as inextricably bound together as they are for any other species.

The nested hierachy view is not in any way incompatible with that of the developmentalists. Indeed, it is able to incorporate the best of the developmentalist position, and to bolster it by adding an explicit historical dimension. It also provides the basis for resolving one of the oldest arguments in psychology, which is whether human intelligence is some general-purpose device that can be turned to acquiring and mastering anything, or whether intelligence is really a set of relatively discrete skills. Chapter 4 is where this will be considered.

Just words or a real resolution of the problem?

At the start of this chapter I suggested that the nature–nurture problem is of particular interest to an evolutionist because it is the crucible within which psychology's relationship to evolutionary theory will be forged. It is now possible to understand what was meant. The nature–nurture issue is not an option for social scientists; it isn't a conceptual game that we can either choose to get involved in or refuse to play. The nature–nurture problem *is* the central and essential issue that has to be settled for *every* aspect of human behaviour and psychology. It encompasses historical cause, the processes of development in a species in which the individuals are born altricial (that is, with no locomotor ability, very limited sensory capacity, and quite unable to fend for themselves) and which has an unusually prolonged period of developmental change, and the mechanisms of learning, memory, reasoning and decision-making – the very agencies of nurture – which themselves feed back to become causal in both individual development and the evolution of the population to which the individual belongs. Unravelling the nature–nurture issue is what psychology, properly done, is about. It constitutes the complete explication, a total causal explanation of everything that we are and all that we do. Take any psychological problem, from how we are able to see in depth, through why we come to like one person and dislike another, and on to how we are able to write or understand a poem: for a complete explanation, each problem must be decomposed into those constituent causal nexuses that give rise to it. The nature–nurture issue is the unavoidable way by which evolution gets into every psychological nook and cranny.

Now, it isn't just a matter of grand words and waving arms. The nature–nurture question also prescribes an empirical programme. It must do so if it is science. What does it mean to say that nurture has nature? It means understanding exactly what a predisposition is, and how that predisposition was formed. If, as will be argued in a later chapter, we think well in certain ways and poorly in others because we are innately disposed to do so, the fact of it is no more than that. It is merely descriptive. We do or we don't. But *explaining* the predisposition requires a developmental account at a minimum, and clever experiments that aim to root out historical antecedence. Sometimes comparative studies of different species can help. There are case studies that we can learn from, like face recognition in humans and song learning in birds (both to be discussed in later chapters).

So Plato's question doesn't just teach us how to put a complex causal story together. It also tells us what kinds of observations and experiments we should be doing. It points to what a truly successful science of psychology should look like. And it brings with it an account of how to marry the biological and social sciences. Far from being trivial, old hat or resolved, the nature–nurture question is where all the action is, or should be, all the time. It's the only conceptual game in town – the only way to understand why the human mind is what it is.

Suggested Readings

Boakes, R. (1984) *From Darwinism to Behaviourism.* Cambridge, Cambridge University Press. (An excellent history that documents many of the guises in which the nature–nurture problem has appeared.)

Elman, J. L., Bates, A. E., Johnson, M. H., Karmiloff-Smith, A., Parisi, D. and Plunkett, K. (1996) *Rethinking Innateness: A Connectionist Perspective on Development.* Cambridge, Mass., MIT Press. (One of the most important books written in recent years about the nature–nurture question.)

Freeman, D. (1984) *Margaret Mead and Samoa.* London, Penguin.

(Whilst largely a controversial re-assessment of Mead's work, which has been so important to the nature–nurture debate this century, it also contains a detailed general review of the issue.)

Oyama, S. (1985) *The Ontogeny of Information*. Cambridge, Cambridge University Press. (One of the stronger formulations of the developmental resolution of the nature–nurture problem.)

Plotkin, H. (1995) *Darwin Machines and the Nature of Knowledge*. London, Penguin. (An exposition on the nature of all nurture, and hence the resolution of the nature–nurture argument preferred in this chapter.)

3

The Revolution in Our Neighbour's House

During a relatively brief period in the 1970s, the study of animal behaviour changed so radically that it can best be described as a revolution. Classical ethology virtually ceased to exist and was replaced by a potent mixture of sociobiology, often popularly referred to as Selfish Gene Theory, behavioural ecology and Game Theory. Long-established and excellent teaching texts were quickly replaced by books that addressed these new approaches; the scholarly journals devoted to animal behaviour were rapidly colonized by these novel ways of thinking and the older, more descriptive comparative studies effectively driven out of existence. Undergraduate teaching was changed so completely that a course in animal behaviour taught in, say, 1973 or 1974, simply bore no resemblance to one delivered in 1978 or 1979. These most profound changes in thinking all revolved around shifts in emphasis and interpretation of evolutionary theory. Nothing bears greater testimony to the extent to which psychology remains aloof from evolutionary thinking than that these momentous events in what, in effect, is our intellectual and scientific neighbour's house, passed almost unremarked in psychology. Psychology's most important and influential scholarly journals over the period 1975 to 1990, which incorporates the rise and peak of the new thinking about animal behaviour, carried almost no reference to this change. Now, the scholarly papers that appear in journals like *Psychological Review* are extremely influential with academic psychologists. These are the journals that not only reflect current thinking in scientific psychology, but most influence that thinking. The indifference to the new ways of theorizing about, and doing, animal behaviour science is reflected, therefore, in the general textbooks that are the principal vehicles for teaching psychology. The net result is that most students will graduate with degrees in psychology and know either little or nothing about these interesting new theories and whether they have any bearing on the workings of the human mind, or combine that ignorance with antipathy to these new ideas. Well, this chapter aims to remedy the situation in some small way. And it is the antipathy and hostility that form our starting-point.

The problem is that evolutionary theory is often portrayed as having an unpleasant message for humans. It tells us that, at least to some degree, we cannot help but be what two million and more years of evolutionary history have made us, especially the last one or two hundred thousand years which roughly make up the long eras of the middle and upper palaeolithic period during which our species, *Homo sapiens*, appeared and then evolved into what we are today. (Palaeolithic is the word used to refer to the cultural stage of human evolution that covers the period of around two million years before the present to around 10,000 years ago; biologists and geologists use the word pleistocene to refer to the same period.) If modern humans are taken to date from the time of the agricultural revolution of about 10,000 years before the present, then the 500 or so human generations of this period represent less than half of 1 per cent of the two and a half million or so years when the first species of the genus *Homo* appeared on Earth. Ten thousand years, it is argued, is very little time in evolutionary terms. Our biology can have been little altered since the invention of agriculture and the first appearance of city states. What we are now is what we were a long time ago. I will call this the thesis of ancient provenance.

Well, this cannot be true, not entirely at any rate. Human intelligence is an extraordinary feature of our species and it has allowed us to change and adapt, even as it has simultaneously been the engine of change of what it is we have had to adapt to – our intelligence is at once both originator, and adaptive solution to, the new world we have invented. However, there may indeed be parts of the human mind, just as there indubitably are large parts of our corporeal selves, that are just as they were 20,000 or 50,000 years ago. There may, then, be some truth in the notion that we are products of (certainly), victims of (rather more tendentiously), the selection forces that shaped the human mind in previous ages. Of course, a strong evolutionary view asserts the ever-present reality of historical causation, and insists that our minds now *are* the products of evolution and *must* be understood in this light. That was the message of Chapter 1. However, the 'may' of the previous sentences is a caution born of the possibility that our intelligence and our culture are forces so strong in the here-and-now that they 'may' neutralize or alter these ancient parts of our minds.

A variant of this thesis of ancient provenance has most recently, and controversially, been expressed by sociobiology, and one just cannot write a book that surveys the place of evolutionary theory in scientific psychology without considering this school of thought. There is one aspect of sociobiology that must be swiftly mentioned and then disposed of, as it concerns some of the criticism and deep hostility to sociobiology. It is not new that biology, and especially evolutionary biology, has been used by ideologues of different kinds to support their socio-political thinking. Sociobiology, and ethology before it, have been used in this way by both non-scientists and, alas, scientists. As a result, sociobiology as a subject has been sometimes branded as racist, anti-women and anti-working class. It is, of course, none of these things, just as no other scientific discipline is any of these things. There are individual sociobiologists about who may dislike women, I don't doubt. But then there are also racist physicists and anti-working-class botanists. So, without dwelling any longer than we need to on this rather silly claim, let's see what the sociobiological position really is, and on which parts of psychology it may bear.

What is sociobiology?

This is not an easy question to answer. There are different kinds of sociobiology, there are different kinds of sociobiologist, and what they have been saying has changed across the period from 1975 to the present, partly as the subject was advanced internally, and partly in response to the intense critical barrage directed at sociobiology from the outside by social scientists and biologists alike. Crudely, the whole discipline can be divided into three parts. First, there is what has come to be called Selfish Gene Theory, after the title of a highly influential book by Richard Dawkins published in 1976. Second, there is behavioural ecology with its use of what are called optimality models, that try to understand and explain behaviour relating to a particular environment in terms of the benefit that it confers on individual survival and reproduction – what, in other words, is the role of behaviour within the total economy of an animal's life and exactly what form do behavioural adaptations take in different environments? Third, there is the use of Game Theory, an interesting case of an inverted flow of influence. It has usually been the case that biology has been imported into the human sciences, but Game Theory was developed in the 1940s to explain how people come to make economic decisions for themselves and why they dispose of their resources as they do. Some sociobiologists have made powerful use of Game Theory to model competitive interactions between organisms, including social interactions and behaviour. I leave out of consideration here what has come to be called Darwinian or evolutionary psychology, which is concerned with the supposed universals of the human mind which evolved as adaptations to the pleistocene/palaeolithic environment. These are the subject of later chapters.

There are close links between all three strands of sociobiology, and it is somewhat artificial, and also a little difficult, to keep them separate. However, in order to keep this account down to a manageable size, this chapter will focus on selfish genery. This is the aspect of sociobiology that most observers see as central to the enterprise. It certainly is the issue that has attracted greatest critical fire. Some mention, though, will be made of Game Theory as well because one of its implications for human intelligence is striking.

One of the reasons why Darwin was a great scientist was that he was always looking for what he called 'difficulties' and 'objections' to his own theory. Whole chapters of *The Origin of Species* are given over to painstaking appraisal of phenomena that might wreck the theory of evolution by natural selection. One such difficulty lay in the existence of neuter and sterile insects. Darwin believed that the great problem posed by sterile insects was that they display striking behavioural adaptations, instincts in his language, as well as morphological adaptations, often widely different from those of the fertile insects that are their parents 'and yet, from being sterile, that they cannot propagate their kind'. Oddly enough, even though his theory was built upon the central conception of the individual, of individual variation and individual survival and reproduction, it wasn't the sterility that really bothered him, and this was because he explained the sterility issue by shifting ground to what would now be called a group selectionist position. He wrote:

How the workers have been rendered sterile is a difficulty; but not much greater than that of any other striking modification of structure; for it can be shown that some insects and other articulate animals in a state of nature occasionally become sterile; and if such insects had been social, and it had been profitable to the community that a number should have been annually born capable of work, but incapable of procreation, I can see no especial difficulty in this having been affected through natural selection.

The crucial words are 'profitable to the community'. There are thousands of instances, in *The Origin* and in Darwin's voluminous other writings, where it is clear that his theory was firmly built upon the individual: 'each organic being is striving to increase in a geometrical ratio', and 'there must in every case be a struggle for existence, either one individual with another of the same species, or with individuals of different species' are typical examples from his 1859 book. *Individual* variation, *individual* fitness and *individual* selection are at the heart of Darwin's theory. Yet, in the case of the sterile insect castes, his explanation slid from the individual as the unit of selection to the group. That is, the adaptations of the sterile workers are not for the good of the individual sterile insects but for the good of the larger community or group of which they are a part. He had to make this move. After all, if a creature is unable to bear offspring, yet is replete with specialized adaptations and behaves with great purpose, for whom or what is the purpose? Why the adaptations? Darwin's answer was that the purpose and good were that of the group, the community.

The sterile insect castes, none the less, did seem to be the exception, and individual selection the more general rule; and so it was that when the synthesis of genetics and Natural Selection Theory was written in the 1920s and 1930s, it was on the basis of individual fitness and selection. There were occasional lapses into group selectionist language, Konrad Lorenz being one who sometimes referred to 'the good of the species'. But the language only signalled group selectionist thinking when 'the good of the group' became the cause, not just the effect, of individual characteristics. Lorenz often argued that ritualized aggression, which are aggressive encounters in which physical contact between combatants is reduced and regulated by displays that minimize actual injury, is a set of adaptations that is for the good of the species to which the individuals belong. If by this he meant that the adaptations increased individual fitness, and consequently the survival of the species was ensured, then he was no group selectionist. But if he meant that it is variation and selection of the characteristics of different groups or species that cause the traits of the individuals making up the groups or species, then indeed he would have been a group selectionist.

Lorenz was not clear on this point – it actually seemed unimportant to him, as it probably was for most evolutionists of the 1940s and 1950s. The difference between what G. C. Williams later referred to as 'a population of adapted insects and an adapted population of insects' must have seemed obscure and subtle and irrelevant. For some, though, it was a matter of real significance. Some theoreticians considered the issue in terms of the characteristics populations would most likely have if group selection really did occur. Others, like the Scottish biologist V. C. Wynne-Edwards, considered specific examples of traits that might be considered to be for the good of the group rather than the individual. In 1962 Wynne-Edwards published a book in which he surveyed the many cases where animals appeared to act in ways which actually or potentially reduce their own fitness, that is, their own chances of survival and reproduction, whilst increasing the fitness of others. This, of course, is the case of Darwin's sterile insect castes. But it had become apparent by the 1960s that such 'altruistic' behaviours are much more widespread than biologists had previously realized. Typical examples concern the winter groupings that many species of birds and mammals form. Group selectionists like Wynne-Edwards argued that the function of such grouping or flocking is to modulate the reproductive output of the group as a whole in the coming breeding season, this being achieved by the magnitude of the stress responses of individual animals to the conditions of crowding and reduced local resources. So, in a cold winter with many animals in the group competing for few resources, the numbers of offspring in the spring will be less, but that is good for the continuing success of the group which currently has too many individuals in it to be adequately supported by the diminished local resources. Equally, if the weather were milder or the numbers of animals less great, then the resultant reduction in stress responses would lead to higher subsequent breeding rates, and that too is good for the group because the conditions are favourable to larger group numbers. The important point is that the evolution of the stress response and its effects on reproductive behaviour have not, by the group selectionist account, evolved because of its benefits for the individual animals, but because of the benefits it bestows on the group as a whole.

The questions raised by group selection are technical and often difficult, hingeing as they do on what is occurring in variant forms, what selection forces are acting on, what exactly is being selected for, and what is being transmitted across generations. In other words, the questions all revolve around what these various possible units (of variation, selection, replication and transmission) are. Since living things, especially multicellular, sexually reproducing, social living things, are structurally highly complex entities (a social animal has genes inside cells and cells within organs and organ systems; and is also an individual creature that forms part of a social group and many social groups form larger social aggregates), the issue of what is a part and what is a whole becomes proportionately complicated to resolve. For the sake of consistency, and to some extent for simplicity as well, for the rest of this chapter I will adopt the gene-centred position that became the dominant way of thinking about this problem over a period of about twenty or more years, and probably still is the way most evolutionary biologists think. However, in recent years another view tolerant of group selection has begun to emerge as evolutionary theory may apply to humans. This will be taken up in Chapter 6.

So, then, the opinion of several authoritative biologists in the 1960s was that while Wynne-Edwards was running a beguiling line of argument, it could not be correct. This was because the explanation offered by group selectionists hinged upon an assumption about the world of living things that, it was argued, is so unlikely to occur that the position makes little sense. Consider again the example of some species of bird that flock in the winter, as do many common species such as starlings. Now, assume that the Wynne-Edwards position is right in the initial stages of the history of that species, and the breeding behaviour of individual birds has been selected on the basis of what is good for the species. Now, in the fullness of time, and geological time is very full indeed, a mutant bird will be born in which the response to stress is different, perhaps greatly reduced or entirely absent, or in which the linkage between stress and reproductive output has been severed in some way. This uninhibited mutant bird will breed year after year without regard to the stress-inducing conditions that are affecting the other birds in the flock, and will be likely to have more offspring overall than the average of the other birds. Now, if the alteration in morphology (or psychology) that decouples the breeding behaviour of the bird from the winter flocking conditions is heritable, that is, it is passed on to offspring, then not only will the mutant bird, on average, have more young than the other members of the flock, but so too will its offspring, and the offspring of the offspring, all of whom are flat-out breeders. Very soon the flock, or the group, or the species, will be taken over by the mutants and the original good-for-the-group individuals driven to extinction. In every case, apart from humans (more of whom later), species whose adaptations are good for the group (an adapted population of birds or mammals, to paraphrase G. C. Williams) are vulnerable to invasion and eventual takeover by mutant individuals whose adaptations increase individual fitness without regard to the well-being of the group (a population of adapted birds or mammals).

Evolution is a giant statistical machine that crunches numbers over immense stretches of time. In such a world almost anything is possible. There is general agreement among evolutionary theorists that there are certain, unlikely but possible, conditions under which group selection could occur. So perhaps there have been, or there are now, one or two species in which the initial conditions for establishing traits that are good for the group but not for individual fitness of the individuals making up that group, were present, and good-for-the-group traits actually did evolve; and perhaps, by extraordinary chance, mutant individuals whose traits would eventually take over the group have never arisen. Unlikely, yes, but possible. The chances of this being the case for all the many species that display good-for-the-group traits are, however, vanishingly small – so small that no scientist would accept that this is an explanation for all traits that appear to be good for the group or species. There has to be another explanation. Either flocking really does enhance individual fitness, perhaps by helping individual animals to maintain body temperature or by improving foraging efficiency, or something else is driving the behaviour.

The difficulty is the breadth of the failure of group selectionist ideas as the explanation for the existence of behaviours that go way beyond just that of the sterile insect castes or the winter flocking of starlings. There are many other examples of specific behavioural acts which conform to the definition of being altruistic, that is, which reduce the chances of survival and reproduction of the animal doing the behaving (the donor) while increasing the fitness of others (the recipients). And in most cases the explanation seems to be beyond the reach of conventional individual-based evolutionary theory.

In some cases the altruism is of an extreme kind and may result in the actual death of the donor animal. The standard example of this is the likely death of honey-bees once they attack and sting intruders to the hive, as they instantly do. Because of the anatomy of the bee, the stinging mechanism, when activated, may fatally damage the bee that is doing the stinging. In this case the fitness of the donor is reduced to zero, while that of the recipients, its fellow hive-dwellers, is raised in so far as the sting drives off the intruder and safeguards the resources of the hive. But what is in it for the individual bees? Why has not a mutant bee evolved that is somewhat less eager to attack intruders? In other cases, the behaviour of the donor may not put its life at the same degree of risk, but a risk element is involved none the less. All warning signals of danger put the signaller at risk because what alerts others, usually conspecifics, of the presence of danger may be detected by the source of that danger and direct the attention of a predator to the signaller. Why do so many species have warning calls, albeit often shaped by evolution to be hard to localize, when silence in the presence of danger would be a safer strategy? Silence promotes individual fitness and endangers others. Warning signals threaten the fitness of the signaller, but enhance the fitness of conspecifics who receive the signal.

Then there are many well-known cases of helping behaviour in different species of bird and mammal. A famous study of the Florida scrub jay showed that over half the breeding pairs of these jays have one or two helpers who assist in feeding the young birds and help guard against predators. The black-backed jackals of East Africa have been extensively studied and found to have remarkably similar life-styles to the Florida jays. The jackals form monogamous breeding pairs, and each pair, more often than not, has several helpers who render services such as feeding the young animals, and sometimes even feeding the lactating mothers. On occasion the assistance given is distinctly dangerous, as in helping to drive off formidable predators like hyenas. Again, why does this happen? Helper animals are using their own energy resources at the least, risking their own lives at most, in order to rear the offspring of other animals. Exactly what is it that has driven the evolution of this 'anti-Darwinian' trait? Helping behaviour can also take unexpected forms. Social mammals can be divided into species the individuals of which form exclusive nursing relationships between mother and young, and those species that have non-exclusive nursing relationships. In general, non-exclusive nursing exists in species with high predation rates, the trait having evolved, probably, because if the mother is killed this does not mean certain death for her pre-weaning offspring if other females in the social group are also nursing those young animals. In fact, traits like non-exclusive nursing are traits of reciprocal, mutual aid, which are wide open to invasion by cheating mutants who just don't play by the rules – they will take the benefits but not pay the costs. This takes us into the territory of Game Theory, more of which later. But it remains a puzzle as to why animals will nurse the young of other animals and not conserve all their own resources for channelling into their own off-spring. The issue becomes even more puzzling in the case of lions, who are an interesting exception to the rule. Lions, prior to the appearance of humans and even then not until this century when hunting rifles became commonplace across Africa, suffer little or no predation. Lionesses really should not have non-exclusive nursing relations with the cubs of other lionesses in the pride, and yet they do have just that. Well, in the case of species under high predation pressures one can produce the somewhat contorted argument about non-exclusive nursing having evolved because survival of one's own young is ensured, even if the cost is having to nurse the young of others, and this is a situation where the benefits outweigh the costs. However, lions are a clear-cut case where such an argument could not be run. There would, at first blush, seem to be no advantage at all for lionesses to help nurse the lion cubs of others.

The most spectacular case of all helping behaviour, of course, is that of parents towards their own offspring. This really is widespread across many animal phyla. Being the kind of mammal that we humans are, we are steeped in the seeming naturalness of parental care. So it will seem to be an odd question to ask, but just why has parental care evolved? Blackbird mothers in the spring almost work themselves to death pursued by plump, bloomingly healthy young blackbirds who are rapaciously insistent on being fed by their mothers whose nutritional state is vastly inferior to their own. Why does the mother blackbird oblige? As we will soon see, parental care is not always given unstintingly and ungrudgingly, but the fact that it is given at all is not easily explained by Darwinian theory because the parent certainly does reduce its own fitness in some, often several, way(s) in order to raise the fitness of others, even though those others are their own offspring. Classical definitions of fitness in terms of individual survival and reproduction only beg the question. Reproduction, yes, but at what cost?

In all such examples the issue is one of explaining how altruism evolved and why it is so widespread in the animal kingdom – what E. O. Wilson, at the beginning of his 1975 book, referred to as 'the central theoretical problem of sociobiology'. Well, legend has it that it was the great evolutionist J. B. S. Haldane who first indicated the solution to the problem in rather informal circumstances, but it was first done so formally in a series of separate and seminal publications by W. D. Hamilton and G. C. Williams in the 1960s, and then made widely accessible by the Wilson and Dawkins books of 1975 and 1976 respectively. The key to it all is that most altruistic behaviour involves donors and recipients who are genetically related. Let's reconsider all the above examples of altruistic behaviour. The scrub jay and jackal helpers are usually older offspring of the parents they are helping – their behaviour is improving the fitness of their siblings or half-siblings. Honey-bee genetics is more complicated than the genetics of birds or mammals because the females arise from normally fertilized eggs and so have two of each chromosome, which is the structure in the nucleus of every cell, including the sex cells or gametes, which carries most of the genetic information; males develop from unfertilized eggs and so have only single chromosomes. The results are complicated, and not a little bizarre – male honey-bees have neither fathers nor sons, whilst the females, more to the point, are more closely related to their sisters than they are to their mother. This strange form of genetics, called haplodiploidy, is common to many of the social insects that have intensely altruistic behaviours. And what of the strange nursing behaviour of lionesses? Lions have a social structure built around the leaving of the natal pride by young males, the females remaining behind. So the females in a pride are quite closely related genetically – they are mothers, daughters, aunts, and so on, of one another. On average, the females in any lion pride share about a quarter of their genes, and so a lioness nursing the cub of another female of the pride is nurturing an animal with whom she shares a significant proportion of her genes. The resources that she puts into the young of others, in this case, are helping to propagate her genes. The males, incidentally, on average are even more closely related, and male lions are remarkably tolerant of, and sharing with, their fellow males in the pride. As for warning signals, in the many species where individual warning signals have evolved, the social groupings are such that the recipients of warning signals are genetic relatives. Finally, in birds and mammals, of course, parents and offspring share half their total genetic complement – more correctly, they share almost half, because a small amount of genetic material lies outside of the chromosomes.

The heart of what has come to be called Selfish Gene Theory is Hamilton's Rule. This rule normally takes a mathematical form, but what it means is as follows. Every altruistic behaviour has certain, in principle measurable, actual or potential costs for the donor and benefits for the recipients. A particular behaviour will evolve if the cost of the behaviour to the donor is outweighed by the benefits to the recipient, those benefits being weighted by the degree of genetic relatedness between donor and recipient. Technically, because of the complex way in which the genes are divided up among sex cells, relatedness refers to the probability of sharing a particular gene. As a crude shorthand, relatedness can be thought of as the percentage of genes shared overall between animals. They do not always yield the same results, and if one is doing the sums they should be worked out on the basis of probability of shared genes. But for ease of expression I will talk here in terms of percentage of shared genes.

Consider the example of a warning signal. Giving a call that signals a predator costs a few calories in the actual execution of the behaviour. It may, say with a probability of one in twenty, result in the predator locating the caller and attacking it. This could be very costly in terms of flight (many calories), injury and recovery from injury (even more calories), or death. The benefit, though, is that on nineteen out of twenty occasions that the caller calls, it possibly saves some of its neighbours from death or injury. Now, if your neighbours, the ones who can hear the call, comprise on average some immediate family (parents, offspring, sibs), as well as a sprinkling of aunts, uncles and cousins of various degree (as well, inevitably, as some genetic non-relatives), then the caller, though risking itself, is saving relatives. This means that even the (statistically unlikely) ultimate sacrifice is offset by the caller's genetic relatives, that is, those who share some proportion of the same genes as the caller, surviving and themselves having offspring who will further propagate those shared genes. J. B. S. Haldane's famous aside was that he would sacrifice his life for two or more full brothers or sisters (we share, on average, half of our genes with our sibs) or eight or more first cousins (with whom we share one-eighth of our genes).

Hamilton thus expanded the notion of individual fitness to one of inclusive fitness: that is, it is not just the individual's own genes and their propagation into the future that count. It is the shared genes that are also present in others, who by definition are genetic relatives, that are equally important. Hence the concept of individual selection gives way to kin selection. It doesn't matter how genes get to be propagated, just so long as they are. This was the point of Haldane's quip. It isn't the individual that matters – three siblings are better than you or I, the argument goes, because three siblings will propagate yours or my genes better than you or I could do. The name of the game is maximizing inclusive fitness, and there will be selection for behaviours that do this. All instances of altruistic behaviour are behaviours that have been selected because they maximize inclusive fitness, not individual fitness – they result in genes surviving and being propagated into the future in genetic kin, and they may do so at the expense of the individual.

It is clear from all the 'on average' and 'possibles' of the previous few paragraphs that Nature works in a probabilistic fashion. Even though one of the advantages to scientists of the new science of animal behaviour is that, unlike classical ethology, it lends itself to the precision of mathematical formulation, Hamilton's Rule is actually quite complicated and subtle in its workings. For example, animals like ourselves are equally related genetically to our offspring as to our parents. Are we likely, then, to be as altruistic towards our parents as we are towards our children? This would be biological nonsense because our offspring (on average, of course) are biologically more fit than our parents, that is, they are likely to survive longer and reproduce more offspring in the future. It can be expected, therefore, that Hamilton's Rule will have a kind of 'fitness conversion factor' attached to it. Altruistic behaviours directed to offspring are more likely to evolve than altruistic behaviour directed towards parents – although, as we have seen, helping behaviour that assists in the rearing of sibs (who include, after all, possible future offspring of one's parents, hence it might seem worth keeping parents around to produce them) does evolve, but that is sib-directed altruism rather than parent-directed altruism.

Another complication is what is known as the 'gambler's fallacy'. This is the mistake inexperienced (or stupid) gamblers make of distributing their stake, say in a horse race, on the basis of the odds offered on the individual horses. It is a simple arithmetical task to demonstrate that, provided the odds are an approximate match to the likely outcome, then gamblers should repeatedly put all of their stake on the favourite, and not spread their bets across the field in proportion to the odds. Now, as already said, evolution is a giant statistical machine that operates on very large numbers over exceedingly long periods of time. It is unlikely that Nature would commit the gambler's fallacy and evolve altruistic behaviours that are somehow apportioned on the basis of degree of genetic relationship. In an uncertain world, what should have evolved is the concentration of certain forms of altruistic behaviour on those with whom the animal shares the largest fraction of its genes and who is most likely to propagate those genes in future generations; there should be relatively little altruistic behaviour directed towards animals sharing a smaller proportion of genetic makeup, or who are less likely to propagate them.

Despite these elaborations and complications, and there are many others – there is nothing simple about Selfish Gene Theory – the main point to understand is that the explanation for the evolution and continuing existence of altruistic behaviours, biologically defined, is because of the tendency genes have to propagate themselves in the future. It is not the individual who is the unit of selection. It is the gene. Gene selection, then, explains the phenomena that at first sight seem to be explicable in terms of group selection but not individual selection. We have seen, though, that group selection cannot be the explanation for so much and such widespread altruistic behaviour, and individual selection certainly fails to explain it. The concept of gene selection does, however, do the explanatory job. It is what has been called a 'gene's eye-view' of evolution.

It must be said that selfish genery is not the only explanation of altruistic behaviour. There are other possible reasons why animals might behave altruistically to one another. Reciprocity between animals that are not genetically related, a kind of 'I'll scratch your back if you scratch mine', does appear to be present in some species of animal. There is good evidence that chimpanzees, for example, will form mutual help alliances with non-kin in which assistance given now becomes a promise of a return favour some time in the future. Again, this is better understood in terms of Game Theory, which will be briefly considered at the end of this chapter. Another example comes from studies of vampire bats. Bats that had obtained a blood meal during the night have been shown to feed in turn those in the roost who have failed to feed successfully in that same period. Some of the beneficiaries are genetic relatives but some are not. This kind of reciprocity, though, may just be a case of poorly directed and hence inefficient selfish genery that further evolution in time will eliminate. Then there is mutualism in which co-operative behaviour has immediate payoffs for all concerned, for instance by improving foraging efficiency or defending against predators. In both cases, reciprocity and mutualism, one has to switch conceptually back to individual fitness and individual selection to understand them. This switching back and forth may be hard to do, and critics sometimes see it as an inconsistency, a kind of sloppy thinking, that reduces the credibility of sociobiology. It isn't clear why this should be so. There is nothing contradictory or incompatible in both individual and inclusive fitness operating together as forces in evolution, which is a highly opportunistic process. It remains the case, though, that reciprocity and mutualism are peripheral to sociobiology. It's the selfish gene that really counts.

Is sociobiology a reductionist exercise?

The morning that I chanced to begin writing this section started with a quick scan of the Sunday papers. The arts review section of the *Observer* newspaper contained an interesting account of the Snow–Leavis clash over Snow's conception of the two cultures (the arts and the sciences, and how the two, supposedly, never meet). The writer, normally an interesting and amusing commentator, ended his piece thus:

the things that really matter to us – the secrets of the heart, of what it means to be an individual, the depths and heights of human experience – all are accessible, if at all, only through literature and the creative arts. Science has no purchase on them, and precious little to say about them beyond the posturings of reductionists. A knowledge of the biochemistry of the brain tells us nothing about the mind of its owner. And even when the whole of the human genome has been mapped, we will still not know what makes us tick.

In the same cavalier spirit as the piece had been written, I dismissed this last paragraph as fatuous nonsense. But what struck me, as so often in the past, is that when someone wants to strike out at science for some perceived misdemeanour or failure, it is the accusation of reductionism that so often leads the criticism. 'The posturings of reductionists' is a phrase that tells us quite clearly that scientists who are reductionists are the worst of a bad lot. Reductionism has a very bad press, and the most virulent of sociobiology's critics have always had the charge of reductionism near the top of their list of sociobiology's misdeeds. Well, just what exactly is sociobiology guilty of? Let's begin with a brief examination of the concept of reductionism.

There are, in fact, several different kinds of reductionism. Writing on this subject is not helped by different people having different classifications and different names for the same things, and sometimes using the same names with different meanings. It depends in part on whether the reductionist exercise is taking place in the more general context of biology, or the more restricted (and difficult) domain of the mind–body problem. What follows will be more quickly recognized by those who know something of the argument from the point of view of the former rather than the latter. The most fundamental form of reductionism is *ontological* reductionism, sometimes referred to as materialism (or physicalism by some philosophers of biology). Ontological reductionism is now virtually the universally held position in science. This is the view that all things are physical things and nothing else. Take a living creature, any living creature, and it comprises only physical processes and mechanisms. There is no mysterious, ineffable, undefinable, untouchable or unmeasurable force or property of life beyond a very complex organization of chemicals which is described by the laws of chemistry and physics. There is, in other words, no *élan vital*, no life force beyond physics and chemistry. The same argument is run in psychology. Take a person, any person, and while the complexities of their mind might be orders of magnitude greater than the complexities of the chemistry of a cell, the mind is not some non-physical essence that follows that person about. The mind is the workings of the brain, and the connectivity of billions of individual brain cells is of a complexity probably greater than any other known thing, bar one. None the less, no matter how complex that connectivity, the mind and the brain are just chemistry and physics. There are simply no dualist psychologists in existence – nobody thinks that what psychologists study is some kind of immaterial spirit.

The same argument runs with regard to culture. Culture *is* the most complex thing in the known universe because it is some kind of complex organization of (often large numbers of) very complex organizations, namely minds. But culture is not some sort of non-physical essence that fills the spaces between the people making up a society. And, of course, in line with what is preached in Chapter 1, all living things, all minds and all cultures – especially all minds and cultures – are replete with historical causes. Minds and cultures are immensely complex *now* because they are sensitive to and products of complex histories that determine what they are now. But it is all chemistry and physics. As the philosopher and critic supreme of human sociobiology, Philip Kitcher, says: 'Physicalism is true. No antireductionist should deny it.' Whatever sociobiology's errors, it cannot be criticized on the grounds of its ontological reductionism, which it shares with all of science.

The complexity of life, minds and cultures is the reason why reductionism is ever an issue at all. Most forms of reductionism are not just a matter of assuming that one kind of thing can be explained by other kinds of things. There is always an ordering involved and what is thought of as more complex and less fundamental is being explained in terms of the less complex and more fundamental. Take the example of headaches. What constitutes the proper explanation of headaches? There is a considerable psychological literature on the causes of headache and examples are easy to conjure up. 'Mary is an ambitious, hardworking person trying to get on in a world largely controlled by men; her partner resents the amount of time she spends at work and the added demands it makes on him to increase his share of the household chores. So Mary suffers quite a lot of stress coming at her from several directions and her headaches have a pattern that correlates with that stress.' The study of headache, and a causal account of it, in psychological terms is one way to understand headaches. Now, it is also known that headaches correlate with certain changes in the blood vessels in the neck and in the membranes that cover the brain. So a vascular theory of headaches is another way of understanding this condition. Then there is the neurological basis of pain in general, and in particular of the pain that we feel in our head when our cranial vasculature is contracting and dilating following a row with our partners or associates. A neurological theory of headache, then, is also available.

Well, are three separate theories necessary? Might not one theory encompass the psychological, the physiological and the neurological explanation of headache? *Methodological* reductionism gives the answer that in a complex system like the human head the only really 'good' or most 'complete' science is done by studying the most fundamental level of that system. So, in a world where science budgets are limited, we should only fund work on the neurology and neurochemistry of headache. The choice is predicated on the intuition that a phenomenon like pain, though a psychological state resulting from tissue damage or change, *at bottom* (here is the ordering) is a matter of patterns of firing of nerve cells; and that nerve network activation patterns are really the common phenomenon and metric of all psychological states and processes, including having rows with our partners. A surprisingly large number of natural scientists subscribe to this view, which a short period of reflection should reveal as plain nonsense. If nothing else, a psychological study of headache is often both more practicable and therapeutically more useful than a neurological study of headache. There is no compelling argument whatever that science should be directing its attention and resources only to the most fundamental level of any complex system. If there were, then most of us scientists would be retraining for other jobs and leaving all of science to the physicists and chemists. A biochemical study of an ecological system that discounted whole organisms or communities of organisms, or the neurochemistry of consumer choice that eschewed notions of people wanting or needing, would be absurd forms of science.

Now, sociobiology is often accused of some form of genetic reductionism. Well, it can't seriously be thought of as preaching genetic methodological reductionism because there has never been an injunction issued by any sociobiologist that the study of social behaviour be abandoned and replaced by some attempt to trace what parts of an animal's genome are involved in the formation of social behaviours.

On the other hand, while it may often not be practical or useful to study the most fundamental level of a complex system, *explanatory* reductionists argue that the 'best' or most 'complete' understanding of such phenomena comes from an account cast in the terms of that most fundamental level. So, they argue, working on the psychological factors associated with headache is understandable for a number of reasons. But the right explanation, the ultimate explanation of headache, has to do with the chemistry and connectivity of nerve cells. There is no doubt that there is an element of explanatory reductionism in sociobiology's assertion that many social behaviours, including altruistic behaviours, are the product of evolution by natural selection; and that since what is selected are genetic differences between animals that influence their social behaviour, therefore there must be some element of genetic cause in social behaviour that occurs in the here-and-now. However, this is not a belief that is confined to sociobiology. More importantly, no sociobiologist argues that genes alone cause social behaviours. The whole range of causal determinants of behaviour is freely acknowledged, including development, individual intelligence and, in the case of humans, culture. Sociobiologists may not construct interesting or compelling causal stories when it comes to, say, individual learning, and they certainly haven't provided an architecture of these causes in a manner that is new and original to their discipline. That is why it was claimed in Chapter 2 that sociobiology has had nothing of significance to say on the nature–nurture problem. But not having anything original to say about these other sources and causes of social behaviour does not mean that they are out-and-out genetic explanatory reductionists.

It could be argued that when, early in the controversy, Wilson hinted that traditional sciences like physiology and psychology would eventually disappear and be replaced by two major divisions of biology, namely sociobiology and molecular biology, that this was a supreme instance of both methodological and explanatory reduction. That, however, was and is not a typical view – Wilson, more than most sociobiologists, shifted his position markedly over a period of about a decade. Anyway, it hasn't happened, and what sounded like a silly position then reads as even sillier now as subjects like psychology continue to thrive.

Before considering just what kind of reductionism sociobiology subscribes to, completeness requires brief mention of *theory* reduction. This is a form of reductionism that has been quite extensively investigated by philosophers of science and concerns the extent to which different theories relate to, perhaps even displace, one another. Can a psychological theory of headache be related to, reduced to, a vascular or neurological theory of headache? Much of the work on theory reduction concerns the formal study of deducing one theory from another, or of establishing what bridging statements have to be constructed in order to effect such deduction. One thing can be said with certainty about sociobiology. It has not indulged in, or made any contribution to, theory reduction. Whether the older forms of theory, such as they were, of, say, parental behaviour can be formally reduced to an inclusive fitness account is not an issue on which scientists of any kind have spent their time.

None the less, while sociobiology is correctly ontologically reductionist, but no more so than any other science, and while it cannot be seriously labelled as reductionist in any of these traditional ways, neither as methodological, explanatory nor theory reductionist, there is a strong and unusual flavour to the discipline that strikes everyone as being reductionist in some sense. But in what sense? Let's go back to the definition of sociobiology, or at least of its selfish gene part, first given in the previous chapter. Sociobiologists believe that, while there may be additional strands or layers to explaining social behaviour, what must never be lost sight of is the idea that such behaviour evolved in the service of the perpetuation of genes. This most fundamental position of selfish gene sociobiology is part of a wider view that the perpetuation of genes is the engine that drives all of evolution. In his remarkable 1966 book, G. C. Williams wrote that 'the real goal of development is the same as all other adaptations, the continuance of the dependent germ plasm'. In 1975, Wilson said much the same thing: 'the organism does not live for itself. Its primary function is not even to reproduce other organisms; it reproduces genes, and it serves as their temporary carrier.' In the same paragraph he repeats the point with 'the organism is only DNA's way of making more DNA'. (DNA, remember, is the complex chemical structure from which genes are built.) In a famous passage in his 1976 book, Dawkins talks of genes as having 'created us, body and mind; and their preservation is the ultimate rationale for our existence', and by implication they are the ultimate rationale for the existence of all living things. In a later essay published in 1982, Dawkins wrote that 'all adaptations are for the preservation of DNA; DNA itself just is'.

Well, these are striking and deeply interesting claims. And they certainly smack of a kind of reductionism, but it is of a kind created by these writers in recent times and unlike all other forms of reductionist arguments. The claims allow any degree of elaborate other theories about, or studies of, phenomena in biology. It lays no restrictions on what might be said about development, individual intelligence or culture. Let them all exist – they obviously do and they are important – and let theories about them flourish. But always remember, in the end, underlying all the biological and social sciences, the reason for it all, is the 'need' (how else to express it, perhaps 'drive' would be better) for genes to perpetuate themselves. This is a metaphysical claim, and the reductionism that it entails, if it is reductionism at all, is best labelled as *metaphysical* reductionism. Because it is metaphysical it is neither right nor wrong nor empirically testable. It is simply a statement of belief that genes count above all else.

Sociobiology in action

During the last two decades, sociobiology has been at the centre of animal behaviour science. There are few aspects of animal behaviour that have not been interpreted, or reinterpreted, through the theoretical eyes of some or all of the three strands of sociobiology. I want to give the flavour of this work by briefly describing just one aspect of it, which is parent–offspring conflict.

First, the theory. Before the advent of sociobiology, and in particular the analyses of the American biologist R. Trivers, theories on the relationship between non-human parents and their offspring were anthropomorphic ideals focussed upon the nurturing relationship of mothers in particular and the passive reception of resources, especially food, by the young animals. But the ethologists had told us how important it is to observe behaviour over prolonged periods of time in natural environments. This is because many of the important things that animals, humans included, do occupy quite brief episodes and would be, and had been, missed by casual observation. So in the 1950s, 1960s and 1970s, animal behaviour came under more intense scrutiny than had ever been the case before, and as a result many of the received views on what various animals 'are like' had to be changed. Chimpanzees turned out to be hunters and eaters of meat; lions were discovered to have distinctly un-'king-of-the-beasts' characteristics, like killing the cubs of others when they first take over a pride, and being rather incompetent hunters; crocodiles are now known to care for their young; some species of song-bird have regional dialects and accents; and all manner of birds and mammals show a limited degree of tool use. What was also reported in a variety of different species of bird and mammal was quite intense conflict between parents and offspring that did not fit with previous theory. Instead of dedicated parents and compliant, accepting young, a picture emerged of something much more conditional and complicated. Sometimes parents do indeed seem to be uninhibited in the care given, usually soon after hatching or birth. But later they become increasingly reluctant carers, and eventually they reject their offspring. The young, in turn, are far from passive. They urgently press their case for care and attention and may become almost violent when rejected. The noisy and visible conflict which develops may become quite dangerous, revealing their presence to predators and occupying their attention when they could be earning their living more productively with foraging and the like.

Trivers, in a series of early 1970s papers, especially one of 1974, provided a gene's eye-view as an explanation for such conflict. A simplified account of Trivers' theory will be given using mammals as the example, because for a time after birth, in mammals it is usually only the mother who can feed the young. It must be stressed that, as with so many issues in contemporary behavioural biology, the theory of parent–offspring conflict has become both very complicated and highly mathematized. What follows is a greatly simplified account.

Consider first the notion of parental investment. Parental investment refers to 'the investment by the parent in an individual offspring that increases that offspring's chances of survival (and hence which increases the parent's actual inclusive fitness) at the potential cost of the parent's ability to invest in other offspring (and hence which might decrease potential inclusive fitness of the parent)'. The essential point about parental investment is that what a parent is doing now, with this offspring, may affect her ability to nurture offspring in the future: and the doing now certainly is costly in terms of the energy involved in the growth of the foetus and its birth, and the costs of protecting and nursing the young once born until independence from the mother is reached. Now, if a parent has only one offspring in a lifetime, then there is no conflict deriving from the concept of parental investment. All investment is centred on that single offspring and both mother and offspring increase their inclusive fitness. But very, very few species of mammal have only one offspring in a lifetime; the average is closer to double figures, and, of course, in many cases the number is far higher than that.

Consider the situation now from the point of view of the genes and their relatedness in the different animals under consideration. Parents and offspring are 100 per cent related to themselves (an odd, but necessary, part of the calculation). In mammals, parents and offspring share 50 per cent of their genes; and full siblings are on average 50 per cent genetically identical to one another. (Remember, technically, we should be doing the sums in terms of the probability that specific genes are held in common; so, for example, there is a probability of 0.5 that a parent shares a particular gene with its offspring.) From a gene's eye-view of the situation, if the mother's ratio of costs to benefits in nurturing her young offspring is less than one, that is, the benefits outweigh the costs at that moment in time, then both mother and young are at one in their goal, which is one of maintaining the well-being of the offspring. It is to their mutual inclusive fitness gain that the mother cares for the young animal. If the parent's cost:benefit ratio is greater than two, that is, parental care has become very costly to the mother, then because Hamilton's Rule always weights the cost to benefit difference by the degree of genetic relatedness of donor and recipient, which in this case is a half, then the inclusive fitness of the offspring is also threatened if the mother continues to invest in that offspring at the possible expense of other, future, offspring. Genetic self-interest means that when the costs to the mother exceed a certain level, then for the young animal it is other, future, siblings who become important because they may gain more for the young animal's inclusive fitness than that young animal is worth to itself. Once again, the mutual inclusive fitness benefits of both mother and young mean that they are not in conflict with one another, but now the circumstances dictate that parental care should cease for her present offspring, because parental investment in this young animal now may be to the detriment of future offspring and siblings. So when the cost:benefit ratio for the mother is less than one or greater than two, the inclusive fitness benefits for both parent and offspring drive them down the same road – care for the young animal in the former case, or termination of care in the latter case.

But what if the cost:benefit ratio for the mother is greater than one but less than two? At this intermediate level of cost, the inclusive fitness considerations of mother and offspring are in conflict. This is because when the costs exceed the benefits for the mother she is in danger of reducing her inclusive fitness by reducing her chances of successfully rearing young in the future; but for the young animal, it is still in its own inclusive fitness interests that it keep the mother's parental care centred upon itself. It is only when the threshold of the cost:benefit ratio of two for the mother is crossed that the young animal should, as it were, say, 'Go forth and invest in other offspring because they will bear some of the same genes that I have and that will increase my inclusive fitness.'

Every species of bird and mammal should have, during the development of the young, a period when parental care occupies this zone of conflict. What the age of the offspring will be when the care of the young becomes sufficiently costly for the mother that she should turn her attention to the business of future offspring, but is not yet so costly that it is also in the genetic interests of the young that she should do so, and how long this situation of conflicting interests lasts, will vary depending upon species characteristics. Among others, these will importantly include the extent to which care of the young is shared, whether the young are born altricial (that is, in a relatively helpless condition) or precocial (relatively well developed), the rates of development, and the number of offspring born in a unit of time like a breeding season. Documenting the period and intensity of the conflict is an empirical matter for any one species, although one can make quite good predictions if one knows some of the species characteristics just listed. But the theory tells us in broad terms that conflict should always occur.

In their elegant study of the vervet, which is a small species of monkey found widely in sub-Saharan Africa, the American biologists Hauser and Fairbanks showed how the Trivers theory cashes out into behaviour in the same species but living in two different ecologies. They studied conflict between mothers and their offspring in two populations, one of which lives in a swampland environment, and the other inhabits woodland. They recorded significantly higher rates and intensity of conflict between mothers and young around the third and fourth months after birth in animals that live in the swamp compared to their woodland conspecifics. Why? It was not because of any differences in infant mortality rates or predation pressures, because these were shown to be the same for both populations. However, what is significantly different is the availability of food and water, the animals living in the swamp being nutritionally much better off than the woodland animals. As a result, the swamp-dwellers are able to produce twice as many young animals in a year than are the animals living in woodland. This means that the parental investment calculations for each population are different because the difference in nutrition means that much faster breeding is possible, but the rates of development of the young are not accelerated in anything like the same degree. So the swamp mothers potentially lose more inclusive fitness than do the woodland mothers by spending too much time with, and lavishing too much care on, young now, when they will have, on average, twice as many future young as the woodland mothers. At first sight it seems as if the calculation must be the same for the young animals' inclusive fitness as for the mothers', but remember that developmental rates are less dramatically altered by changes in the availability of resources than are the abilities of the mothers to conceive and rear young. So the swamp-dwelling mothers, driven by the consideration of their inclusive fitness gains, are impelled to leave their young earlier than do the woodland mothers, whereas the young of both populations require a minimum period of parental care. Hence the greater degree and intensity of conflict.

The Hauser–Fairbanks study shows how the powerful forces of inclusive fitness operating in both parents and offspring interact with the conditions of the environment to result in differences in the same species living in different circumstances. There have been many other studies of parental behaviour whose surprising results are understandable only in terms of the inexorable arithmetical logic of inclusive fitness theory. For example, Stephen Emlen, an American behavioural biologist, has shown that in a common species of East and Central African bird, the white-fronted bee-eater, the males often actively harass and disrupt the breeding attempts of their own male offspring. This frequently results in the sons joining the fathers' nests as helpers. The reason, once again, is that both fathers and sons increase their inclusive fitness in this way. No other theory will come near explaining such seemingly odd behaviour. So carefully conducted studies such as that of Hauser and Emlen are as nice examples as one can find of work that combines both the selfish gene and behavioural ecology strands of sociobiology. And they demonstrate that one can indeed empirically establish patterns of conflict, and plot the course and nature of such conflict between parents and offspring, depending on ecological and species differences.

Recent reviews have argued that empirical support for the Trivers model is more limited than previously thought, especially in humans where children's tantrums are not tightly linked to weaning. Yet rather than arguing that the theory should be abandoned, commentators like the English ethologist Patrick Bateson suggest that the difficulties arise not because of failings in the basic suppositions of the theory, but rather in its not being sufficiently elaborated with the complex details of observed parent–offspring interactions which are much richer in species like humans than just conflict over resources. Yet, overall, parent–offspring conflict is an instance of sociobiology theory and practice working very well indeed, and it is not an isolated example. The theory would not have come to dominate the animal behaviour literature so quickly and so completely were it not perceived as having very wide application across many behaviours and virtually all species.

But does it work in humans?

Sociobiology's success in helping us to understand the behaviour of animals is no guarantee, of course, that it will succeed equally well when applied to humans. Comparisons across species of the underlying psychological processes and mechanisms that drive behaviour are always hazardous. As we will see in later chapters, the presence of behaviour that, on the surface, appears to be identical in, say, a chimpanzee and a human, says very little about whether that behaviour is caused by identical psychological mechanisms supporting a particular function, or even whether they serve the same function. On the other hand, there is widespread communality across many different species of some psychological mechanisms and processes underlying behaviour, such as associative learning. But the relative importance of associative learning in the overall structure and economy of the minds of different species almost certainly varies; and such basic processes are anyway irrelevant when it comes to the question of whether and how sociobiological theory is important to the understanding of human behaviour.

Let's be clear about the heart of the selfish gene thesis. It asserts that all is in the service of the perpetuation of genes, and that natural selection will have resulted in organisms having behaviours that increase inclusive fitness. Such behaviours could only be selected and retained in a species over long periods of time if they are caused at least in part by arrays of genes that result, during development, in a brain so connected that it will give rise to these behaviours. Roughly speaking, the implication of a genes–brain connectivity–behaviour link, forged in an appropriate developmental environment, is correct if we are considering an animal that can only receive information via its genes. Humans, however, are not like other animals. We differ, amongst other ways, in having an extraordinary individual intelligence that includes the ability to transmit, extra-genetically, large quantities of often complex information between one another. This is the essence of culture, and while little will be said in this chapter about what culture is, how to understand it, and how it might have influenced the evolution of our species – because the whole of Chapter 6 is given over to these matters – one thing is immediately obvious: humans have evolved an additional information transmission system that profoundly influences what we are, what our beliefs and behaviours are, and which may generate causes for what we do and how we behave to one another which might be to some extent independent of the information that we receive from our genes.

That is the nub of the problem of applying sociobiological theory to humans. In fairness, it must be said that sociobiologists either have been aware of this difficulty from the beginning (as in the case of Dawkins, for instance), or have come to it in time (for example, Wilson). None the less, awareness of it must inform all our thinking and judgements about just how applicable the tenets of animal sociobiology are to our species. There is no more stark illustration of the problem than the existence of celibate priests. Biologically speaking, these are people of very low inclusive fitness, yet culturally they are persons often of high social standing and power. It is possible to spin a contorted tale about the evolution of celibacy in a small number of people in a social group because their teachings, which have a greater impact because of their sexual abstinence, raise the fitness of others, and hence their own inclusive fitness since such people will often have genetic relatives in the community. But this is just a story and a not very convincing one at that. The simple point, that results in untold complexity, is that our behaviour has at least two causal forces acting upon it, and sorting out what influence is coming from where is exceedingly difficult. It is the old nature–nurture problem writ large.

None of this denies the possibility that inclusive fitness is indeed a factor that reaches across time through our genes that build our brains whose ultimate objective is the preservation and propagation of our DNA. Perhaps. But how strong that force is, and to what extent the message has become muddied, even overridden, by cultural forces is another matter. An analogy might be useful here. Our ancestors first evolved a bipedal gait some five to seven million years ago, presumably because of the advantages it gave in terms of the reduction in the total body surface area exposed to the harmful effects of the sun, the improvement in speed of movement, enhanced vision, or the freeing of our front limbs to allow them to develop in turn into exquisite instruments for the precise manipulation of small objects. However, the anatomy of our lower backs never did evolve into perfect instruments for walking on just two legs. The result is lower back pain for large numbers of modern humans. Could inclusive fitness be a factor like back pain, an unpleasant vestige from our evolutionary past that we can't quite get rid of?

Let's consider some examples. There are no clear-cut and indisputable demonstrations of Hamilton's Rule operating in humans. Part of the problem is that the evidence, such as it is, comes from observational and interview studies, for example the distribution of wealth to surviving relatives and friends in the wills of people who have died, or who works with, or exchanges information with, whom in fishing communities. The other side of the coin of Hamilton's Rule is what is sometimes referred to as spiteful or exploitative behaviour, that is, behaviour which imposes a cost on the recipient to the gain of the donor. One would expect such behaviour to have a distribution which is the opposite to altruism; it should be differentially directed to those only distantly related genetically to the donor, or to those not related at all. The extreme form of spiteful behaviour is murder. Robin Dunbar has examined Viking sagas and reports that murder of unrelated people was committed for relatively small gains, whilst close relatives were much more rarely killed, and then only if the gains were very large. Provocative as such a claim is, it is not firm evidence.

Cleared of the fog of uncertain history are the data on the pattern of murder in contemporary families collected by M. Daly and M. Wilson of McMaster University in Canada. Whilst it is a commonplace that a high proportion of the overall violence in Western societies occurs in a family setting, these psychologists made specific predictions based on evolutionary theory: they expected that 'genetic relationship is associated with the mitigation of conflict and violence' and that sociobiological theory does 'predict and explain patterns of differential risk of family violence'. Well, the first claim is certainly borne out by the figures. The relationship between murderer and victim is between three and eleven times more likely to be non-genetic than genetic. Overwhelmingly, then, it is husbands and wives, partners, who are being killed by the other, rather than it being parents and children or other genetically related individuals who are victims and killers. Furthermore, when it is the much rarer case of it being parents and children who are the murderers and victims, the results again conform to sociobiological expectations. There is a very steep drop-off in age of mothers killing their children, which can be interpreted in terms of parental investment – younger women have a longer child-bearing period in front of them and so lose less inclusive fitness by destroying their children when they, the mothers, are younger than is the case when they approach the age when they can no longer have children. Similar reasoning accounts for the fact that the murder of children by fathers declines less steeply with the father's age because, it is argued, the reproductive potential of men declines less steeply than that of women. And when children kill their mothers, the figures show a significant relationship with the age of the mother at the time of the birth of the child, older mothers being much more likely to be killed than younger mothers. This is interpreted as being due to the decline in the potential of the mother to increase the child's inclusive fitness by having more children – the older the mother, to put it bluntly, the less she is worth to her present children in terms of having other children in the future. It should be stressed that no one envisages people sitting down and thinking these relationships and consequences through, and then killing some member of their household, or not, on the basis of the calculations they make about their inclusive fitness interests, any more than that is what is thought to occur in non-human animals. What is assumed is that natural selection has put in place devices that govern the direction of spiteful and altruistic behaviours which operate unconsciously and without our having to think about it.

These are a small selection of the facts and figures that Daly and Wilson present, and they have sometimes been challenged for technical reasons that are of no importance here. What is important is that while the statistics do, in general, support the sociobiological thesis in every case, in every case there is an alternative explanation. Consider the fact that the murder–victim relationship is one that is predominantly non-genetic. The alternative explanation is that the 'spousal' relationship is quite different in terms of age differences, competition for resources, and the disruptive intrusion of others into the relationship (sexual jealousy, in short), when compared to the relationship between a parent and its child. In other words, relationships differ along many dimensions, and the degree of genetic relationship is only one of them. The success of sociobiology in accounting for animal behaviour certainly is one small reason why a sociobiological explanation might be considered correct, or partly correct, when weighing which of these dimensions might be the real contributing causes. But it doesn't mean it necessarily is the correct explanation, and its success with other species does not rule out alternatives when it comes to humans. This is the problem with observational studies, which is what collecting the data after the fact is. Collecting the figures from various agencies makes it extremely difficult to hold things constant, to eliminate differences except one which is then systematically manipulated. To do that would be to carry out experiments, which, of course, is not possible when one is studying murder. So one ends up with lots of correlations and complex statistical techniques and arguments, but not much chance of putting a finger on the causes of what one is trying to understand.

Similar arguments, and difficulties, hold for the interpretation of the figures on parents killing children, and vice versa. Young women are frequently less securely placed in their communities and have fewer resources, including experience and other psychological resources, to draw on than is the case for older women. That is at least one alternative, and to many people a very plausible alternative, explanation of why it is that younger women kill their children more frequently than do older women. As for the age differences of women who are killed by their children, that very difference encompasses dissimilarities in mores and values which will be greater between a fifty-year-old and a fifteen-year-old than between a thirty-five-year-old and her fifteen-year-old child, and which will lead to greater tension and conflict. Once again, there are other ways of interpreting the figures, and no good yardstick by which to determine which is the better or more likely explanation.

A particularly chilling figure discussed by Daly and Wilson concerns the killing of children by step-parents. Apparently, in Australia, Britain and the United States, step-parents are about 100 times more likely to kill a child in their household than is its natural, genetic, parent. 'Living with a step-parent is the single most powerful risk factor for child abuse that has been yet identified.' Nor is this an Anglo-Saxon phenomenon, but rather it exists in all cultures, many of which have specific procedures for protecting children following the death of a parent, especially the father. The obvious explanation is that step-parents have no inclusive fitness connection with step-children, hence are less inhibited in their reactions to them. This may seem to be a compelling statistic and argument. However, the step-parent situation provides sociobiology with a big problem. Whatever the increased risks attaching to step-parenting, humans are not lions who kill all the cubs in a pride when they first enter it after driving out the previous resident males. The overwhelming majority of step-parents do not abuse their step-children in any way, and usually provide such children with a loving and supportive home. There is no obvious sociobiological account of such lack of genetic self-interest apart from contorted reasoning about reciprocal altruism (you scratch my back and I'll scratch yours) and the benefits that this will ultimately have on the inclusive fitness of the step-parent.

Murder in families may be thought of as a somewhat grotesque and obscure part of human activity on which to test the adequacy of the sociobiological position. In the minds of those who think about these things, sexual behaviour and sexual strategies are much more central to evolutionary biology and evolutionary theory, for the obvious reason that sexual choice and activity is redolent of biological fitness and the production of offspring. After all, whilst altruistic and spiteful behaviours may raise one's inclusive fitness in the absence of any sexual component to that behaviour, the most common and direct impact on the propagation of genes comes from sexual behaviour. However, most analyses of sexual behaviour by social scientists have not been rooted in evolutionary biology. The maintenance or enhancement of worldly goods, the formation of alliances, closeness in space (sometimes referred to as propinquity theory), or the matching of mates to parents or others of significance in one's life, are some of the sorts of explanation that anthropologists and psychologists have given to explain the patterns of human sexual behaviour.

In recent years, though, some people have begun to turn explicitly to evolutionary theory as a more focussed and precise instrument for explaining our sexual behaviour. Especially prominent in this has been David Buss, an American academic psychologist. Buss derives his position in large part from Trivers' writings on parental investment, briefly considered earlier in this chapter, and partly on sexual selection theory, which centres on the notion that one sex is a limited resource and makes choices that act as the selection force on the characteristics of the other sex, which is a less limited resource. Trying not to do too much violence through oversimplification, one can describe his argument as hingeing on the differences in investment that human males and females have to make in order to propagate offspring, and on the effects that such differences had during human evolution – this is very much a thesis of ancient provenance. In a nutshell, the average human male produces vast numbers (many billions) of sex cells in a lifetime, and at least initially has only a restricted role to play in nurturing offspring. Females provide a much greater investment. They have orders of magnitude fewer sex cells and so have much more to risk than do males in turning some of those cells into viable offspring; they must carry the child internally for around nine months, which is a very long gestation period and a not insignificant proportion of a lifetime which in the palaeolithic period lasted maybe thirty or forty years on average; and they must nurse it following birth, perhaps for up to four years according to evidence from contemporary hunter–gatherer societies. Producing offspring, therefore, cost palaeolithic human females far more than their production cost males. As a result, human females evolved a particular set of sexual strategies of choosing mates who would provide them with the resources with which they could rear their children. Male sexual strategies, by contrast, will focus upon choosing mates who are fertile and healthy enough to cope with the physical stress of child-rearing, on preventing their being cuckolded because putting resources into the offspring of others is a serious cost (and, of course, by the same reasoning, a significant gain for the male whose offspring is raised on the resources of another), and on competing with other males for the control or ownership of the limited resources that determine female mate choice.

Now, because this is a thesis of ancient provenance, the point that Buss and others of a similar view are making is that these sexual strategy differences were selected over long periods of human evolutionary history; that there are genes that build brains that express these strategies in sexual choice and sexual behaviour, and that we all have them. So these are strategies that should be present in all humans of every culture. Well, the somewhat older, comparatively well-off man (carrying the promise of stability and lots of supporting resources) seeking, and often winning, the affections and loyalty of a younger, healthy and attractive woman is almost a caricature of sexual strategies in Western industrialized societies. Literature, films and television soap operas are replete with this image. But is it true, and more importantly, is it true for all humans whatever their culture?

A trawl through the Lonely Hearts columns of British and American newspapers does, it is claimed, support this picture. More importantly, Buss carried out a celebrated survey of sexual preferences in thirty-seven cultures across the world, and produced evidence which he argues supports the position of universal and different male and female sexual strategies. Females are looking for mates who are older than themselves and who either already have the resources to support them and their future children, or who have personality traits like ambition and industriousness, which bode well for their future acquisition. Males, on the other hand, are unconcerned with the resources that women have, seek women younger than themselves, usually in their mid-twenties which is close to the peak of female fertility, and who are healthy and attractive.

There have been many criticisms of the Buss study. The most significant is that the great majority of the purportedly different cultures studied was, in fact, made up largely of cultures that are European, or European-influenced, 'urbanized, cash economies'. Similar responses to Buss's questions might merely reflect similar cultural influences and might have had nothing at all to do with palaeolithic natural selection and genetics. As one critic, David Rowe, put it, even in different cultures 'the use of business suits is now nearly a cross-cultural universal, at least in cities', yet one would, of course, find no evidence of a genetic cause for the adopting of this form of dress. Among other objections, widely accepted, is that a statement of preference cannot be assumed to be equivalent to what people actually do – all men may say they prefer beautiful (whatever that means, which is far from clear) women, but who they marry is a different matter; and that what people say, especially in response to questions about their sexual behaviour, may not be the truth. A nice example of the latter comes from a British psychologist, Dorothy Einon, who has pointed out the strange discrepancy in numbers of sexual partners in a lifetime claimed by men and women. The former consistently give figures three to four times higher than the latter. But every new sexual partner for a man is also a new sexual partner for a woman. The difference in the claims, therefore, can only be accounted for either by the existence of enough sexually hyperactive women (including prostitutes) to make up the difference, or people are not telling the truth. Einon's evidence and calculations, based primarily on Britain and France where the most recent extensive surveys have been done, and which both have populations around or in excess of fifty million people, hence where the numbers or activity of sexually hyperactive women would have to be astonishingly high to close the gap between the claims of men and women, cast serious doubt on the likelihood of a small number of extremely sexually active women accounting for the disparity. It is much more likely a combination of the boasting of men and the overly modest answers of women.

Anthropologists like Mildred Dickemann are especially scathing in their criticism, asserting that Buss's findings are a consequence of poor methodology, and that his results are simply not congruent with the majority of in-depth anthropological studies which reveal widely varying sexual behaviour and practices in different cultures. The existence of such diversity, writes Dickemann, is contrary to Buss's central assumption

that human reproductive behaviour is a set of invariant responses arising from some set of invariant evolutionary dicta. Yet everything we know about human biology and social behaviour tells us that our 'adaptedness' consists of a capacity to grade and modify responses in relation to socioenvironmental circumstances, a highly evolved phenotypic plasticity that is central to Darwinian behavioural biology, human and other . . .

It must be said that Buss has subsequently extended his theoretical position, and published it as one of the few articles on evolutionary psychology to appear in recent years in *Psychological Review*, although he has not improved on the evidence to support it. One of the ways he has moved is to introduce a somewhat more flexible theory that will account in a small way for the diversity that Dickemann is pointing to. However, one simply cannot discount his central ideas about evolved sexual strategies in humans, even in the face of diverse cultural practices. The argument in defence of Buss has been most strongly made by Tooby and Cosmides, both highly influential figures in the declaiming of the evolutionary case on the American academic psychology stage. Tooby and Cosmides made what might turn out to be a very important distinction. Drawing on the differences between a genotype (the total store of genetical information of an individual) and a phenotype (the expression of some of that genetic information, through the complex processes of development, in an individual), they make an analogous distinction between 'an individual's innate psychology and an individual's manifest psychology and behaviour'. The variation in sexual behaviour and strategy between individuals and across cultures is the result of the same evolved innate psychological processes developing within different environments. There is at least one well-known example of an evolved innate psychological process, the capacity of acquiring language, that finds a degree of different expression in different environments that will be discussed in a later chapter. It is perfectly conceivable, then, that Buss is tapping into a similarly innate device that governs human sexual strategy. However, we will only know this to be the case when we have evidence for it. Right now it's a plausible hypothesis, but without some clever experimentation which is able to unpick the way that our beliefs and behaviours have been stitched together, and which will reveal the different causes, including possible innate psychological processes, a plausible hypothesis is all that it will remain. These are genuinely complex matters that are not just confined to questions of sex and sex differences with regard to sex, so we will return to them several times in the chapters that follow.

There have been many other attempts to apply sociobiological thinking to human behaviour. Some of them, such as considering the ways in which certain cultural practices correlate with the degree of monogamy and polygyny within those cultures, are serious and interesting exercises. Others, such as attempts to explain homosexuality, rape or ethnocentrism, are contrived and utterly unconvincing. This chapter, though, is growing too long, and the reader must seek further material in the list of suggested readings. In summary, then, the selfish gene side of sociobiology is proving difficult to demonstrate in humans. Inclusive fitness may be a causal force in human psychology. In principle I cannot see why Hamilton's Rule should not be operating in us. But in the face of powerful cultural forces, the influence of inclusive fitness on our behaviour may be so reduced as to be undetectable by the gross methods of observation and questionnaire studies. This is not a problem confined to obscure and rare practices like celibacy in priests. Almost ten years ago, Daniel Vining of the Population Studies Center in Philadelphia pointed to what he termed the 'central theoretical problem of human sociobiology', which is that in contemporary urbanized societies, with the exception of a unique period from 1935 to 1960, there is an inverse relationship between reproductive fitness, measured by numbers of children actually produced, and endowment, measured by wealth and social status. People at large are not cashing out their resources into producing as many children as possible, which seems to be at variance with the expectations of sociobiological theory. The riposte from Dawkins, among others, was along the lines of the thesis of ancient provenance. Natural selection, he argued, favours 'behavioural rules of thumb which, without the behaver being aware why, tend to have the effect, in the environment where most of the selection took place, of maximizing reproductive success. Change the environment and, of course, you'll be lucky if the rule of thumb works.' Urban, industrialized society bears little resemblance to the conditions of palaeolithic times in which *Homo sapiens* was evolving. Dawkins particularly lit upon the prevalent monogamy of contemporary Western societies as one of the most significant differences from the circumstances of ancient humans, and he challenged Vining to analyse data from contemporary polygynous societies, of which there are many, betting that in these a strong positive association will be found between wealth and status on the one hand, and numbers of children on the other.

Well, perhaps. But that simply does not address the crucial point, which is why large numbers of humans behave in ways which are contrary to maximizing their biological fitness. Are the 'rules of thumb' so weak or delicately poised that they are destroyed by the changed environments in which people now develop and function? And if so, why should they be so weak when what is at stake is the correct operation of a fundamental rule of biological fitness? A recent study of French-speaking Canadian males by the Canadian anthropologist Daniel Perusse makes the point nicely. Perusse has shown that, at least in the population he studied – though there is no reason to doubt that it would also apply to men in other industrialized societies in the West – reproductive and cultural success are not correlated, which is what Vining had pointed out. However, Perusse was able to show that mating success does correlate with cultural success. In short, men of high social status have sexual encounters with more women than do men of low social status. *But for contraception*, it might be assumed that mating success in culturally and materially better-endowed men would indeed translate into higher reproductive success. So, in the case of sexual behaviour, it is contraception which in large part is defying the sociobiological expectation. But contraception is a product of contemporary culture which, as Dickemann points out, has been developed as an adaptive response to reduce fertility and raise parental investment.

It would be too crude and inaccurate to characterize the story on human sexual strategies as one in which culture wins out all the time over biology. If nothing else, this is early days in the argument. However, what must be understood is that culture is a part of our biology, and the central issue is how to bring about a synthesis of sociobiology, so successful in accounting for much of animal behaviour, and perhaps applicable to humans provided the evidence for it stands up to scrutiny, with the social sciences that try to understand human culture.

Playing games with Game Theory

In the mid-1960s a popular science book was published by Lorenz. Entitled *On Aggression*, it came to have a significant influence on the thinking of those of the general public who have an interest in matters scientific as they relate to human nature. In the book Lorenz presented in some detail a view of the adaptive nature of aggression and the way in which aggressive interactions are modulated and softened in their effects by ritualization, which serves always to reduce actual physical damage between combatants – with one exception. Humans are a species in which such safeguards, for some reason, have disappeared, and so we are a uniquely murderous kind of animal. This idea gained much popular currency, which it still retains. In fact, it is factually wrong and theoretically flawed and limited. In many species of animal, individuals will kill others of their own species under certain circumstances. This stretches across wide reaches of the animal kingdom. It includes many vertebrate as well as invertebrate species, and includes perennial favourites like the chimpanzee. So much for the generalization that only humans uninhibitedly kill one another. And that is what was wrong with the theory. It was just a general, blanket statement with little analytical force, and no explanatory power at all when intensive animal behaviour study revealed more and more violence in the animal kingdom. Lions kill other lions under particular circumstances, being neither indiscriminate killers of their own kind all of the time nor mere adopters of aggressive postures (ritualized behaviours) without ever hurting one another. Adult rabbits will kill the young of other rabbits, but only on certain occasions.

In the early 1970s, John Maynard Smith, of the University of Sussex, developed a framework for understanding the 'iffy', the conditional, nature of such aggressive interactions. It was based upon an extension of Game Theory, which was first established in the 1940s and 1950s by the mathematician John von Neumann and the economist Oskar Morgenstern. Von Neumann and Morgenstern's central assumptions about interactions between people who are exchanging goods or competing for a resource were that people, players in Game Theory language, are rational and self-interested. In turning Game Theory into a framework for understanding the biological principles that govern behaviour more widely, Maynard Smith assumed that the latter characteristic is subsumed by the notion of Darwinian fitness, and that the former, rationality, could reasonably be translated into the assumption that population dynamics tend towards stability and don't fluctuate wildly and randomly.

The central idea in the application of Game Theory to behaviour is that behaviour is functional only in the context of the behaviour of others. Using the young of your neighbours as an easily accessible and cheap form of nutrition is a good idea if almost no other animal in the warren is doing it. But as the frequency of infanticide increases in a social group, then your own young are at risk when you are not there to protect them. This frequency dependence is at the heart of what Maynard Smith called an evolutionarily stable strategy, which is a strategy with the property that if all the members of a population have it and use it, then no mutant strategy can arise which will successfully invade and drive out the old strategy. In some species like rabbits, a strategy of no infanticide is not stable because mutant infanticidal animals will arise in time and successfully invade a colony; and a strategy of all-out infanticidal behaviour by all members of a colony is equally unstable because the attrition on young animals would be such that the colony would not be sustained. Depending upon the ecology, which would include factors like the availability of other food sources and predatory pressures, infanticide will be a behaviour adopted by the members of a social species like the rabbit at a frequency which is evolutionarily stable.

Though much of the early work on the application of Game Theory in biology concentrated on aggressive behaviour, because the theory gives rise to quantifiable models, is more in tune with the observed complexities of social interactions, and is mindful of the real ecology in which animals live, it quickly became one of the dominant themes in the study of animal behaviour at large. Widely differing behaviours became grist to the mills of the Game Theorists.

One of the most interesting applications of Game Theory has been in trying to understand how co-operative behaviour could evolve and be maintained. As we have already seen, inclusive fitness is one way in which behaviour that benefits both the recipient and the donor will evolve. Game Theory demonstrates another, and quite different, process by which altruism, reciprocal altruism, can evolve. The problem with reciprocal aid is that it is vulnerable to cheating. Only human culture has put in place the structures of coercive laws that ensure that, for example, reneging on a debt or on a promise of a return of help in the future as a price of receiving assistance in the past, does not occur. However, whilst direct economic exchange in humans may be safeguarded by legal sanction, most co-operative behaviour in humans, and all co-operative behaviour in animals, cannot be protected in this way. Yet it most certainly does occur. Reciprocal co-operation is widely assumed between friends, neighbours or work-mates when no genetic kinship is present. We all know that cheating can occur and are sensitive to the possibility of its occurrence, but mostly it does not. Similarly, reciprocal aid has been reliably reported in all manner of non-human animals, including the vampire bats mentioned earlier in this chapter. And reciprocity is prominent in the social behaviours of monkeys and apes. How can the evolution and maintenance of such vulnerable behaviour be explained?

One of the principal ways of understanding reciprocity uses a particular form of game called the Prisoner's Dilemma, which was first devised nearly half a century ago. The name of the game derives from the predicament of two prisoners, friends, being held in separate cells by the police, who think that they were accomplices in a crime. An officer visits each prisoner in turn, and informs them that the offer now being made to them has been, or will be, made to the other prisoner. The offer is that if they will give evidence against their alleged accomplice then they themselves can go free and the accomplice will receive a heavy jail sentence. If neither implicates the other then there is enough evidence for them to be found guilty on a lesser charge and receive relatively light sentences; but if each implicates the other then a more serious charge will be brought against them and they will be jailed for quite a long time, though not as long as will be the one who was fingered by the other and who did not himself betray his friend. So the ordering of possible punishments is 'none' if you betray your friend and are not in turn betrayed; 'some' if neither betrays the other; 'quite a lot' if each betrays the other; and 'a great deal' if you have been pure in spirit and not betrayed your friend and he has betrayed you. As a result, each prisoner, knowing that the other has been made the same offer, reasons that if they betray the other, then they might get off completely; however, each realizes that the other prisoner must be having the same thoughts. Each knows that the best outcome is that neither betrays the other, but each understands that they cannot take the risk of not betraying the other because the cost of being a 'sucker' in this situation is the heaviest of all, and first prize goes to the one who betrays and is not himself betrayed. So each betrays the other because of the peculiar logic of their predicament and each goes to jail for much longer than would have been the case if they had trusted one another and neither had betrayed the other. That is the dilemma. In a Prisoner's Dilemma game of just one episode, the 'best', the 'safest', response is always to defect rather than co-operate because although the gain for mutual co-operation exceeds the costs of mutual defection and betrayal, the reward for one-sided defection is greatest of all.

However, the picture changes completely if the Dilemma is repeated again and again, when it becomes known as the Iterated Prisoner's Dilemma game. Consider the situation where a student comes to me and says that she knows that I am venal and corrupt and £10,000 is mine if I let her see the final year's examination papers – before the exams are sat, of course. I reply that this is a fine idea but we must be discreet in our arrangement and not meet again. Instead, when I have all the examination papers gathered together, which will be on a specific date that I name, I will place them in an envelope which I will, that evening, tape under the bench at the top of Parliament Hill; you, the student, in turn will at the same time leave the money under a stone in Gordon Square in Bloomsbury. Now, if this is just a once-in-a-lifetime exchange, then we are back in the situation of the Prisoner's Dilemma. This is because we both go away and ponder the relative benefits of betrayal. I think that the student may cheat me and collect the examination papers without leaving the money – and I certainly could not approach some higher authority to plead that an injustice has been done. So perhaps I should not leave the examination scripts under that bench. Indeed, the more I think about it, the better an idea this seems, because the best possible outcome is that the student leave the money and I don't hand over the questions – after all, in that case the student equally would have no public claim to make against me without impugning her own honour. The student is harbouring mirror-image thoughts of betrayal, because the best deal for her is not to deliver her part of the bargain and hope that those examination questions are under that bench on Hampstead Heath. This is precisely the dilemma of those prisoners in police custody, but transplanted into a different situation. So, despite the fact that mutual co-operation would have left us both happier, me with the money and the student with wonderful results in the final exams because she had prior sight of the papers, in the end we both betray the other and no one gains at all.

But think now of a fantasy world of the future where computers do all the work and fifty-year university degree programmes have become a major leisure industry. The student and I enter into a relationship of 'mutual help' as before, but with one difference. Examinations are now a monthly event and we hope to 'help' each other each month for many years. This is now the iterated form of the game, and co-operation and defection begin to look very different. After all, why defect early on in the game, when it might incur retaliation? On the other hand, it seems to me, as it may to the student, that defection is always a tempting option because on that exchange, especially an early exchange, the defector may feel she will likely gain something for nothing because the other member of the relationship might not yet be thinking in terms of betrayal, so the defector may gain a reward without incurring an immediate cost. The cost of betrayal is always in the future in an Iterated Prisoner's Dilemma game and always involves the partner ratting on their part of the deal. Well, what is the best strategy? Always defect from day 1? Or co-operate until one has been betrayed and then defect for ever? Or, once betrayed, renege on the deal oneself on, say, three occasions before returning to co-operating again? Or turn the other cheek? And if so, for how long? Even with just two possible responses, co-operate or defect, the number of possible strategies is huge. How can one know which is the best one to adopt?

One way of finding out the answer is to simulate the game on a computer. In a famous study carried out at the University of Michigan, this is what political scientist and Game Theorist Robert Axelrod did. He set up a computer tournament, inviting prominent Game Theorists and others with an interest in the subject to submit entries of their strategy for an Iterated Prisoner's Dilemma game in which each strategy, in effect a little automaton that either defects or co-operates in each encounter in computer space with another little automaton, played every other strategy several hundred times. Each interaction between any two strategies resulted in certain losses or gains, depending on whether the co-operation or defection was mutual or not, and the overall score for each strategy was added up at the end of the tournament. Now, while the extreme strategies of 'always co-operate whatever has been done to you in the past', which is always a losing strategy, and 'always defect', a highly aggressive and, under certain conditions, successful strategy, need no supporting psychological processes, all other strategies in an iterated game do have a minimum psychological requirement in the form of memory. At the least, each little automaton must be able to remember whether the other automaton that it is interacting with now defected or co-operated the last time they met. For example, the strategy that won the Axelrod tournaments, called 'Tit-for-Tat', always begins its first play with a rival strategy by co-operating. Thereafter it does to each opponent what had been done to it in their previous encounter. Tit-for-Tat is characterized by Game Theorists as being 'nice' (it is never the first to defect), 'forgiving' (it does not hold a grudge) and 'provocable' (Tit-for-Tat never turns the other cheek). It was also astonishingly successful, despite its simplicity – the strategy itself required just four lines of computer programming and needs to remember just one thing with regard to each other contestant in the game. A variant on Tit-for-Tat is a strategy, called 'Joss', which co-operates at the start, responds to a prior defection with a defection and usually replies to co-operation with co-operation. But this strategy consults a random-number generator to decide when to pull out the occasional surprise defection. Another variation, known as 'Generous Tit-for-Tat', is the reverse of Joss. It is just like Tit-for-Tat, except that it occasionally responds to a defection with co-operation, so it is even more forgiving than its parent strategy. Experiments subsequent to the Axelrod tournaments have shown Generous Tit-for-Tat to be an outstandingly successful strategy when played against other strategies. And just recently a strategy named 'Pavlov' has been shown to be even more successful. Pavlov uses a win-stay, lose-shift strategy, that is, if its previous interaction with a particular other strategy had a high payoff, then on the next trial it does the same thing, and if not it switches. So Pavlov too requires a relatively limited memory capacity. Not all strategies, of course, are 'nice'. Joss is a little nasty and others can be downright mean, for example, one might co-operate until defected against, and then defect for all time. Pavlov is a decidedly nasty character because confronting a strategy that is nice and which seldom if ever defects, Pavlov keeps on defecting – remember, the highest payoff in the game comes from defecting when the other player co-operates.

An important point to note is that which strategy accumulates the most points depends on many things, for example the precise makeup of the other strategies, the balance of 'nice' and 'nasty' strategies, and how many iterations (trials) are played. These tournaments have also been run as 'ecological games' in which the scores are converted into numbers of offspring, thus simulating the changes that might occur in a biological population. In this case, a high-scoring strategy will increase in frequency in a population whose constitution is changing, and a low-scoring strategy decreases in frequency.

Axelrod's tournaments quickly became famous because of the surprising victories of Tit-for-Tat, and later of Generous Tit-for-Tat. It seemed that these experiments showed that nice, co-operative strategies could and would evolve, even in a world initially dominated by nasty strategies. The appearance, and the success, of Pavlov rather changes the picture. Perhaps being nice isn't good enough. Perhaps the evolution of co-operation is more complicated than the outcome of the Axelrod tournaments suggested. What is certain is that introducing Game Theory into the study of social interactions has been immensely interesting and fruitful. Game Theory does have one other interesting implication, though it is no stronger than an implication. It is this. In Chapter 5 we will consider what is known as the social function of intellect hypothesis. In a nutshell, this suggests that the engine behind the evolution of intelligence is the complexity of social interaction and understanding that is necessary if one is to get on well and thrive in a social group. This seems to be a plausible view. Yet the Game Theory tournaments have shown that the most simple of social strategies with the most limited of memory requirements will thrive and evolve. It could be, of course, that the Game Theory tournaments are just hopelessly inadequate test-beds for the evolution of co-operative social behaviours. But it may also be that they point to inadequacies in the social function of intelligence hypothesis.

Overview

Even a chapter as long as this one does scant justice to the elegance and conceptual power of contemporary animal behaviour science. Too little has been said about behavioural ecology and there are so many other interesting examples of the use of Selfish Gene and Game Theory that illustrate the range and strength of this approach. However, as already pointed out, the success of what I have been calling sociobiology when applied undiluted to humans is much more questionable. I do not doubt that some of the causal forces operating in the behaviour of animals are also present in humans. But there may be few, if any, aspects of human psychology and behaviour that can be understood without reference to the causal forces of human intelligence and culture.

Suggested Readings

Axelrod, R. (1990) *The Evolution of Co-operation*. London, Penguin. (Classic Game Theory account of the origins of co-operation.)

Buss, D. M. (1995) 'Evolutionary psychology: a new paradigm for psychological science.' *Psychological Inquiry*, vol. 6, 1–30. (An overview by someone who believes in strong application of sociobiological theory to humans.)

Dawkins, R. (1989, 2nd edition) *The Selfish Gene*. Oxford, Oxford University Press. (The original popular account of Selfish Gene Theory with two chapters added to the 1976 edition, one of which concerns Game Theory and co-operation.)

Horgan, J. (1995) 'The new social Darwinists.' *Scientific American*, vol. 273, 150–157. (A sceptical look at the new evolutionary psychology.)

Kitcher, P. (1985) *Vaulting Ambition: Sociobiology and the Quest for Human Nature*. Cambridge, Mass., MIT Press. (Best and most detailed critical review of the application of sociobiology to humans.)

Nowak, M. A., May, R. M. and Sigmund, K. (1995) 'The arithmetics of mutual help.' *Scientific American*, vol. 272, 50–55. (Explaining why tit-for-tat doesn't always win.)

Rose, S., Kamin, L. J. and Lewontin, R. C. (1984) *Not in Our Genes*. London, Penguin. (Strongly argued case against genetic reductionism being applied to any aspect of human function.)

Williams, G. C. (1966) *Adaptation and Natural Selection*. Princeton, NJ, Princeton University Press. (The original reductionist attack on group selectionist thinking, and the most elegant and influential book written on evolutionary thinking in the last half century.)

4

The Structure of the Mind

Does the human mind have a structure, and if so what is it? Some people find this an odd question. Everyday experience suggests that the mind is some unitary entity without internal boundaries. If I am hungry I may go to a sandwich shop, choose what I want, pay for the item of my choice and then eat it. I do not have a sense of using one part of my mind to move my legs, another to navigate my way through streets, and yet another to calculate whether the change I am given is correct. The seamless quality of normal experience, however, may be an expression of just how well the different parts of our minds work together. Less normal experiences that have their origins in disease, accidents or the effects of drugs tell a different story. Alcohol, for example, if used to excess will excise certain forms of memory and leave others intact, as surely as will the scalpel of a surgeon. Surgery, carried out to control the spread of epilepsy or to remove tumours, will sometimes eliminate visuo-spatial skills but leave all of memory untouched. Even the entirely normal condition of development in the infant and child tells us, for instance, that the analysis of raw sensory data, from our eyes, say, and the constructions based upon that data, is in some important sense different from, bounded off from, the understanding and use of language. There is a very large body of evidence of this kind. So while the mind is very good at hiding its structure because its constituent parts usually articulate so well with one another, all the evidence points overwhelmingly to a structure of some kind.

Others will think this a truism. In one sense everything has a structure and the mind can be no exception. Furthermore, unless one holds the dualist position that the mind has an existence independent of our bodily selves – and few scientists are of this view – then the mind must in some way relate to the brain, and the brain certainly does have a structure. However, accepting that the mind must have a structure does not answer the question as to what that structure actually is. More importantly, it does not tell us when the issue of structure is a trivial matter and when, and why, it becomes a question of profound importance which encapsulates some of the most interesting and fundamental theoretical problems, and hence sources of disagreement, within all of psychology. What I aim to do in this chapter is consider through an evolutionist's eye-view this most basic of all psychological issues as it applies to one broad area of psychology, namely cognition, because it is with respect to cognition, the 'knowing' parts of our mind, that structure is at the centre of the most fierce and most fascinating of disputations.

Let's first get rid of the issue of structure when it is a matter of little current significance, even if in the long distant past it warranted much thought and analysis. In the nineteenth century, the mind was thought to have three major components: the emotions (the feeling components of mind), conation (the willing part of mind) and cognition. Nowadays the partitioning of mind is somewhat more closely resolved, and every general psychology text has chapters or larger divisions on specific topics, for example, perception, emotion, learning and thought. These, by and large, are a reflection of the currently held view of the structure of mind. Of course, there will also be chapters on integrating themes such as development and pathology. But such higher-order conceptions apart, the fact is that psychology has non-arbitrary divisions within its subject matter which reflects current understanding about where the suture lines lie that mark off the structure of mind. Just as in medicine where people may specialize in the functioning and pathology of specific organs or organ systems, be it brains, livers, bones or whatever, which represent the structure of the entire body, so a parallel situation exists within psychology.

It must not be thought that a structural description of a complex system implies functional separation. It doesn't. Quite the contrary. Brains and cardiovascular organ systems are structurally separate components of our bodies. But what happens in the one can, and usually does, have an effect, sometimes a profound effect, on what happens in the other. Well, what applies to the structures of the body applies also to the structures of the brain and the mind. Emotional states can and do have an impact on what we attend to, how well we are able to carry out complex tasks of motor co-ordination, and what kinds of decision we make when facing choices. Emotion, attention, motor control and decision-making are quite different parts of our minds with separate neurological linkages, but functionally they are closely stitched together. The stitching, of course, is also a part of the structure.

So, then, the psychological and neurological evidence of many kinds demonstrates that whilst functionally linked, emotion and attention are different structures of mind sited in separate divisions of the brain supporting specific processes and mechanisms. This is undoubtedly important knowledge about the structure of mind. However, because it is presently not a matter of dispute at all, it is not the kind of issue that receives much attention at all; most psychologists would happily agree that emotion and attention are separate, if interconnected, parts of the human mind. Pretty much the same acceptance would apply to the assertion that emotion and motor control, for instance, are discrete psychological divisions. Where the picture changes is when structures are postulated as existing *within* domains of function that are already widely accepted as being separate structurally from other domains of function. The devil of disputation, in other words, lies in the detail.

This is not too surprising. After all, claims about structural details at anything other than the gross level that demarcates one structure off from another, are detailed claims about what it is one is trying to understand. Yes, yes, we may say, of course emotion is different from attention, but the big questions about emotion are about the details within the realm of emotional function. This is where the big arguments about emotion are and where the big questions are settled. Now, throughout the history of psychology, but particularly in the last couple of decades, this has been especially the case for cognition. What exactly is the structure of the knowing mind? Do the various words that we have for possibly different forms or aspects of cognition, like learning, language, spatial orientation and thinking, to name but a few, reflect real differences, discrete functions and structures of the knowing parts of our mind? And when we come to have different kinds of knowledge, for example of a language as opposed to the spatial layout of our homes or neighbourhoods, are these the end-products of different processes and mechanisms sited in different structures, or are they the result of some single process of knowledge acquisition? These are the questions that bring out the crowds because, to some at least, while it might be overstating it to say that this is the only game in town, it certainly is the biggest and it relates to the nature–nurture problem. It is the question that lies at the heart of much of contemporary scientific psychology. Because this is such a dominating issue, I will devote the rest of this chapter to a consideration of it; and because language has been the psychological characteristic over which the battle has raged most fiercely and where the issues are defined most clearly, it is language that will take up much the greater part of our attention.

Is language an instinct?

Language is an extraordinary human psychological trait. In the second half of this century our understanding of what language is and how we come to acquire it has been one of the principal conceptual battlegrounds in psychology fought over by two broadly defined and seemingly very different approaches. The one, the older of the two, says that language, complex though it may be, is acquired and then used by the same general cognitive processes and mechanisms, the same intelligence if you like, that humans use to acquire other information and skills. The two most prominent proponents of this position were Jean Piaget, the Swiss developmental psychologist, and B. F. Skinner, the American behaviourist. The other, which leaped to prominence in the 1950s and 1960s, based initially upon structural linguistic analyses of language, asserts that language is an innate organ of mind operating in different ways and using different processes and mechanisms from other cognitive functions. Intelligence, in other words, is not just one thing. This second approach owes most to Noam Chomsky, the American linguist. A recent prominent spokesman for this view is the psychologist Steven Pinker, whose book *The Language Instinct* is the source of the sub-heading above.

Consider first what language is not. It is not just a signalling system equivalent to smiling, dilated pupils, a slumping posture, or other such non-verbal forms of communication. There are aspects of language that take on this emotional signalling function, such as loudness and vigour of voice and intonation; however, this is simply a case of non-verbal signalling attaching to language. However much importance non-verbal aspects of language have both in the acquisition of language by infants and for its subsequent function as a channel of communication between people, and some psychologists accord them very great importance in these roles, they are not the defining features of language. Unlike language, non-verbal communication is widespread among animals, and is especially rich in primates. Nor is language merely a linear sequence of unitary elements, from the most basic (phonemes) to the most complex (sentences), that are acquired as a string of such elements and invariantly sequenced in the same way on all future occasions of use. Nor is language limited in its referential qualities. These last two points, relative fixity of surface structure and limited reference, again are characteristics of signalling found in other species. For example, the ethologist Von Frisch showed many years ago that honey-bees communicate specific spatial positions of food sources or potential new hive sites, and even their quality, to their fellow bees by performing a 'dance' on their return to the hive. But that is all they communicate. More recently, the African vervet monkey has been discovered to have several specific calls warning of different kinds of danger and fellow vervets respond in ways appropriate to the threat to which the call refers. Here again, the reference is very limited indeed. And then there are the attempts over the last thirty years or so to teach language to apes.

Following earlier failures to train chimpanzees to speak, and the realization that such failures may simply have been due to the animals not having the requisite peripheral structures, such as an appropriate vocal cord apparatus and its neural control, experiments were begun which attempted to teach chimpanzees American Sign Language. The reasoning behind this work was that some species of ape might indeed have the cognitive abilities necessary for the learning and use of language, but to demonstrate this it is necessary to marry such putative language capacity with an appropriate peripheral effector system, and perhaps the language input should come via a channel better developed in chimpanzees than is hearing. Well, chimps have good manual skills and highly developed visual systems. Might it not be that such animals could acquire language in much the same way that deaf children are able to do? Using either sign language, or physical tokens, or symbols generated on computer screens, several major research programmes extending over many years have given us the answer, which is no. The animals certainly were adept at learning hundreds of signs, most of which were for objects (like water), much the smaller number being for actions (go, for example) and action modifiers (such as more). This does not, however, in my view, constitute language.

Having language is having the ability to use a limited set of symbols to generate a virtually unlimited number of combinations to form utterances, each of which has meaning. It is very unlikely that I have ever generated the previous sentence in precisely that form before. And that sentence is just one of an estimated 10^{30} that you and I and every other normal human being are potentially capable of producing – potentially, because 10^{30} is a very large number, so large that in our allotted three score years and ten of life, even if we never stopped speaking, we would utter only the tiniest fraction of the sentences of which we are capable. *Creativity* of symbol use, despite that creativity occurring in the context of a system of rules that constrain the structure of all languages, is the *sine qua non* of language. Symbol use *per se* does not define language. Apes seem to acquire limited numbers of symbols, though whether they function as symbols for them is entirely unclear. But there is little sign of structure and none of creativity. Even the most celebrated of pygmy chimpanzees, Kanji, would produce 'sentences' like 'Ice water go'. Well, this *may* be interpreted as meaning 'Bring me some cold water', but even such liberal acceptance of possible meaning cannot hide the poverty of the utterance. Every human being beyond a certain age could ask for water, cold or otherwise, in hundreds of different ways, all of which would be well formed and precise in their meaning: 'I want some water', 'Get me some water', 'Water is what I want', 'Please would you be so kind as to bring me some water' and 'Water now!' are just a very small sample. Furthermore, Kanji, as described in a recent book by Savage-Rumbaugh and Lewin listed in the references at the end of this chapter, is reputed to be able to respond to sentences containing conditionals, transformations and other complexities in a manner indicating understanding. But the evidence appears to be anecdotal and either non-replicable or unreliably replicable. Whatever interesting light these studies throw on the cognitive abilities of chimpanzees, they do not demonstrate the presence of language in these animals.

People like myself who draw this conclusion are not making doctrinaire claims intended to protect the special nature of man. Nor, of course, is it an anti-evolutionary position. There is no doubt that chimpanzees must have psychological processes and mechanisms (a' features in the symbols of Chapter 2) that are either the same as, or have evolved from, certain features (a features) in the minds of the ancestral apes that were the common ancestors of both contemporary humans and chimpanzees, and from a evolved the features (a'') that give humans their language characteristics. This is an absolute requirement of the theory of evolution. But the theory does not say that we have to share *any* traits, in the sense of having identical features, with contemporary related species, though close relatedness (and we do share most of our genes with chimpanzees) increases the likelihood that some traits will indeed be shared. So we draw the conclusion that apes don't have language because the evidence does not support the claim. It is to the credit of those who have carried out these studies that the work has often been of a high standard and at great cost of effort and time. Other studies, some of which will be reviewed in Chapter 5, that have attempted to show different human qualities in other primate species, have often been without these virtues. What the ape language studies do seem to share with experiments on the likes of 'mind-reading' and 'self-awareness' in other apes is a prejudiced stance among many primatologists who want to see such 'upper'-level human cognitive abilities in other primates, and hence make inflated claims for what their studies show.

Now, in contrast to our nearest animal relatives, human beings communicate through some 5,500 documented languages. All of them are characterized by a phenomenal creative richness, and all are characterized by grammatical and syntactical constraints. Any human infant is able to learn any one of these languages. Take a baby born to French parents and raise it in the northern Transvaal and it will grow into a fluent speaker of Shangaan. There is no link between genes and the specific language that an individual will come to speak. There most certainly, however, is a link between the ability to acquire language and genes, just as there is for any trait in any species when that trait is species-specific; and there is an obvious link between the environment and the specific language we come to speak with native fluency. In fact language is a beautiful example of how to unravel the nature–nurture issue. Consider first the developmental pattern of language acquisition which is common to all children.

At about one year after birth, all children have a vocabulary of just one or two words. Given a normal linguistic environment, by five years of age children are revelling in a language comprising between 5,000 and 10,000 words. What is more, the language of a five-year-old conforms to most of, some argue all, the structural (syntactical and grammatical) rules of the language that has been acquired. From the age of five onwards there is a steady, if less spectacular, increase in the number of words known, and so the richness of meaning continues to develop. But the rules of language structure change little thereafter, even if the fluency of some transformations increases.

There are several revealing, and sometimes astonishing, aspects to language learning in children. First, the general pattern of acquisition is universal without regard to the language being learned. The progression from babbling, through the shaping of babbling to a form consonant with the phonetic structures of the native language, to single-word expression, then two-word combinations which are not random but conform to specific structure, then multiple-word sentences and onwards occurs in the same manner and at approximately the same age, be the language that is being learned Cherokee or Swahili. Most extraordinary is the evidence from deaf children. When deaf children are raised in a normal linguistic environment provided by deaf parents, hence a world in which significant adults are using sign language all the time, both among themselves and to their children, the children acquire the language using signs at the same rates, if not faster, and in the same order as do hearing children who acquire spoken language. Even when deaf children are raised in linguistically impoverished environments of parents with normal hearing who will not sign to them, such children show relatively minor retardation in the acquisition of signs, and the concatenations of signs as they develop are never random, but conform to structural rules.

Second, the learning of language structure, that is, the grammar and syntax that characterize every language, occurs without the child, and subsequently when the child grows into an adult, without the adult having any idea at all what it is they have learned. I know that I know certain people's faces and names. I do not know that I know how to use the conditional subjunctive because I do not know what the conditional subjunctive is, yet linguists tell me that I must know it because I use it correctly. Most adults would struggle to tell an adverb from an adjective. The vast majority of fluent language users would have no idea what a noun phrase is or what constitutes a case marker; they certainly would not know that to turn a declarative sentence (The zebra that is spotty is confused) into its interrogative form (Is the zebra that is spotty confused?) requires a transposition of the verb following the noun phrase (which is why no speaker would ask, 'Is the zebra that spotty is confused?'). Yet we are all able to accomplish such a transformation, and all other forms of transformation, without thinking about it. In this most extraordinary way, then, native speakers of whatever language possess a great deal of knowledge about the rules that govern the structure of their language. They must do, otherwise each of us would produce non-permissible sentences a great deal of the time, and yet we almost never do this. Yes, spoken language is often less than perfect as we trail off and don't complete sentences, or suddenly switch into a new sentence before completing the one we were on. But there is a difference between incomplete speech, or jumpy speech, or speech that intertwines different topics and sentences, and non-permissible language. In spoken language incomplete and intertwined sentences all conform to the structural rules of language. Yet we don't know that we know these rules.

The third point to note is that the rules are really very complicated. Anyone who doubts this should look at a text on English grammar (or Greek grammar or Kivongo grammar); even more complex are the possible general rules of many different languages, perhaps all languages, that linguists devise. It is difficult to make the comparison, but my intuition is that the rules governing the transformation of active (The zebra ate the grass) into passive (The grass was eaten by the zebra) utterances is at least as complex as those for carrying out long division in arithmetic. And this really *is* the point. The acquisition of the rules of grammar and syntax seems to occur effortlessly, and without any formal tutoring. No parent ever teaches their child the rule for transforming active to passive sentences – if for no other reason than that few parents consciously know the rule. Even quite gross errors of grammar made by children (The zebra eated the grass) most often, we now know, go uncorrected. Parents just do not hold tutorial classes in correct language use for their children. The same goes for vocabulary. On average, children learn four or five new words every day. This is not done explicitly. Adults don't say to their two- or three-year-old toddlers, 'Today we are going to learn the following new words.' Children just do it. They seem to learn language so easily.

Contrast this with the difficulty of teaching a child to read, or to ride a bicycle or to carry out long division. Illiteracy is a serious problem. Yet given some minimal linguistic environment, every normal human being becomes proficient in their native language within just a few years. This characteristic of learning complex material with seeming ease is not unique to language. Making coherent sense of a mass of information coming through the eyes, or how to perform everyday but highly complicated motor manoeuvres, presents us with a similar problem. Language, however, demonstrates the difficulty in its most acute form. It is also the case, of course, that we learn simple things, like the association between two events, with apparent ease, and I will turn to this issue later. For the moment, though, I want to stay with complexity because it makes the point more strongly.

Now, cognitive psychologists have a powerful conceptual tool in their tool-box of ideas which they use to justify their claim to be a far better approach to understanding how we humans come to know things and act on them than anything the behaviourists ever offered. As we saw in Chapter 1, the behaviourists eschewed non-observable causes. They claimed that the only way we can really understand how humans, and other animals, come to have knowledge of the world is by observing and documenting all the inputs to a person or animal and all outputs. Nothing else need be known or invoked for an adequate explanation of what any creature knows or does. In effect, the behaviourists believed that psychological explanation reduced entirely to a rather fancy theory of reflexes. Cognitivists, however, thought differently. Arguing from a range of data from studies of perception and memory, they concluded that there could be no reduction to a simple, if extended, input–output reflexology. This is because perceptual and memory outputs contain more than is present in the input. For example, take a list of words, scramble them into some random order, and ask someone to look at the list. Then ask them to recall as many words as possible. What you will find is that the words recalled are grouped in some way, perhaps by beginning letter, or the sound of the word, or their meaning, or whether they are nouns or verbs, or one of many other possible orderings. The output, the memory of the list, is 'richer' in its patterning, it contains more 'information', than was present in the input. Many perceptual phenomena, for example perceptual constancies, demonstrate the same failure of output to reduce simply to input, or to a history of input–output relations. It is not easy to say precisely and in measurable terms what is meant by 'richer' or 'more information', and so an absolutely watertight demonstration is difficult to come by. None the less, the general notion that cognitive output is greater than proximal input had by the mid-1960s and onwards been widely accepted, and became known as the Argument from the Poverty of the Stimulus. 'Modern Cognitivism', wrote the philosopher–psychologist Jerry Fodor, 'starts with the use of Poverty of the Stimulus Arguments.' The Poverty of the Stimulus Argument says that if the output is different from, richer than, the input, this must mean that some kind of work, transformation, computation occurs that alters and enriches the input. This 'work' constitutes hidden or unobservable causes that cannot be seen directly by just observing behaviour. These causes of cognition are what make cognition 'smart'. They are the causes of the subtlety and delicacy of cognition. They are, if readers cast their minds back to Chapter 1, the kind of thing William James was looking for – something that frees our minds from a slavish coupling to the world and gives us an intelligence and creativity that go beyond immediate experience.

Well, Chomsky drove a particularly strong form of the Argument from the Poverty of the Stimulus. He contended that the Argument is such a commonplace of biological thinking that everyone takes the main message for granted and never thinks to articulate it explicitly. The proximal inputs to the human foetus and infant constitute a set of nutrients and chemicals that do not provide an adequate explanation for the exquisite differentiated forms that make up the human body, or that of any other animal or plant. It is just not possible to provide an explanation for the internal combustion engine of the cell or the form of the human hand simply in terms of these proximal inputs. A child's face cannot be accounted for in terms of meals eaten and liquids drunk. Proper understanding of the human organism as a whole has to include the 'innate factors [that] permit the organism to transcend experience, reaching a high level of complexity that does not reflect the limited and degenerate environment'. In other words, no account of human form, or that of any other creature, can leave genetics out of the story. There has to be some other source of order and information apart from a partial and unreliable proximate experience, and that source must lie in the genes. Well, of course, this is correct and no biologist would dream of arguing against this position. They might want to add in notions like principles of self-organization, but would never deny the importance of genetic information.

Okay, asks Chomsky, so why should the human mind and brain be any different from the rest of our bodies? Why should we not think of the mind as being made up of some number of discrete, intricate and complexly structured organs that are at least to some extent innately determined? Why should we think that the mind is a unitary and indivisible entity? To help make his case, Chomsky draws a useful distinction, which is not unlike similar distinctions drawn by others, it should be said. The distinction is between the shaping and triggering effects of the environment. An example of the former is instrumental learning where, as a result of contingencies between behaviour and reinforcement (the technical term for rewards and punishments), the behavioural product comes to fit and in some sense resemble the conditions of the world. It is an interesting point that there are relatively few examples of characteristics that owe their form to shaping. Chomsky contrasts shaping with triggering where the environment, perhaps in the form of nutrients or temperature or other sensory inputs, initiates an intrinsically determined process that results in an end-product that bears little or no resemblance to the triggering conditions. For example, the complex form of our hands does not resemble in any way the foods that we eat or the kinds of object that we habitually manipulate. No biologist of any kind would ever claim that the structures making up our vascular systems are shaped by the proximate features of the world in which development occurs. Much the greater number of characteristics of animals are due to triggering.

Language, for Chomsky, is the prime example of an organ of mind that is subject to the Poverty of the Stimulus Argument, and whose complexity and conditions of acquisition point to a hefty component of innate, genetic causation. The problem, at this point in the argument, is that we have no data which tell us exactly *how* language is acquired by the child. We do know, as pointed out earlier, that the acquisition is unstructured. We do know that what is acquired is complex. And we do know with rare experimental certainty that there are aspects of language that are not learned by some form of shaping in Chomsky's sense of that word. An early, and famous, study by Berko in the 1950s showed this using what is known as an elicited production task. Children were shown a picture of an unusual object – one they were unlikely to have seen before. 'This is a flunk,' they were told. Then they were shown a picture with two or more of the objects and told, 'Now there are two (or more) of them. So now there are two . . .' and the great majority of five- or six-year-olds would say, 'Flunks.' Or they would be shown a picture of a child carrying out some very clear action with a novel object and be told, 'Jessica is grunding. She really loves grunding and does it as often as she can. For example, all day yesterday she . . .' and the children said, 'Grunded.' Now, the point is that flunk and grund are not English words. The children could not have acquired the responses 'Flunks' and 'Grunded' by any process of shaping, for instance, imitative or instrumental learning. This is because they could never have heard the words uttered by parents or others around them, and in the very unlikely event of the children themselves having produced these words spontaneously or mistakenly in the past, they would not have been reinforced for doing so. Obviously, what Berko was demonstrating was that children acquire certain *rules* which they express as regularities of spoken output that go beyond the limited language input that they have experienced. This is what Chomsky means when he talks about an impoverished or degenerate environment. Now, children may well be acquiring a lot else, like how to produce the acceptable phoneme sounds of the native language, how and when to use prosodic elements of speech, and what words actually refer to, in part at least by one or more shaping processes. But the acquisition of language structure, it is asserted, must be triggered. True, this latter claim rests only on circumstantial evidence, even if very strong circumstantial evidence. It is conceivable that children acquire all possible grammatical constructions of their native language by some painstaking trial-and-error form of learning. This is the difficulty with studying human development. You can't do the experiments that will establish causation beyond doubt. But it is so unlikely on the basis of the circumstantial evidence as not, in my view, to warrant serious consideration. As we will see later, there is an alternative explanation now on offer from the American neuro-biologist Terrence Deacon, but it does not rest on any assumption of trial-and-error learning of grammar and syntax.

So, once again, what we have here is a nature–nurture issue, but one which seems to be nicely resolvable because of the seeming clarity of the evidence. The story is that humans come into this world with parts of their brains already structured by genetic information and a supportive prenatal developmental environment. We are primed by our genes and development to acquire language. But not *any* language: only one of the 5,000 or so, and variants on these, that occur on Earth. These existing languages are a tiny set within the space occupied by all possible languages, which is huge. This is a very important point to understand. The human languages that exist are just the tiniest fraction of all possible languages. Indeed, and this is the point, Chom-skians claim that actually all languages are really just variations on one language. Chomsky considers this the single truth that must illuminate all studies of language. The argument goes as follows. If language has an innate component, which it must have; and if any child can learn any language on this planet, which it can do; then it must be the case that all humans carry the same innate component for the single human language. Russian isn't Spanish on the surface, but both conform to a single universal grammar, and that universal grammar is why, as Chomsky puts it, Martian explorers returning home will report on *Homo sapiens* as having just one language with surface variations on that basic theme. It's those surface differences that drive second-language learners to distraction, the difficulties of learning a second language after a certain age being a part of the explanation of how universal grammar unfolds into a native language or first language.

Just what that universal grammar comprises is something that linguists have argued about for nearly forty years, and the ideas have changed a great deal during this time. The framing of these ideas is always within a highly technical linguistic context, the details of which need not concern us. For example, one of the most recent and minimalist formulations says that universal grammar is made up of a set of principles. One such might be word order freedom. Some languages, like English, are very strict in their word order requirements; others, Russian for instance, are a bit more permissive and have a small set of possible word orders; and yet other languages, like Warlpiri, have a large set of permissible word orders. Another example from Pinker is 'whether or not a given language allows the speaker to omit the subject in a tensed sentence with an inflected verb'. The formation of these principles, which must be a property of the neural networks subserving language, are triggered during development such that at birth, or shortly after it, these principles are present within the child's mind as the essential basis for their subsequently being able to use language. After birth the child is exposed to a specific linguistic environment. This environment is, in effect, a linguistic space within which the child generates hypotheses about the language it is hearing, these hypotheses being constrained by the characteristics of universal grammar. The child, hearing a language and selecting the hypotheses that best fit that experience, thus sets the parameters within which the principles of grammar will operate for that child. So a child hearing English as its native language has the parameter for word order set to 'strict', and the null subject parameter is set to 'off'. Once these parameters are established for a first language, it becomes much more difficult to alter them for the learning of a second language, which is why we all find acquiring languages other than our native tongue difficult. The child is also, of course, acquiring other features of a language. At least one of these, the phonemic structure of that language, seems to be subject to a phenomenon known as sensitive period learning, which means that whatever is being acquired is best done so within a certain period in development. From around eight years of age onwards it is almost impossible to learn a language and not have a 'foreign' accent.

Now, as Pinker puts it, because

the rules of grammar interact tightly ... a single change (to a parameter setting) will have a series of cascading effects throughout the grammar. On this view, the child only has to set these parameters on the basis of parental input, and the full richness of grammar will ensue when those parameterized rules interact with one another and with universal principles. The parameter-setting view can help explain the universality and rapidity of language acquisition: when the child learns one fact about her language, she can deduce that other facts are also true of it without having to learn them one by one.

In other words, the architecture of the network of principles is a feature of universal grammar that facilitates acquisition. The principles are triggered. The parameters are shaped.

Is there any supporting evidence for language as a discrete and innate organ of mind? Well, while everything that any animal, human or otherwise, is or does in some, albeit remote, way has a genetic basis, the species-specific nature of human language points to a clear genetic basis. We may be only 1 or 2 per cent genetically different from chimpanzees, but that is still a very big difference (in the region of thirty million base pairs); and somewhere in that genetic difference between ourselves and our closest living relative lies the genetic basis of language that is triggered to result in the innate organ of mind that constitutes universal grammar. But just what that genetic basis is, involving which chromosomes, is entirely unknown. There may be familial language disorders, which supports the argument of 'genes for language'. But it is only going to be possible to get some kind of handle on this issue when we have begun to master the more general problem of understanding how genes, and almost certainly complex suites of genes will be involved, relate to the neural network structures of the brain. This is a problem for twenty-first-century science.

Now, whatever that genetic basis might be and however genes might map on to neural structure, an innate organ of mind must be something one can literally put one's finger on, or scalpel if one were a brain surgeon. And for this there is a great deal of supporting evidence, even if at present of a rather crude kind. Areas of the brain that appear to be dedicated to language functions were identified as far back as the 1860s. The effects of brain tumours, damage caused by projectile injuries to the brain, the administration of drugs, and direct stimulation of the brain by surgeons, all implicate specific regions of the left cerebral hemisphere of the brain in most people. These same regions are implicated in the use of sign language by the deaf. In recent years neuroscientists have developed methods of imaging the brains of conscious people. It is possible literally to see which parts of the brain are active when people are performing different kinds of task and activity. Such functional imaging studies confirm that language is connected to those regions of the cerebral cortex that had been pointed to in many previous studies. It must be said that as in so much of psychology and neuroscience, the picture that has emerged over the last twenty or so years is not as clear-cut as earlier models of brain function would have had us believe. There are more areas of the brain involved in language than was previously thought. The general view, though, remains that there are core areas for language comprehension and production. But as yet we have no way of understanding exactly how the brain, and the activity of the brain, relates to complex psychological processes like stringing words together according to specific rules and thereby generating meaning. That too is twenty-first-century science. However, within the limits of our crude knowledge of brain structure and function, there do seem to be regions of the brain that are specialized for language production and understanding.

There is one problem for this whole picture which concerns brain injury in young children. If the damage is to those areas of the cerebral cortex close to the Sylvian fissure, which is the region normally associated with language function, then often enough language recovers, indicating a plasticity in the way the brain organizes itself. Such plasticity has long been known about, and that it happens in the case of language attests to the fundamental importance of this most human of traits. But it does detract from the 'simple' story of genes coding for innately determined wiring of anatomically specified brain regions with dedicated neural network structure specialized for the functions of language. Somehow the genes coding for language, which would presumably not be activated in neural networks outside of the Sylvian fissure region, do become switched on when the normal language centres of the brain are destroyed. Right now there is no obvious way of marrying this fact to a Chomskian-type theory of language.

Chomsky has had an impact on psychology which spread much wider than language. His view of language as the product of an innate organ of mind was an important influence in the formulation by Jerry Fodor of the conception that has come to be known as modularity of mind. Fodor suggested in a 1983 book (see end-of-chapter reading list) that information entering the mind is initially dealt with by specialized, dedicated and innately specified information processing modules that are 'smart', that is, they demonstrate the properties from which is derived the Argument from the Poverty of the Stimulus in that they bring information to their processing tasks that does not exist in the input they are receiving from the world. That information is coming from the genes. Fodor's book has been one of the most significant pieces of writing in psychology of the last fifteen years. The conception has now been much expanded upon, what Fodor refers to as 'modularity gone mad', and is now a term with a somewhat different meaning from that originally given it by Fodor. Roughly, it now refers to any cognitive device that is specialized, computationally dedicated and innate. In this guise it looks like a cognitive adaptation and as such the modularity thesis has become important to evolutionary psychology.

Folk psychology and scientific psychology

At this point, readers who are newcomers to psychological science might be seriously puzzled by the general drift of this chapter. How can it be possible, why would anyone want to think, that our minds function on the basis of processes and principles buried so deep that we are not in the least aware of their existence? If there is such a thing as universal grammar in the form of the principles and set parameters just described, it has been ticking away in the minds of humans since language first appeared in our species, which is a long time ago, and no one knew it was there until the linguists told us about it a few decades ago. This seems to conflict with everyday experience and common-sense notions of what is in our minds, what we know, and how and why we do things. And indeed it does conflict with ordinary experience because the goals and methods of contemporary psychological science are not to produce something that maps neatly on to ordinary experience. This is such an important point that it is worth a diversion from the main storyline of this chapter.

There is no doubt but that every human being is an acute observer of all other human beings. We watch what others do with keen interest and we make inferences about their attitudes, motives, abilities and predict their future behaviour. We even construct 'theories' about others, and doubtless have been doing this ever since our species evolved – perhaps even our ancestors, like *Homo erectus*, did this as well. We are, in other words, each and every one of us 'natural' psychologists, and for an intensely social species of animal like ourselves, there are good evolutionary reasons for being this. Our very survival may depend on it, and the quality of our lives in terms of the resources that we can gain from, or share with, others most certainly does depend upon it. An important part of being natural psychologists requires introspective knowledge of how each of ourselves works 'in our minds', and then inferring similar states in others as a means of predicting how they will behave. This much is unarguable.

However, our evolution as natural psychologists skilled at constructing folk psychological theories does not mean that everyday experience, and the need to act as natural psychologists, gives us access to the processes and structures of our minds that allow us to observe ourselves and others, and to draw inferences from these observations. Indeed, one can construct an argument that this would be too wasteful, inefficient and expensive. It is much better that we have access only to the end-products of such complex processes, rather than the processes themselves. After all, it has taken psychology 100 years to get to where we are in understanding the human mind, and that isn't very far at all. If each of us had consciously to work out early on in life the basic principles and processes by which our minds work because that is the only way we could get ourselves to function psychologically, and then put them into operation every time we had a thought or a percept, we would spend all our lives being scientific psychologists and have no time for anything else – assuming that we could bootstrap such processes into existence in the first place. There is an obvious analogy with computers. In this day and age many people are skilled at using software packages, for example the wordprocessing package that I am using as I write this. Yet I have no real understanding of the program that my computer runs which allows me to type these sentences, or of the hardware of the computer itself, nor need I have such understanding. Indeed, to have acquired such knowledge in order to use a wordprocessor would have taken me years, in effect studying for degrees in electronic engineering and computer science. I would, I am sure, have elected to stay with my old-fashioned type-writer.

There can be no certainty that our minds evolved in the way that they have because natural selection eliminated human variants who did have access to the processes and principles underlying our talents as natural psychologists, because such 'process gazing' is an inefficient way of constructing a natural psychologist. But what is certain is that the computational load attaching to the most ordinary event, like getting out of bed in the mornings, which involves the co-ordinated contracting and relaxing of large numbers of muscles on the basis of information flowing in from joints, eyes, balance senses and so on, is so large that if we had to work it out each time, we would never get out of bed.

Contemporary psychological science just doesn't have an interest in folk or natural psychological explanations. We are all very good at the latter, and that is why it is often the case that people from outside the discipline who don't understand the objectives of contemporary psychological science sometimes feel that it is a waste of time and simply tells us what everyone already knows. Well, if all that psychology is concerned with is what we all already know, then, of course, they would be correct. But that is most certainly not what psychology is about. Underneath the awareness that we have of what is at the surface of our minds, or of what people are doing, that is their behaviour, are deep layers of processes that drive the surface awareness and behaviour. It is getting at these deep processes that is what contemporary psychological science is about.

Freud, 100 years ago, and in *this* respect decades and decades ahead of his time, understood this and tried to teach us what a proper science of mind should look like. Well, in a way, Chomsky is not too different from Freud. He is trying to understand and uncover deep-lying processes and principles that cause the surface phenomena. The process as cause should not be confused with the surface phenomena as effect. Unfortunately, at times in psychology's history we have been guilty of just such confusion. The behaviourists were especially guilty. Chomsky once remarked that a definition of psychology as a science of behaviour is at about the same level of silliness as a definition of physics as the science of meter-reading. He was quite correct. Just as physics is concerned with understanding processes, structures and forces that are utterly remote from ordinary experience but fundamental to the nature of the universe, so psychology is equally concerned with processes and structures remote from, perhaps entirely removed from, ordinary experience.

The moral of this diversion is simple. Universal grammar may or may not exist. This is an empirical matter and time will tell. But universal grammar, or the complex laws of association, or the way in which visual scenes are constructed, or how we carry out complexly co-ordinated acts, are the bread-and-butter conceptions and problems of a scientific psychology. They simply cannot be judged in terms of whether they make sense in the light of ordinary experience.

The opposing argument: language learning is a consequence of a general process

There is a long history in psychology to the idea of general processes of learning, going back at least to Pavlov and Thorndike at the start of this century. Discussion on the issue has been constantly bedevilled by a failure to draw a quite basic distinction, so that is where we should begin. In biology the word 'general' has two quite different meanings, which psychologists have always conflated. It can mean general in the phylogenetic sense of being a process or structure that occurs widely across species, usually because of evolution from a common ancestor for whom that process or structure was a trait. Such generality means similarity or identity because of homology as defined in Chapter 2. For example, haemoglobin is a complex protein molecule that serves to transport oxygen and carbon dioxide in the blood of all vertebrates, and many invertebrates as well. There are three other respiratory pigments, as they are known, in the animal kingdom, but haemoglobin is much the most widespread phylogenetically. Well, is there some learning equivalent, at least amongst vertebrates? It almost certainly would not be a molecule, no matter how complex; but it might be some particular architectural or microstructural form of nerve net, as will be briefly considered later. This is the first sense that the word general might have, and we will know when it is being referred to in this book because it will always be prefaced by the word phylogenetically.

The second sense of the word general is in the sense of 'generalist' or all-purpose. Take the haemoglobin example again. This is a molecule with very specific function. It does not serve as a general, all-purpose transport mechanism that carries all manner of nutrients and waste matter (other than carbon dioxide) around the body. So haemoglobin is phylogenetically general, but not functionally general. It is dedicated to a specific task.

Now, some psychologists, indeed most, have hypothesized that, unlike the gas transport mechanisms in the blood, learning of almost every kind is served by a general, all-purpose mechanism. There has been a tendency for most people who assume that learning is functionally general to assume that it is also phylogenetically general, partly because they seem not to have realized that the one need not imply the other. This has been the assumption of many, perhaps most, supporters of the notion that apes can learn language; that is, they believe that apes and humans learn language using the same mechanisms that are used to learn other things, and that these mechanisms are phylogenetically general. I have yet to see anyone suggest that chimps and humans are using different learning processes and mechanisms to arrive at the same state, which is supposedly one of having acquired language. And since under normal conditions apes do not learn or use language, then under the very special circumstances of being taught language (but do remember, I don't think any ape has ever been taught language), they must be recruiting to the task learning processes and mechanisms that are normally employed to acquire other sorts of information.

It is, however, perfectly possible to argue that the two forms of generality do exist, but independently of one another. Thus a species like the honey-bee, perhaps, may have learning processes that are generalist and able to acquire all the information that honey-bees use, but which are processes unique to honey-bees. Or the specific task demands of a particular form of learning, say the position of objects in space, combined with the fact that species never evolve but carry with them many of the characteristics of their ancestral species, may result in the processes of spatial learning being phylogenetically general, present in, say, most extant vertebrate species, but different from other forms of learning in vertebrates that are specialized for the acquisition of different kinds of information. The latter possibility may certainly combine with the possession of other generalist learning capacities, so a learner might conceivably have some combination of both phylogenetically general learning processes and other, different, generalist learning processes; or even some mix of phylogenetically general but functionally specific, and also species-specific generalist, and perhaps even more species-specific and functionally specific learning processes and mechanisms. This last case may well describe the mix of learning forms present in humans. The final possibility is that learners may exist who have neither form of generality, that is, they have more than one learning process, each different from the others and none shared with other species.

Psychologists who argue against the position that language is an innate organ of mind are generalists of one sort or another. Few, though, believe that humans acquire language using learning processes that are both entirely generalist and phylogenetically general. A possible exception to this was B. F. Skinner.

Skinner, heir to the extreme behaviourism of a previous age, was one of the most extraordinary figures in the history of psychology. Only Freud bears comparison with him in terms of attention received, citations and critical damnation. Indeed, within the academic community I would guess that Skinner surpassed Freud on all these measures. Freud, after all, was an instinct theorist and a developmentalist, both perfectly respectable things to be in his time, and subsequently. Freud's early career in neurobiology was distinguished and he came close to being the originator of the neuron doctrine, which is the seminal conception of the nervous system as being composed of separate nerve cells. By contrast, Skinner was rooted intellectually wholly within academic psychology and he had none of the conceptual ballast that comes with being steeped in related sciences. None the less, Skinner's impact on psychology has been enormous. This is not because there are now, or have ever been, many followers of Skinner. There are not and never have been. It is because he articulated in a powerful way so provocative a viewpoint that his heuristic value was immense. One might want to think that had he not existed, someone would have had to invent him in order that the extreme behaviourist position be represented. It is fair to say that his greatest achievement as an outspoken representative of extreme behaviourism was to demonstrate quite conclusively the intellectually bankrupt nature of this school of thought. And a not insubstantial part of behaviourism's failure revolved about language.

Skinner invented in the 1930s a conditioning chamber, usually referred to as the Skinner Box. This apparatus served as the vehicle by which Skinner developed his approach to the functional analysis of behaviour. His subjects early on were laboratory rats. Protruding from one of the walls of the chamber was a lever, which was connected to a food pellet-dispensing device. When the lever was depressed, a small pellet of food was delivered into a feeding tray. Usually a small light bulb or loudspeaker was present near the lever. In conditioning chambers such as these, Skinner and his disciples – and he did have some very devoted disciples – worked out some of the basic features of operant conditioning, which previous workers had called trial-and-error learning or instrumental learning. At the heart of operant conditioning is a three-term relationship: in the presence of a stimulus (the light bulb comes on) the response (pressing the lever) is followed by a reinforcement (a food pellet is delivered to the food tray). In time, the stimulus (light) becomes the occasion for the response (lever-pressing) which is controlled by the reinforcement. The relationship between the response and the reinforcer is the absolutely critical feature of operant conditioning – it was *consequences* that were crucial to Skinner's thinking about operant conditioning, a theme that was expanded in his later writings to something much larger than trial-and-error learning. Skinner did not claim that the stimulus elicited the response. The cause of the response was always something of a mystery for him. What he did claim was that understanding the relationship between response and reinforcer was of the essence for a science of voluntary behaviour; that this relationship could be studied and understood only one way, that is, by observing all inputs to the behaving animal and all its behaviours (outputs) and relating the one to the other – this is what was meant by a functional analysis; and that the observed relationships would be shown to be the same in all species that demonstrate operant conditioning, certainly all vertebrate species. As the English psychologist Geoffrey Hall put it, the central doctrine of Skinner's work was that 'what an organism does can and should be explained entirely in terms of what happens to it'.

In some respects Skinner's work was highly significant. The controlled environment of the conditioning chamber proved an excellent 'test-tube' for investigating operant behaviour in rats and, later, pigeons; it led to the discovery of the schedules of reinforcement, that is, the precise ways in which the distributions of reinforcers in time or according to the animal's response rate or pattern lead in turn to characteristic features and patterns of behaviour. These were robust and easily replicable findings, and as such they were and still are important. The big questions that came from this work were, and remain, as follows. First, how far, phylogenetically and in terms of what is being learned, can the operant behaviour of a rat or pigeon in a conditioning chamber be generalized? Second, is the functional analysis developed by Skinner in such a limited environment and using such relatively simple behaviour adequate for understanding more complex behaviours in less limited environments? Skinner was an ardent advocate of the power of functional analysis, whatever the behaviour and whoever the behaver. In order to maintain consistency of stance, this meant that for Skinner all explanations couched in mentalistic or physiological or genetic or any other kind of language depicting entities not immediately available to the functional analysis espoused by him had to be rejected. He did not deny the existence of mental states or genetic dispositions. He simply denied the adequacy of explanations of behaviour couched in such terms.

Well, Skinner liked to practise what he preached and in 1957 he published a book entitled *Verbal Behaviour* which comprised a very lengthy analysis of human verbal behaviour within the framework of operant conditioning and the functional analysis of behaviour. It really doesn't matter that Skinner claimed the work to be 'an exercise in interpretation' rather than 'extrapolation of rigorous experimental results'. The world took it as a test case of how far a functional analysis of behaviour can be taken when you are dealing with something as complex as human verbal behaviour, and the judgement was not very far at all. In a famous, some say infamous, and devastating review of the book published in 1959, Chomsky destroyed Skinner's thesis that a functional analysis of verbal behaviour based on the operant could be successful and yield important insights into human psychology. There is absolutely no point in presenting any details of Skinner's case because 'mands', 'tacts' and 'autoclitics' simply did not survive Chomsky's criticism. It would be like giving details of phlogiston theory in a text on modern chemistry. It is important, though, to examine generally and briefly why the world at large took Chomsky's critique to be an effective killing of Skinner's approach to a complex human psychological trait.

The criticisms were of three kinds. First, the literal transplantation of a functional analysis of operant behaviour in the rat in a conditioning chamber to that of the verbal behaviour of humans in their normal environments simply fails. One much discussed instance of this is the application of the concept of stimulus control to human verbal utterances. In the case of the rat in a chamber, the experimenter arranges things such that the bulb near the lever lights up periodically, and it is only when it is lit that pressing the lever results in reinforcement. In this case the lever press is under the control of the light stimulus, and this is clearly and easily demonstrated. One of the questions Chomsky asked was whether the notion of stimulus control could be *meaningfully* applied to human verbal behaviour. His famous example was the response 'Dutch' by a speaker to a painting, rather than 'clashes with the wallpaper', 'I thought you liked abstract work' or 'never saw it before' amongst the hundreds, nay thousands, of possible utterances that a painting might bring forth. The response 'Dutch' is given according to the Skinnerians because it is under the control of a particular feature or set of features of the painting. Had the speaker said, 'It reminds me of a picture my Aunt Sarah used to have' it would have been because that utterance is under the control of other features of the painting. But unlike the conditioning chamber where we manipulate the conditions and can say with certainty that behaviour X is under the control of stimulus Y, in the case of human verbal behaviour in a natural setting all that we can do is identify the stimulus (whatever that is, and in the case of Aunt Sarah's picture it might not be easily identified) after the response it made. This means that 'since properties are free for the asking' in Chomsky's words, we are headed back to some kind of mentalistic account because the stimuli are as much a part of some aspect of the speaker's mind at the time of the utterance as they are of the world outside of the speaker. All the objectivity and predictiveness found in the conditioning chamber disappear when we observe and try to explain the verbal output of someone looking at a painting.

The second criticism of Skinner's account is that in losing the objectivity of the conditioning chamber, the use of language appropriate to that situation degenerates into a kind of scientism, 'a kind of play-acting at science' to quote Chomsky again, when applied to people speaking. The notion of reinforcement is a good example of this. *Verbal Behaviour* is remarkably full of examples of reinforcement that according to Skinner is automatic and internal. People are reinforced for talking to themselves (how? Why? We are not told), copying the words of others (are we?), by anticipating future events (saying something now that will have an effect later – well, this is really getting complicated and deeply cognitive, you might say), and even not emitting verbal behaviour. Well now, in his early writings Skinner was very precise about what is and is not a reinforcer, and none of those just listed fits his definition. The word reinforcement assumes in his book on verbal behaviour a kind of ritualistic function serving to remind the reader that 'This is SCIENCE'. But the word has lost all objective meaning and has no connection whatever with the way the word is used when studying the behaviour of animals in conditioning chambers. The whole exercise certainly no longer counts as behaviourism of any kind. Indeed, reading *Verbal Behaviour* impresses one with the extent of Skinner's appeal to non-observable causes. This is no functional account. The word 'reinforced' simply replaces the 'wants', 'means', 'refers to' and 'expects' of more traditional explanations. All the supposed rigour of behaviourist functional analysis quickly goes out of the window.

The third criticism is perhaps the most important. It is nicely posed by the Belgian psychologist Marc Richelle when he points to what to many behaviourists is or was 'the crucial alternative: are so-called cognitive processes part of behaviour (are they anything other than behaviour) or do they have a mental status of their own, with behaviour being merely their by-products?' (The sentence in brackets is Richelle's own writing.) Skinner, answers Richelle, opted for the first of these. Indeed he did, but it is a position that beggars understanding. If taken literally, it is simple nonsense. To assert, for example, that an association or perception is behaviour, is to fail to use language properly. However, if the assertion that an association is behaviour really is a shorthand for something like 'an association is something that may have or has given rise to a behaviour', then no one could object. Certainly no cognitivist would object because the assertion is that certain inferred, directly unobservable, event or entity causes behaviour. Now transfer Richelle's question to language. The Chomskian asserts that the child's ability to transform a declarative to an interrogative sentence, verbal behaviour in both cases, occurs by way of the functioning of some hidden language organ of mind. But Skinner refused to countenance such explanation (despite all those curious unobservable reinforcers) because an unobservable language generator is a cognitive process that cannot be directly observed. It just doesn't appear, it isn't visible, in a functional analysis. Yet if an association can be equated with altered behaviour, i.e. it *is* the altered behaviour, then why can't a device that transforms language structure be equated with the behavioural transformation? That is, why can't the language generator *be* the behaviour? Both, of course, are equal forms of nonsense, but at least the position would have been consistent if it had been maintained, which it wasn't.

Unable to accept that there is something inside of a child that contributes significantly, and crucially, to the verbal behaviour of that child, a functional analysis, properly used, is left only with mopping up some of the peripheral questions relating to language behaviour; like how it is that certain words and word forms with certain meanings come to be uttered in certain circumstances. Thus it leaves us without any explanation of what is so striking about human language, which is its beautiful complexity and astonishing creativity. It misses the point, to paraphrase Skinner's own comment on his reading of Chomsky's review.

Piaget was another general-process theorist who thought language is acquired by general-purpose cognitive processes, but only in their adherence to the general-process view can he and Skinner be grouped together. Piaget was essentially silent on the issue of phylogenetic generality, and so should be considered to have been the advocate of functional generality but not phylogenetic generality. Unlike Skinner, Piaget was a cognitivist through and through whose major work was accomplished in Europe during the era when behaviourism was so dominant in American academic psychology. His writings were also deeply affected by a somewhat unusual biological orientation, and unlike most other cognitivists whose thinking tended to start at the sensory-perceptual end of psychological things, Piaget's approach centred upon action: 'In the beginning was the response,' he wrote. This combination of response-oriented cognitivism and the idea that cognitive processes are an extension of fundamental, organic, auto-regulatory processes is what makes Piaget such a unique figure in psychology's history. He was a truly original thinker, a person of genius, but one whose writings are formidably difficult to understand.

Piaget's thinking is rooted in the concept of autoregulation. Living things, he asserted, are in a constant state of dynamic interaction with the world in which they live. Success, that is, survival, depends on achieving a state of equilibrium between any organism and its environment. This comes about through a web of complex information flows between the organism and its environment by which the former regulates its activities and functions on the basis of fluctuations in that environment, one of the principal sources of change of environment being the activities of the organism itself. Intelligence was conceived as essentially one thing, and that thing is an adaptation. Cognitive processes are at once the outcome of organic autoregulation and the most highly differentiated organ of autoregulation. The activities of the organism in its environment, and the operation of its cognitive processes, constructs both that environment and, through autoregulation, the changes that occur within those cognitive processes. Piaget often referred to this dynamic exchange as a dialectic – something changes in the world which directly leads to changes in the organism which leads to further changes in the world, and so on forever. The general position is anti-Darwinian with a strong feel about it of Lamarckian evolutionism, which Piaget was happy to acknowledge. So, in general, Piaget's ideas hinged about this view of a very dynamic exchange between organism and environment in which autoregulatory and self-organizing processes find expression in a *construction* by the knower, the individual, of both the world to be known and their own cognitive processes by which they come to know the world. It is for this reason that Piaget's system is often described as constructivism.

Piaget assumed this general stance to be true of all living creatures, single-celled or multicellular, plant or animal. However, he had virtually nothing to say about cognitive processes in animals. The territory of his writings was the development of intelligence in children; his primary themes were actions and schemas on the one hand, and assimilation and accommodation on the other – there were some others but they cannot be pursued here. A schema is a cognitive structure, hence not directly observable, which generates and shapes actions and is shaped and changed in turn by the action itself and its effects on the world of the child. Schemas are highly flexible, and though initially relatively simple, as the child develops they grow complex in form and number and the way in which they become integrated with one another. Action, it must be understood, is not merely the literal response of the behaviourist, but includes all of perception and reflection. A child may grasp a rattle, and that certainly is an act, but so too is the listening without any visible behaviour to the sound made by the rattle. Later, when the child or adult can reason and think mathematically, the reasoning and doing of mathematics constitute the integrated functioning of large numbers of schemas, all of which originate in the simple actions of the infant. Now, when the infant grasps the rattle, it incorporates into that grasping schema the features of the rattle, its shape, texture, and so on. The notion of incorporation is central to Piaget, and indeed in variant forms, to all of cognitive psychology. Those features of the world that come to be known are incorporated into the structures of the knowing mind. Cognitivists generally refer to the product as a representation. Piaget called the process assimilation. However, in assimilating the rattle into its grasping schema, the schema is changed by the very act of assimilation, and this Piaget termed accommodation. So you know something by incorporating its features into your cognitive structures, yet that very incorporation changes those structures, hence what is known, hence those features of the world that are known are changed – here is Piaget's dialectic operating in the cognitive sphere specifically.

The difference between Piaget's brand of cognitivism and that of most other cognitivists lies in this endless, dynamic exchange between the knower and what is known, between assimilation and accommodation. The result is endless regulation of cognitive structures, for it is the latter, and the actions of the child, that are so dynamic and flexible. Yes, the world literally changes. But not nearly as fast as does the child, and it is the child, the schemas of the child, that are what really drives the changes for that child. The action schemas of listening assimilate the heard properties of the rattle, which accommodate to those properties. In time these schemas will become integrated into a higher-order schema, which will also incorporate other schemas, for example grasping and pulling, hearing and seeing. Exactly the same thing is happening to you, the reader, now, but at a very high representational level within an immensely complex, hierarchically structured set of schemas that all adults possess. You are assimilating the words and meanings portrayed on this page, these high-level schemas accommodating to the contents, and hence altering for yourself what is written here – and integrating these schemas with others you have acquired. That is how we eventually come to have knowledge and understanding of all of the world.

Piaget described a strict sequence of cognitive development. The first stage lasts about eighteen months after birth and is a period of very 'literal' actions. Through grasping, sucking, pulling and pushing the most basic and pervasive features of human intelligence emerge, for example the understanding of means–ends relationships, causality, the permanence of objects, and spatial relationships such as 'on top of' and 'contained within'. Towards the end of this sensorimotor period, the literal actions begin to merge into more autonomous, self-regulated functioning of schemas which no longer have to find expression in actual behaviour. The child becomes capable of interiorized action, though it is still action. At this stage the child enters the stage of symbolic thought, which lasts until about four years of age; later, between the ages of five and seven years, the child arrives at the stages of pre-operational intuitive thought, the stage of concrete operations between seven and twelve years, and finally the stage of formal operations when, with the emergence of general propositional thinking, the child assumes adult intelligence. Because it is language that we are concerned with here, these later stages must be sought out by the interested reader from other sources.

Language first appears during the transition from the sensorimotor to symbolic thought stage, and for Piaget language is 'all of a piece with acquisitions made at the level of sensorimotor intelligence'. He utterly denied the idea that language is substantially different from other features or forms of human intelligence. Language, he said, is 'a particular case of this (symbolic or semiotic) function, but it is *only* a particular case ... but a limited case within the totality of manifestations of the symbolic function'. (Piaget emphasized 'only' in the original.) When the child shows linguistic concatenation (stringing words together in a temporal sequence) and categorization (using different words as members of a class of words, for example wall and flower are both nouns) this is based upon schemas developed in the sensorimotor stage; specifically, schemas relating to temporal sequence, all actions having the feature of temporal sequence, and grouping schemas which emerge because objects are grouped in terms of the similarity of actions performed upon them. And when the child develops the ability to embed clauses within spoken sentences and to understand embedded clauses when heard, it is because this is built upon the schemas developed during the sensorimotor stage when the spatial embedding or object containment schemas emerged as these kinds of spatial relationship became understood. There is nothing special or domain-specific about language. All its features are either contained in, or are elaborations of, sensorimotor schemas already established, or they are closely related to the other elements of the symbolic or semiotic function.

According to Piagetians, language is but one of several elements of the symbolic function. The first is the elaboration of symbolic play, by which the child will 'pretend' that objects are other things, that is, they stand for or represent other things (a leaf represents a boat or a doll a child) or that whole situations are not what they actually are (a bedroom becomes a hospital). The quasi-isomorphisms (dolls look quite a lot like small children) give way to the purely symbolic, words as signs being only arbitrarily and conventionally related to their significates (there is nothing about the word dog that bears physical resemblance to the animal, but woof-woof clearly does). The conventional social aspect of language is important, Piaget thought, because it plays an important role in shifting the child's egocentric symbolisms towards shared experiences and shared meanings. Other elements of the symbolic function are imitation, by which the child assimilates sounds and gestures and accommodates schemas to their reproduction; interiorized imitation, whereby internalized imitations result in the elaboration and grouping of their appropriate schemas; and deferred imitation, which is imitation that occurs in the absence of the model. All these additional semiotic functions, Piaget asserted, are being elaborated in tandem with language and contribute crucially to its development.

In 1975 a famous debate was held near Paris between Chomsky and Piaget and their various followers, the proceedings being published in Piattelli-Palmarini (see the end-of-chapter reference list). What is striking about the debate is that while the concept of universal grammar has, as yet, only circumstantial evidence to support it, albeit and as already pointed out earlier in this chapter that evidence is none the less powerful, the Piagetian account has no supporting evidence of any kind. The strict sequencing of developmental stages is central to the Piagetian thesis, and the fact that language emerges at the end of the sensorimotor stage was claimed by Piaget to be strong evidence of the growth of the one from the other. Yet the fact that language first appears when the sensorimotor stage is coming to an end does not in itself prove any link between the two. Furthermore, the insistence of Piagetians that language in the child is multiply caused (different schemas deriving from different functions) is similar to Skinner's argument, but irrelevant when weighed in the balance against Chomsky's position. Chomsky's theory of universal grammar does not deny some, if small, contribution from imitation or even operant conditioning. But the imitation of sounds by a child in no way negates the concept of a universal grammar.

What is also remarkable about the Chomsky–Piaget debate is the general vagueness of Piaget's arguments compared to the wealth of detailed examples given by Chomsky. There is, quite simply, a considerable gap between Piaget's theory of general intelligence and its application to language acquisition and use, whereas Chomsky's ideas fit the indirect evidence so closely. There is, in fact, evidence against Piaget's account of language. At the 1975 debate, the great French biologist Jacques Monod suggested a thought experiment: what would we find if we looked at language development in children with such severe motor disability that their sensorimotor stage of development should be impaired? If Piaget's argument is correct, such children should show corresponding language impairment. There is no good evidence one way or the other on this, but what there is counts against Piaget. However, a related set of observations to that suggested by Monod is to look at language development and use in children with generalized and severe cognitive retardation. This comes in several forms and it is clear that in no case is language seriously impaired. This is not easily squared with the linkage Piaget draws between general intelligence and language.

Above all, there is simply nothing in the Piagetian argument that is able to counter the notion of the innateness of language apart from sheer prejudice. In common with most other general process theorists, constructivists reflexively reject all ideas of the innate. 'This prejudice going . . . so far as to prefer the consideration of a still unformed constructivist hypothesis to an already formed and explanatory hypothesis that has innatist implications,' is how Sperber put it during the debate. This bias against the general notion that the structures and functioning of the human mind have no origins in genetic information and the sequence of selection that makes up human evolutionary history is, quite simply, a profoundly anti-biological stance that no scientist of any worth should ever adopt. Sometimes anti-biological psychologists argue that claiming innate causation is a kind of intellec-tual laziness, a 'cop-out', the declaration of innateness supposedly relieving one of all further empirical or theoretical work. This is plain nonsense. First, the structural linguists of Chomsky's school have been striving mightily for forty years to discover just what universal grammar is. They might be wrong in their goal; they are not idle in their activity. Likewise the centrality of innatist thinking in classical ethology and its successors, like behavioural ecology, has not lessened decades of highly productive empirical and theoretical work in understanding animal behaviour. Second, the claim that something is innate is never ever more than a claim of part causation. The development of innately determined traits is as much a cause of the trait in its final form as is the genetic information from which it begins. Third, the belief in innateness detracts not one jot from studies of how something works, what its function is, how it interleaves with other traits, and what its contri-bution is to the overall economy of a living creature. So, you see, the 'cop-out' assertion isn't just nonsense; it is ignorant nonsense.

A middle way

Now, the story is not so simple as a single innate-trait theory of language winning out over the rival view that all human cognition is the product of a single, generalist, *tabula rasa* type of intelligence. Psychologists have long argued that the problem with linguistic approaches to language in general, and the idea of universal grammar specifically, is that it fails to address the issue of meaning. There are also serious doubts expressed as to the assumptions that have to be made about the evolution of brain structure and the relationship that has to exist between the latter and behaviour as complex as language in any evolutionary account of universal grammar. Basically, it is the complexity and detail of what must be innate in any such explanation of universal grammar that troubles people. Arguing for the form of the hand or vascular system in terms of the innate is one thing. But language is orders of magnitude more complex, hence is a different matter. As a result of this unease, more recent theorists of language have attempted to go some way to occupying the middle ground between the likes of Chomsky and Piaget. Elizabeth Bates, an American cognitive developmentalist, is a good example of a contemporary theorist who is extracting the best of both positions. Bates's position is that the processes and mechanisms underlying human language learning and use are of partial phylogenetic generality and are also driven by devices that are partially general-purpose in nature. She argues that Chomsky does not distinguish between domain-specificity of outcome, language, and domain-specificity of the processes and mechanisms used to achieve the outcome; it is possible that application of general mechanisms to a problem space with unique properties will lead to a domain-specific outcome. For example, Bates argues that the kind of thinking used for playing chess did not, of course, evolve for the purpose of playing chess. So there must be some degree of generality to the problem-solving thought that goes into chess. However, the outcome of such generalized, generalized at least to chess, problem-solving certainly does result in chess-specific thinking that cannot be generalized to bridge, or any other game. Perhaps this is the way we should be thinking about language. Furthermore, whilst not denying that language is a uniquely human trait, Bates suggests that its acquisition occurs by way not of a single general intelligence capable of learning anything, nor just by the unlocking or triggering of a single universal grammar, but by 'a variety of distinct and partially dissociable cognitive and perceptual mechanisms', all innately determined. Some, perhaps all, of these may extend their function beyond language learning alone, and at least some of them may be found in other primate species. Her central data are that 'every major milestone in early language development co-occurs reliably with reorganizations in at least one area of non-linguistic cognition'. For example, word comprehension at nine to ten months is coincident with the appearance of deictic gestures (pointing, showing and giving); word production at twelve to thirteen months occurs at the same time as deferred imitation; and the burst in vocabulary around twenty months co-occurs with gestural combination in symbolic, motor and social play. The same argument used against Piaget still holds, though – sequencing and co-occurrence do not allow inferences to be made about causes. However, the larger the number of coincidences, the less likely they are to be attributable to chance.

Bates suggests at least six different processes that are necessary for learning and using language, some of which are neither human-specific nor language-specific (fine motor control, for example), some of which are both human- and language-specific (object-oriented communication, this being pointing, showing and, above all, giving things, which becomes transmuted into talking about things, that is, reference and meaning), some of which may be specific to humans but not tied just to the domain of language (like imitation). As a psychologist, Bates sees language as more than an exquisitely complex structure that is isolated from the whirl of events that make up cognitive development. Language for her is a nexus of intricately interconnected interactive and constructive processes in the mind of the growing child. And for a *psychological* perspective on language, rather than a linguistic one, hers might be the more satisfying view. She certainly is very different from Piaget, but as in his case, she does not embrace what Chomsky referred to as the 'fixed nucleus' of language, some form of innate universal grammar, at the heart of human language. However, there is nothing in her approach that constitutes any form of negation of the concept of universal grammar. In other words, it is perfectly conceivable that some form of universal grammar does exist, but that for an adequate explanation of the full psychological panoply of language learning and language use, other mechanisms like imitation and fine motor control have to be brought into the picture.

A not unrelated position has been adopted by another American cognitive developmentalist, Patricia Greenfield. Like Bates, Greenfield occupies a kind of partial or midway position on language with regard to its phylogenetic generality and the extent to which it is built on some broader, but not too generalist, intelligence or learning mechanism. Greenfield points to certain similarities between language and the ability to combine motor acts using more than one object. She argues for a common neurological substrate in the infant for both the development of speech and the ability to manipulate objects, which then diverge from one another around the age of two years into two separate modules, each then subserving the two different functions of language and object use. Others have made similar suggestions. The connection with Piaget's sensorimotor schemas is clear. And yet the position has the virtues of being both innatist and explicit about the phylogenetic and ontogenetic origins of language. It remains the case, though, that no one has been able to map the grammar of object manipulation and tool use on to the grammar of language, which is what is needed to clinch the argument.

A recent book by Terrence Deacon (see end-of-chapter reading list) presents the most detailed and most plausible middle way yet. What is so interesting, and unique, about Deacon's approach is that it invokes functionally general, yet innately constrained, cognitive processes and mechanisms, and combines them with evolutionary theory in two different ways to result in an account of universal language features. Deacon's synthesis comes closer to reconciling Chomsky with contemporary cognitive theorists than has been achieved by anyone else. Deacon is no general process theorist. He accepts that there is a 'human predisposition for language' and that there are many different forms of learning. Where he differs from the evolution-of-a-universal-grammar approach is that he does not believe that the predisposition is for a universal grammar. Whatever universal features there are to language are a consequence of other innate cognitive mechanisms interacting with the social dynamic that constitutes the linguistic and social environment of the child, any child anywhere.

Deacon begins with meaning. We have for too long, he argues, been mesmerized by the complexities of grammar and syntax, when what is really significant is 'the common, everyday miracle of word meaning and reference'. For Deacon, symbolic reference is what lies at the heart of human language. He postulates a hierarchy of levels of reference in which the lower levels, iconic and indexical, which are based on the processes of recognition and correlative (associative) learning and hence which are certainly not language-specific processes, are essential to the formation of the highest level of meaning, symbolic reference. Unlike the lower levels, symbolic reference is a stable network of highly interconnected meanings: symbols do not just stand within an unstructured field of tokens that map only on to external referents in the world. Symbols also represent each other (think of how a dictionary or thesaurus works, suggests Deacon) and each has a place within an extraordinarily complex and rich network that grows ever more complex as the child develops. The result is 'a kind of tangled hierarchic network of nodes and connections that defines a vast and constantly changing semantic space'.

Deacon takes it as read that the mind is the product of evolution and hence is innately constrained in terms of basic sensory processing, perception, attention, rates of information-processing, memory, and other functionally general cognitive processes that provide the processing power upon which symbolic reference is built. He then marries this idea of a semantic hierarchy with a quite different conception, which is the passage of language between individuals in much the same way as other ideas and information are passed between people. As will be discussed at some length in Chapter 6, there is a developing body of theory on social or cultural change as cultural evolution. One of the components of such theory is that what is transmitted between individuals in a social group is equivalent to genetic transmission in biological evolution. These 'memes', as opposed to genes, are essential units of a social group's common cultural currency. Deacon views language as a set of memes. The result of a socio-linguistic evolutionary process involving language being played out on the constrained psychological processes such as short-term memory and attention that are universal to all humans, is a convergence in every language on certain universal structures of language. But this is not because universal grammar is built into our brains by our genes and development, but rather because 'language structures at all levels are the products of powerful multilevel evolutionary processes [what in Chapter 6 is referred to as co-evolution], to which innate mental tendencies contribute only one subtle source of the Darwinian selection biases'.

Deacon's is a theory of co-evolution of the brain and mind at one level, and of language at a sociocultural level, with universal grammar an outcome of such co-evolution rather than a predisposition of the mind put in place by a set of language genes by the evolution of the first level alone. It begins to explain universal features of grammar, but gets there by way of a very different route to that followed by Chomsky and Pinker. Either way, Pinker or Deacon, it looks more and more as if evolutionary theory is an essential part to our understanding language.

*

We are now at the end of what has been a long review of the two opposing camps in the great language debate, its length reflecting the importance of the point being made. Although the matter is a long way from being definitively resolved, it is my view as well as that of most contemporary cognitivists that the pure general-process account simply cannot tell the whole story, indeed can't get near doing so. The great weight of evidence is that language is a feature of the human mind that, in its rule-governed creativity, is different from the rest of the mind. Even if some aspects of language can be explained by other, broad processes and mechanisms like attention, memory and imitation, in many respects there is nothing else quite like it. This difference between language and other cognitive functions is the place where I am driving a conceptual wedge. My intention is to show that language cannot be explained by general-purpose intelligence, because once that is demonstrated that is all one needs, just one instance, to make the general case that the knowing mind does not comprise only general-purpose, *tabula rasa*, intelligence that has no structure apart from that written on to it by experience. In fact, as will now be much more briefly discussed, the weight of evidence is that the knowing mind has a much finer-grained structure than just language and the rest – the rest itself has structure, being made up of different modules of function.

The modularity of other cognitive functions

We perceive form, colour and movement because of the ways in which objects in the world emit, absorb and reflect light of different wave-lengths, these light-waves then entering our eyes and exciting different kinds of receptor in our retinas. These retinal sense cells then transmit information in the form of patterns of nerve impulses which are conducted to specific regions of the brain, at least twenty in number, which then in turn project to many other areas of the brain. Since the 1960s there has been a veritable explosion of knowledge about the visual system in the brain. Psychological investigations of vision reach back to the very beginnings of psychology as an experimental science (see Chapter 1), and we know increasing amounts about the effects of brain damage on vision. In other words, we know quite a lot about the human visual sense, and everything that we know, anatomical, cellular, physiological and psychological, all points to a domain of function that is separate from, though integrated to some extent with, the rest of our minds. Vision is not just a sensory system that is obviously different from other sensory systems such as touch and taste. The *psychological* problem involved in constructing a visual scene is simply different from the psychological issues relating to taste, ultimately because each of these sensory domains maps a different energy form and distribution. But this means they are not just different senses. The nature of the information, the energy form, to which each modality is sensitive means that the task demands of the mapping function are different too. The knowledge that we have of the world that comes to us by way of our sense of vision must, therefore, constitute an area of psychological function sufficiently different from other ways of knowing the world, which begin with other senses, that it is reasonable to think of vision as a different structure of our mind from that made up of information coming through those other senses. It is no coincidence that discussions of the structure of the mind must usually begin with our senses.

Now, the ability to construct a stable and meaningful visual scene is an immensely complex task. Yet, like language, it appears to occur with such rapidity that it is likely that we come into the world with another 'fixed nucleus' of function whose innate structure allows the mass of information flowing up into the brain by way of the one million or so nerve fibres that make up each optic nerve to be parsed so that visual scenes can be built according to some 'grammar' of visual scene construction. As with language, no explanation of visual scene construction can be based on a generalist intelligence account. For example, no *tabula rasa* learning device acquires the knowledge that colour is bounded by the edges of light-reflecting objects and that such colour does not bleed or spill over on to neighbouring surfaces or objects. The way in which we construct a scene in which colour is bounded is, in Chomsky's terms, triggered by appropriate developmental experience, not shaped. There is no doubt but that we do acquire by some shaping process, some form of learning, information about the habitual form and colour and movement of specific objects in the world. But the ability to construct a stable visual scene relating to those objects is a quite separate matter. So, like language, there are components of visual knowledge that cannot be accounted for by general-process learning mechanisms, and others that might be so explained. But unlike language, there is no reason to doubt that the innate visual module has at least some degree of phylogenetic generality. This is because the visual systems of other primates are structurally very similar to our own; the ecological conditions and the psychological problems presented by visual scene construction are the same for humans as they are for other apes, and monkeys too; and there seems nothing unique to our species about those of our behaviours that are driven by visual information.

Continuing with the comparison with language, neuropsychological evidence from brain-damaged individuals points to a visual domain of integrated function that can be fractionated into component bits if the machinery gets damaged. Some lesions of cerebral cortex, for instance, result in achromatopsia, a condition in which visual experience becomes drained of colour, leaving a visual world something like that of a 1950s television set – all greys, black and white. Other sites of brain damage will result in the loss of the ability to discriminate the differences in the shapes of objects, and yet other kinds of damage will lead to impaired movement perception or the loss of the ability to localize visually detected objects in space. All the evidence points to colour, form and movement as absolutely fundamental to the way in which we know the world through our visual sense and the way in which we construct stable visual scenes. Rather than thinking of each as a separate domain of visual function, it makes much more sense to think of each as a sub-domain with some kind of parallel modular computation on input which is then integrated to result in the visual scene in its entirety where all three come together to make up that most familiar of all experiences, the seen world.

The picture is complicated, however, by indications from several sources of evidence that higher-level visual functions such as face recognition, unlike the more fundamental components of colour, form and movement, might be considered as separate functional domains within the visual system. For such an intensely social animal as ourselves, but woefully deficient in our smell sense when compared to most other species of mammal, visual recognition of others is an absolutely essential part of our survival within social groups that may number scores, hundreds, and in some unusual circumstances, thousands, of individuals. Now, we know that when humans are interacting with one another and looking at each other, we spend most of the time looking at each other's faces, rather than looking, say, at each other's midriffs or knees. And when we are watching others with whom we are not directly interacting, we look overwhelmingly at their faces. No other part of ourselves is looked at more often than our faces, so it is a much used part of our cognition. None the less, it is not clear that over-use alone can account for some of the unique features of face recognition for which there is good evidence. We are capable of recognizing a very large number of faces, but are really quite incapable of giving such recognition a verbal expression, that is, we are very bad at describing faces with language. In the words of cognitive psychology, face recognition seems to be informationally encapsulated, and this is something that is often used to mark the presence of a cognitive module. Prosopagnosia, the inability to recognize faces, arising from circumscribed damage to cerebral cortex, also supports the interpretation of a separate functional module.

So is face recognition a domain within a domain? If one recognizes that the knowing mind has a structure, in part at least determined by the sensory channels of information, but likely containing sub-domains within each sensory domain, it then becomes a matter of arguing over microstructural detail. That is a matter beyond this book, and will eventually be resolved by better psychological theorizing, as well as greater understanding of how genes find expression in specific neural structures. For the moment, though, the general case is surely made by the detailed examples of language and vision. There is no reason to believe that general-process mechanisms are any more dominant in other areas of cognition, whether it be the mapping of our body surfaces, input from muscles and joints during movement, or any other source of knowledge of our world. The mind is functionally structured, and the knowing parts of our mind are further structured into devices that specialize in acquiring specific kinds of information about the world.

How far can one take structural separation?

Although general-process, *tabula rasa*, learning theorists and adherents to the notion of general intelligence have been much the numerically greater over the last century or so when compared to those who believe in the existence of predispositions to learn only limited features of the world, or in specific intelligences, in recent years the weight of argument and evidence from neuropsychological, developmental and comparative studies has made the extreme opposite view not entirely unthinkable. Perhaps there are *no* generalist learning devices in our minds. Perhaps *some* of these specialized intelligences are phylogenetically general. Is this an arguable position? I believe that it is. However, as in the way of these things, it is neither simple nor straightforward and hinges again on the meaning of the word 'general'.

Earlier in this chapter we drew a distinction between 'general' in terms of general-purpose, often referred to as general-process in the psychological literature, and phylogenetically general. Now we need to look a bit harder at the first of these. Strictly speaking, a general-purpose learning device is one that can learn anything. Well, that has some interesting implications. To be able to learn anything must mean that everything that there is to be learned is actually all one thing; that everything that is learned can be decomposed into common elements. What could this one thing be? The candidate that has been on offer for thousands of years is association. That is, how things connect with one another, how they stand relative to one another in space and/or time, what is linked with what, and how one thing leads to another. The argument has been that association in space or time is what all learning boils down to, and is the fundamental organizing principle of the knowing mind. And it is fundamental because it captures and maps on to the mind an organizing principle of the world. All events and objects in the world can be located in space and time relative to all other events and objects. Learn what that pattern of association between events and objects is, and you have learned everything that there is to know. Beginning with Aristotle, philosophers down the ages have pondered on how one thing stems from or leads to another. The school of philosophy called the British

Empiricists, which included the likes of Locke, Berkeley and Hume, touched on in Chapter 1, enunciated the laws of association, these being organized around factors such as contiguity, frequency, belongingness, and vividness amongst others, all of which have a place in twentieth-century associationist psychology. The work of Pavlov and Thorndike provided laboratory and experimental settings within which the details of the laws of association could be worked out with empirical certainty. The law of effect which describes the relationship between behaviour and rewards and punishments, and the law of classical conditioning which deals with relationships between stimuli, are some of the twentieth-century manifestations of associationist schools of thought.

Now, it is an obvious truth of this somewhat old-fashioned physicalism that everything in the world does indeed bear some kind of spatial and temporal association to everything else. For this reason it is not just likely, but certain, that some species of learner, perhaps all, have evolved the ability to detect such relationships (see next chapter). There is no question but that humans and the individuals of many other species of animals do have associative learning ability. But that does not mean that everything that we come to know, we come to know by way of such learning. After all, a large part of this chapter has been devoted to the failure of Skinner, who espoused one form of associationism, to explain language learning. The problem, you see, is that associationism, at least initially, is a reductionist exercise. Everything must, at the start, be reduced to whatever the learner senses as the most elementary thing that can be associated with other most elementary things. Then these elementary associations can be grouped into higher-order sets, and these higher-order sets into yet higher-order sets, and so on. This is a slow, painstaking and difficult enterprise. Take the example that we will deal with in some detail in the next chapter. Humans acquire knowledge about the knowledge and intentions of other people. Now it is possible, it is always in some sense possible precisely because the world has the structure that it does, to provide an elaborate and clumsy scenario of how we come to know what others know by way of a very long and tenuous string of associations. But it is utterly unimpressive, because it seems to be so arduous, so unintelligent and so unguided. Such accounts are vulnerable on exactly the same grounds as were Skinner's views on language. Learning what other people know by way of long, long strings of associated elements and events is too slow, too hazardous and error-prone, and too inefficient. It is the Poverty of the Stimulus Argument all over again, this time applied to learning about the knowledge and intentions of others. Such vital information must be acquired, and acquired quickly. Dedicated machinery that is tuned to receive chunks of information directly relevant to what it is that others have in their minds, and that is primed to manipulate that information in ways specific to drawing inferences about the intentions of others, is going to do a far better, quicker and more reliable job than a painfully inefficient cobbling together of a primary picture of what elements go with what other elements, initially presumably not even from units of association that are whole people but a scramble of unconnected features, eventually forming a web of associations so complex that somehow, and who knows how, knowledge that other people have knowledge falls out of it. The life of any one of us is too short and the world is too complex. What is a much more likely scenario is that over evolutionary time, which is a very long time indeed, our minds have been shaped by selection forces such that individuals are triggered to acquire certain kinds of knowledge rapidly and effectively. Evolution shapes and individual development mostly triggers. The result is the capacity to acquire complex information of specific kinds quickly.

But that is the case in humans, and very likely most other contemporary species whose individuals can learn. Learning and intelligence, however, is almost certainly nearly as old as multicellularity itself. With multicellularity came the evolution of collectives of cells that were specialized for interacting with one another, and with yet other cells that were sensitive to energy changes impinging upon them from their environment. Such cellular collectives, brains in other words, evolved connections with peripheral organs that were able to change the relationship of these early multicellular creatures to the external world. The details of the evolution of sense organs, nervous systems and effector organs are very little understood. They are all soft tissues that do not fossilize. We can only conjecture and use comparative evidence. What is clear from the comparative evidence is that the architecture of neural networks may be widely shared, and probably evolved from early, common multicellular ancestors. This common neural architecture is the third kind of 'general' that we need to distinguish.

Alert readers will say at once, 'Ah, but this is the same as phylogenetically general.' Well yes, it is, but with a difference that may make a real difference. If there is a commonality of neural architecture, it is *deeply* phylogenetically general. Normally when we talk about phylogenetic generality in psychology we are talking about traits shared by relatively closely related animals, for example colour vision in humans is shared with other primates, but not with non-primate mammals. So yes, colour vision is phylogenetically general in primates but is quite restricted phylogenetically. But what I am envisaging for neural architecture is something so old that virtually every taxonomic group that has now, and has had in the past, a nervous system shares that neural architecture. The architecture is such that it can learn associations of what-goes-with-what. Through deep evolutionary time this architecture has become the 'unit' that evolution has been able to combine in all sorts of interesting ways to produce complex combinations that exploit the basic learning capacity of the 'original' nerve net to give rise to devices that can learn really very complex things quickly. This, of course, is conjecture on my part but it is a story that brings together much of what we know, which is not very much at all, about learning in different kinds of animal including humans, what their nervous systems look like, how they are connected, and what theorists who build models of nervous systems tell us. And it leads us to expect that the basic processes of learning, that original unit of nerve cells that can acquire information, will be *anatomically general* in our nervous systems; but bound now into even more complex architectures of networks whose capacity to learn is dedicated to specific domains of knowledge. In other words, the microstructure may be shared, but there is a macrostructure that has functional consequences.

So there may, in the sense just described, be general-purpose learning devices; they are very old and in some macrostructural configurations shared by fairly closely related creatures may result in phylogenetically general forms of intelligence and learning; they may be found as basic units of neural architecture in all intelligent creatures and be widespread throughout the neural computational machinery of such animals, and hence are anatomically and functionally general; and they may be honed into particular combinations by evolution to result in specific and dedicated forms of learning and intelligence. It is most likely that this most general of microstructures originally subserved an associationist role, but through clever combinations wrought by evolution, they now function in ways quite unrelated to that original function.

In recent years cognitivists and neuroscientists have been very excited by a family of theoretical models of neural architecture that has come to be known as connectionist networks. The reader who goes beyond this present book into any recent account of neurobiology will quickly come upon these models because they seem to bear some resemblance to real neural networks and they do show some mightily interesting learning characteristics. The possibility must be entertained that early on in the evolution of nervous systems some form of connectionist network evolved, was selected, conserved and then transmitted to all descendant populations. If this is so, we may be not that far off a really exciting synthesis that will begin to explain not only what is common to all intelligent creatures, but how deep differences can emerge from such commonality.

One final word must be said on the matter of just how far one can divide the mind into functionally discrete areas or structures. If the mind is not to tie itself into knots of conflicting and competing activities, there must be parts of the mind that co-ordinate its overall activities. These supervisory functions may have attentional oversight on all inputs to our minds; they may have attentional oversight on all outputs from individual domains of information processing and learning; and they may prioritize our actions on the basis of our needs. These kinds of general process, perhaps best referred to as systems-general or systems-common processes, constitute yet another kind of generality that needs to be conceptually distinguished from those other distinctions drawn in the rest of this chapter.

Does evolutionary theory mandate modularity?

I have laid out the arguments about the domain-general and the domain-specific. And I have tried to indicate how the drawing of certain crucial distinctions allows us a glimpse of how these seemingly conflicting notions can be married into a unified view of the structure of the knowing mind. But just what would an evolutionist say about all this? Well, it would depend on who is being asked. The tack taken in this chapter is that the structure of mind is a product, a consequence, of evolutionary forces. And while evolutionary theory says a great deal about the processes that transform biological systems in time, and on which there is quite widespread agreement, it does not mandate much in terms of the products of those transformations, other than that they should not be wholly destructive to the fitness of those creatures possessing these products – even mildly destructive traits can evolve under certain circumstances. In general though, evolutionary theory has two 'pointers' on this matter, 'predictions' being far too strong a word to use in this context.

The first comes from evolution not being a radical seeker after perfect design. Adaptations do a job. They have a purpose and are goal-directed in respect of specific features of the world, facilitating the interaction of the possessor of the adaptation with that feature of the world. For example, many quite different species of animal, independently of one another, have evolved flaps or plates of one sort or another that share the characteristic of large surface areas which then act as heat-exchange mechanisms. The flap or plate facilitates the gain and loss of heat; the feature of the environment towards which the adaptation is goal-directed is temperature. However, a good engineer given free rein would design much better heat-exchange mechanisms than exists in any animal, even if the basic idea being exploited by the engineer is large surface area. Nature, however, does not have a free rein. It never does. It is always constrained by what it already has to hand, and what other functional demands are being made on an animal. Ears might already be a structural trait of a species, and so the enlargement of the external ear flap with an accompanying enrichment of blood supply might be the response that best trades off the gains in terms of heat regulation against the competing costs of the structure. Not all animals have external ears, though. So some species of birds, for instance, have to 'solve' the problem in another way by evolving highly vascularized mouth pouches, some of which can be waggled about to increase evaporation rates, hence regulate body temperature this way. Neither birds nor elephants nor dinosaurs, some of whom had similar arrangements on their backs, evolved completely new structures to do the job. They thriftily modified what they had to start with.

Now, this same logic of conservative tinkering must also apply to the neural structures subserving learning and intelligence. The first mammals evolved about 150 million years ago, and they would have had the same kind of neural architectures as the mammal-like reptiles from which they are descended. At every point in mammalian evolution, including the evolution of primates and subsequently the apes, our ancestors would have been modifying already existing brain structures. It might have been a bit like shuffling cards, with the basic units remaining roughly the same but the ordering and structuring changing. This does not mean that over long periods truly new structures subserving uniquely dedicated learning and intelligence functions could not have evolved. But it does, I think, mean that it is unlikely in the comparatively short period of hominid evolution of the last few million years that such entirely new features of our brains would have evolved. It is much more likely that what evolved must have contained elements of older neural architectures, or a restructuring of basic units of structure. This, of course, is compatible with the suggestion made in the previous section of this chapter that there may be common neural net structures in functionally different domains of the brain. The cautious conclusion to be drawn on this first pointer from evolutionary theory is that even the most functionally domain-specific module of mind might share some of its features with other information-processing modules.

The second pointer from evolutionary theory, most strongly presented in contemporary psychology by the likes of the American evolutionary psychologists Tooby and Cosmides, is that the human mind must be seen as an organ, more correctly a set of organs, of adaptation. We use our minds to interact with the world to our best advantage. But the world makes multiple demands upon us, some seemingly simple and others more complex. The task demands in every case are different. Learning what follows what, which must constitute at least some aspect of acquiring knowledge about the causal texture of the physical world, is vital to our survival. The relative simplicity of the task does not detract from its importance. It may not have the complexity that goes into parsing a heard sentence and then extracting meaning from it, but it surely is at least as significant to our survival. Now, because it is important, there must have been selection for a sensitivity to temporal order and the ability to remember that order. There are parts of the human brain that have just these functional characteristics. And such consistent selection is what must have been responsible for humans, and many other species of animal, having the ability to learn about this aspect of our worlds. A creationist perspective apart, there is no other possible explanation. So, if our sensitivity to detect temporal order is an evolved feature of our minds, and if the task demands are different from, say, learning a grammar or the characteristics of people's faces, then some part of our mind must be dedicated to the acquisition of such information, and this part of our mind must be innate in the sense of being partly determined by our genetic constitution. It does not necessarily mean that such learning ability is present at birth, though it may well be; it does not mean that the trait is not crucially dependent upon developmental processes, which it certainly is; and it does not mean that the task demands are so complex that they could not be acquired without the impetus that comes from having prewired neural structures, that is, the poverty of the stimulus argument may not apply in all of its glory. But it does mean that as an evolved form of learning and intelligence it is functionally and structurally different from other forms of learning and intelligence. The same argument can and must be driven for every domain of the knowing mind. Innateness, and the accompanying structural segregation that follows, is not an optional extra. All functional domains, no matter how general or specific in any of the senses used in this chapter, must be innately given.

How many learning or intelligence modules are there? We don't yet know the answer to this question. It is worth pointing out, though, that the evidence will hinge not only upon analysis of and experimentation on cognitive structures and their neurological substrates. It also requires understanding of how the world changes in ways that are relevant to ourselves, or any species of learner, and how such change is mapped on to specific learning and intelligence capabilities. This is because it is change that drives the evolution of learning and intelligence, which essentially are sets of adaptations goal-directed to the incorporation of change. A static world can be behaviourally adapted to by relatively fixed instincts. The reason why learning and intelligence ever evolved at all was because instincts alone cannot provide effective adaptation to a world where change is a constant feature. So, understand change, observe which forms of change the learner is adapting to behaviourally, look for the cognitive and neurological evidence of a domain-specific module that is acquiring information about that domain of change, and then you have a further cognitive module, a module of knowledge gain, to add to the list.

A final and, perhaps, most important point. While it is relatively easy to be precise about how specific is a particular cognitive domain, is it possible to be equally clear about where the limits of generality are, in the sense of general-purposiveness? Just how general can general-purpose be? Can it ever be so general that a mechanism can learn anything? Is it possible for any learner, human or otherwise (including machines), to have a module that is a blank slate, a *tabula rasa*, upon which can be written any and every form of learned information? The idea of a *tabula rasa* as characterizing the human mind goes back about 350 years to the seventeenth-century English philosopher John Locke. Locke was the founder of empiricism, the doctrine that all knowledge derives from experience, as we saw in Chapter 1. Locke believed that the senses are indispensable for practical life and have, literally, to be trusted. Our senses are also 'the hinges upon which our passions turn'. What Locke rejected was the rationalist view that goes back at least to Plato that there are innate ideas, that we come into this world with knowledge already in our minds. In modern parlance, Locke would have rejected outright the notion of innate, domain-specific cognitive modules. John Watson, the founder of behaviourism, was also a believer in a *tabula rasa* mind.

Well, in evaluating these questions one must first be quite clear that a learner with a *tabula rasa* mind doesn't need any domain-specific learning devices because they would be quite surplus to requirement. Remember, anything can be written on to a blank slate. So a learner who is a *tabula rasa* learner would have evolved with only one module. But is a *tabula rasa* learner possible? The answer is that in theory it might be, but in practice it is not a biological proposition because life is too short. The problem is that the world can be partitioned, described and learned about in an infinitely large number of ways. If you let loose in the world a truly general-purpose learning device that learns entirely without constraint, it will, by chance, set off acquiring information in what is an infinitely large search space along any one of an infinitely large number of search paths. The chances of such a device learning anything that is biologically useful within a single lifetime is vanishingly small. It might just work in an indefinitely long-lived life, but even then the problem of ordering such information is beyond current understanding.

Let me put the problem another way. In a very large search space, if you want to get somewhere specific, you are unlikely to get there if you have no guidance at all. Even if you have a little guidance, but it is too permissive, too loose, in allowing you to adopt specific search paths, you may end up anywhere rather than where you want to be. This problem of the unspecified, unguided, untutored, generalist learner, known sometimes as the frame problem or the combinatorial explosion problem, is widely recognized. There is really only one way to solve what is an almost intractable problem. This is indeed to have vast reaches of time in which to search and the ability to conserve selectively knowledge gained over such massive search spaces. And that is what evolution does. It gains knowledge of the world across countless generations of organisms, it conserves it selectively relative to criteria of need, and that collective knowledge is then held within the gene pools of species. Such collective knowledge is doled out to individuals, who come into the world with innate ideas and predispositions to learn only certain things in specific ways. Every human, every learner of any species, begins its life knowing what it has to learn and be intelligent about – we all come into the world with the search space that we have to work in quite narrowly defined. There is empirical evidence to support this view in a whole range of species. It is a theoretical requirement of any biology or psychology of learning and intelligence. It is a principle that is observed by the community of scientists who work in artificial intelligence. It is a universal law of learning. Plato was part right; Locke was absolutely wrong.

The notion of a *tabula rasa* learner is biologically inconceivable. Evolutionary psychology tells us how the problem of knowing what is important to us, but which is just the tiniest amount of what is contained in the vast ocean of possible information most of which is not relevant to us, is solved by the evolution of domain-specific cognitive modules innately packed with knowledge of what it is that has to be learned. The explanation of cognitive structure is a significant achievement. It remains a possibility that cognitive predispositions may be explained in part as variations on some general neural network architecture, which is somehow tweaked in its connectivity and synaptic weightings such that it works in one way rather than another. Empirical studies will tell. Marry these findings to more general accounts of nervous system structure as these relate to psychological functions revealed in brain-damaged individuals, and we may be in sight of a fairly complete account of the structure of the knowing mind. And that really would be an achievement.

The concept of a collective species wisdom gleaned over immense periods of evolutionary time, which then launches into the world very short-lived individuals with innate predispositions to learn only certain kinds of thing, means that individual people are able to share with one another a rich and complex understanding of the world we live in – or rather of that restricted part of the world to which our innate dispositions give us access. This most certainly would not be the case were we at birth *tabula rasa* intelligences, for then we would all of us enter into some individual and probably unique part of the search space and hence have little shared knowledge in common. So there is an interesting contrast between innate, intrinsic, limiting devices that restrict what we can know on the one hand, and on the other hand how these devices give rise to shared knowledge which, in creatures like ourselves with our remarkable communications skills, allows us entry into those most extraordinary of all psychological domains – self-knowledge, the knowledge of other minds, consciousness and culture. It is entirely fitting that we close this long chapter with Chomsky's own words: 'there is an inseparable connection between the scope and limits of human knowledge.' A move away from innate constraint places an impossibly heavy burden on the uniformity of the environment and on the uniformity of individual experience to lead to sufficiently similar cognitive results that we might share experiences. Increase cognitive constraint and the way is opened for the understanding that there are experiences and minds other than our own.

Suggested Readings

Chomsky, N. (1980) *Rules and Representations*. New York, Columbia University Press. (Middle-period Chomsky, somewhere between language acquisition devices of the 1950s and 1960s and his recently adopted minimalist position.)

Deacon, T. (1997) *The Symbolic Species*. London, W. W. Norton. (A wonderfully interesting and detailed attempt to synthesize both general process and evolutionary accounts of language.)

Fodor, J. A. (1983) *The Modularity of Mind*. Cambridge, Mass., MIT Press. (One of the most important and influential books in the recent history of psychology – and, at less than 130 pages of text, one of the shortest. The précis, in *Behavioural and Brain Sciences*, vol. 8, 1–5, is perhaps the funniest serious piece of writing in academic psychology of all time.)

Harris, R. A. (1993) *The Linguistic Wars*. Oxford, Oxford University Press. (A detailed account of how linguists have homed in on a minimalist position.)

Hirschfeld, L. A. and Gelman, S. A. (Editors) (1994) *Mapping the Mind: Domain Specificity in Cognition and Culture*. Cambridge, Cambridge University Press. (An anthology on modularity which contains material also relevant to the next chapter, notably an essay on agency by Alan Leslie.)

Karmiloff-Smith, A. (1992) *Beyond Modularity: A Developmental Perspective on Cognitive Science*. Cambridge, Mass., MIT Press. (Excellent attempt to reconcile Piaget's general process theory with nativist, modular approaches.)

Meier, R. P. (1991) 'Language acquisition by deaf children.' *American*

Scientist, vol. 79, 60–70. (Details the remarkable parallels in language acquisition in normal hearing and deaf children.)

Piattelli-Palmarini, M. (Editor) (1980) *Language and Learning: The Debate between Jean Piaget and Noam Chomsky*. Cambridge, Mass., Harvard University Press. (Fascinating record of a famous meeting.)

Pinker, S. (1994) *The Language Instinct*. London, Penguin. (Wonderful book that tries to account for the evolution of language.)

Savage-Rumbaugh, S. and Lewin, R. (1994) *Kanji: The Ape at the Brink of the Human Mind*. New York, Wiley. (Easy-to-read account of the most provocative of all attempts to get a non-human ape to use language.)

5

Prediction and Mind-reading: The Evolution of Causal Understanding

Nothing is more important to our sense of a sensible and stable world than the connections that we make in our minds between the component bits of, or events in, that world. We understand the world, the kind of place it is, by way of these connections. This is so significant a part of our knowledge that we are startled by events that seem to be separate or isolated. Everything is usually seen as having some kind of link or attachment to something else – even if at first we don't know the link, we expect that there is one and it is just a matter of time before we discover what it is. One of the most important kinds of connection that we assume exists between entities or events is what we think of as connections of causation, or cause–effect relations.

Cause and effect are correlative terms. In ordinary everyday language what we mean by the word cause is that it seems to give rise to something which we label the effect, and that is why cause and effect are thought of as correlated. Causation implies action, agency and, perhaps, motive. We understand that close proximity to fire leads to, causes, pain and injury, and that is that. Most of us need know no more than the correlation between fire and injury – indeed, the great majority of us could not say in any detail how heat leads to tissue damage. However, as social animals we certainly do have a rather more detailed interest in and appreciation of motive as cause. The reason why someone has acted against our interest and resulted in misfortune for us will be subject to much greater analytical scrutiny than the consequences of being too close to a fire.

Now, human motives considered as causes are for ordinary people much closer to the detailed way in which scientists think of causes. Some theoretical physicists apart, in science at large cause is a specific and crucial conception. The idea of causation is central to the scientific enterprise. Scientists are quite explicit in going out and looking for causal explanations of the phenomena they study. Theories are explanatory nets cast to capture the causal structure of the world. Moreover, whilst in ordinary life, even when dealing with the motives of others, we are fairly lax in the way we think causal relationships through, and do not look too closely at what precisely we mean when we say that this cause has that effect, this is not the case in science. Scientists normally think that the relationship between causes and effects is *generative* rather than merely correlative, and are concerned to hypothesize and then empirically demonstrate the exact nature of that generative link. The scientist will explain the tissue damage that is caused by heat in terms of the excited state of atoms and molecules resulting from increased energy levels leading to the collapse of the intricately balanced and delicate structure of cells. Put plainly, science is the detailed study of the nature of the generative links between causes and effects.

Now, scientists are not the only people who focus on causes. Philosophers have had similar interests, and for much longer. It is certainly no coincidence that those philosophers whose concerns were, or are, very close to science and to matters for which science is of great relevance, are the philosophers who write most about causation. Aristotle is the great example. He argued that four causes can and should be invoked when considering the explanation of any entity. The computer on which I am writing these sentences has material cause, which is what it is made of (plastic, silicon, etc.); formal cause, which is its essence (it is a computational device); efficient cause, referring to how it came into being (the actual construction process in a computer factory); and final cause, what it is for, its end – or goal-directedness (making life easier for humans). Efficient cause is closest to most modern conceptions of causation, though final cause is now also subsumed by science under evolutionary cause in the sense of the function for which a trait has been selected (computers do make life easier; that is why they have caught on – the reason for their having been selected – and are now sold, to the gain of the manufacturers, in great quantities).

Aristotle was the last of the great ancient philosophers. Modern philosophy is closely associated with the rise of science in the seventeenth century and begins with the work of Francis Bacon and Descartes. From that time on significant philosophy cannot be entirely dissociated from science and scientific knowledge, so modern philosophers have laid even greater emphasis on causation than did the ancients. Of especial interest to any discussion of causation was the British Empiricist David Hume, whose importance to psychology was touched on in Chapter 1. Two closely related themes run through the writings of Hume that are relevant to this chapter, both emphasizing the *psychological* importance of cause–effect relations, as well as the importance of *psychological* processes to our conception of causation. This will strike many people as exceedingly odd. Surely, it will be argued by most, our understanding of cause–effect relations reflects what is happening out there in the real world, not what is happening in our minds. Well, Hume begged to differ. His arguments went something like this.

Hume was an associationist, and in many ways one of the first scientific psychologists. He preached the importance of a scientific approach to understanding the mind, and suggested that a science of mind should be modelled upon Newtonian mechanics and be a kind of mind mechanics, a surprisingly modern notion. Knowledge, he believed, comes to us through our senses and from nowhere else – he had little time for the idea of innate knowledge (and was profoundly wrong in this respect). What we know, and this is the first of the Humean themes that are relevant to us, arises from the association of sensory impressions and ideas, there being three kinds of relation driving these associations. Two of these, contiguity and resemblance, are essentially attentional devices that point us to the potentially significant features of the world. The third, cause–effect relations, is the mainstay of our knowledge and beliefs about the world. ''Tis evident,' he wrote in *A Treatise of Human Nature*, 'that all reasonings concerning matters of fact are founded on the relation of cause and effect . . . In order therefore to understand these reasonings, we must be perfectly acquainted with the idea of a cause; and in order to that, must look about us to find something that is the cause of another.' However, according to Hume our belief in cause–effect relations arises merely from the impression of the conjunction of events. There is no 'necessary connection' between them; no actual physical power or force necessarily obtains between what we come to believe are causes and effects. Our belief in cause–effect relations is a kind of psychological compulsion or habit of thought, and not at all a necessary reflection of the structure of the world.

The second theme of relevance to us here is referred to by philosophers as the Problem of Induction (the capital letters are customary and point to the perceived gravity of the matter). In his *Treatise* Hume famously pointed out that our reasoning 'proceed[s] upon that principle, that instances of which we have had no experience, must resemble those of which we have had experience, and that the course of nature continues always uniformly'. In other words, central to the way that we think of the world is the projection into the future of previous experience, on the assumption (as it were) that what occurred in the past will re-occur in the future. Dawn has followed all previous nights, and therefore dawn will follow this night as well. Feelings of well-being and contentment have always been the consequence of a good dinner, and always will be. Even uncertainty is subject to inductive inference and projection into the future. The English weather, for instance, is so uncertain you can never be sure of a game of tennis, even in June. This has been the case in all past English summers and it will remain true of all future summers as well. Now, the important point is that, according to Hume, inductive reasoning can never ever be justified. We simply cannot be certain that the future will be like the past; and philosophers cannot formally demonstrate that induction is inferentially sound. What is more, the uncertainty of induction applies just as much to inferences about cause–effect relations as to anything else.

So, not only are our beliefs in cause–effect relations unsupported by our ability to demonstrate necessary connections between causes and effects, but they are also unsupported as projections into the future because induction cannot be justified. Yet in spite of these twin difficulties, in spite of our inability to prove that all effects have causes, and our inability to be certain that 'the course of nature continues always uniformly the same', none the less we do structure our worlds on the basis of cause–effect relations because the observation of the conjunction of recurring 'matters of fact' gives rise to the mental habit of expecting such regularities to be repeated: 'all our reasonings concerning matters of fact are derived from nothing but custom: and that belief is more properly an act of the sensitive, than of the cogitative part of our natures.' In other words, we are psychologically compelled to believe in a relatively stable cause–effect structure in the world, even if our reasoning cannot support the belief.

More contemporary philosophical approaches have questioned every aspect of Hume's analysis, including whether a belief in cause is indeed a compelling and indispensable part of both science and everyday human knowledge. As already mentioned, quantum physics explicitly eschews the concept of 'push–pull' generative cause–effect relations. None the less, quantum physics apart, all of the rest of science *is* constructed around causal explanations; Humean scepticism *has* had a profound effect on all subsequent philosophical accounts of how and what we humans know; and the weight of opinion today *does* favour Hume's general view that causal beliefs are essential to ordinary human understanding. However, there are two points that any twentieth-century scientist would make in reply to Hume. The first is that he was thinking and writing of these matters some 250 years ago. Late-twentieth-century science is a very different thing from mid-seventeenth-century science. Modern conceptions like the conservation and transformation of energy, the deep understanding we now have of atomic and molecular structure, the unravelling of the genetic code and of the microstructural details of living cells, all repudiate Hume's assertion about the lack of necessary connections. We do know with a high degree of certainty about the *generative* nature of many kinds of cause–effect relations. We can now explain in some detail the necessary connection between the heat of a fire and tissue damage; between the movement and impact of one billiard ball upon the movement (and much else) of another billiard ball; between the existence of a trait in a parent and its appearance in an offspring. Contemporary philosophers themselves continue to refine their analyses of causation, some such refinements being explicitly motivated by, and modelled on, the need to keep touch with flourishing scientific understanding of nature's deep causal laws. Hume was plain wrong on this count.

The second point concerns the evolution of cognitive abilities, but a small digression on adaptations is needed in order to make the point clear. An adaptation, it will be remembered from Chapter 1, is a characteristic of a living creature that adds to the likelihood of its surviving and reproducing itself, which it usually shares with all other members of its species because it is genetically part-determined, and which is the product of a history of evolutionary selection. An adaptation, in the language of previous chapters, is a product of a very long sequence of historical causes that finds expression in the ecological world now. Furthermore, adaptations are end- or goal-directed, and indeed they have the quality of increasing fitness precisely because they are end- or goal-directed. This goal-directedness is a relationship of fit between the characteristic of the living creature that we call the adaptation and some feature of the world of that creature. The shape, colour, stealth or fleetness of foot of a predator such as a lion or cheetah are all adaptations which bear a relationship of fit to the ecologies of these animals, including the features of their prey and the kinds of vegetation and cover in which they live. Adaptations are a remarkable and striking property of life which is responsible for the sense of harmony that life bears to the world; and it is this sense of harmony, and the need to explain it, that has made adaptations so central to all thinking about life and how it is to be understood, whether that thinking has been scientific, philosophical or religious. In a nutshell, adaptations are profoundly important biological phenomena.

We humans are bundles of adaptations too, and all are goal-directed. The form of our fingers is *for* the fine manipulation of small objects; our external ears are *for* the trapping and funnelling of sound-waves into the middle ear. However, two things must be remembered. First, not all traits are adaptations. The colour of blood, for instance, is not an adaptation, though the job done by the chemical that causes the colour most certainly is. Second, as pointed out in a previous chapter, traits are not perfect, indeed are never near perfect, in their adaptive relationship of fit. The external ears of mammals, including our own, are not the best way of trapping and funnelling sound-waves. There are many constraints on the form of any adaptation, and so adaptations always have the quality of 'making do', of being 'satisficing' to use the word of the American social scientist H. A. Simon. So a commitment to the view that some characteristics of animals, including humans, are adaptations is not an endorsement of Voltaire's Dr Pangloss who believed that all is for the best in the best of all worlds, which applied to adaptations would be the view that everything is an adaptation and all adaptations are the best there can be. Only some traits are adaptations, and those that are are never perfect.

Having said that, it remains the case that if you are looking at psychological processes from an evolutionary perspective, then the starting position *must* be that some psychological characteristics or traits are adaptations. It is inconceivable that this would not be the case. What this means is that some processes and mechanisms of mind are part-genetically determined, are common to all members of the species, and are the products of long histories of selection which has shaped them for specific functional ends. But which processes? Which mechanisms? Right now it is the case that we do not have a set of rules, or even very firm guidelines, which allow us to point to this or that characteristic of an animal and make the judgement that it is or is not an adaptation. We have to fall back on one, or some mix, of three possible indicators.

The first is complexity. It has been strongly argued by others, notably by the English biologist Richard Dawkins, that complex traits can only be explained in terms of gradual evolutionary acquisition. The probability of a system as intricate and detailed as, say, the vertebrate immune system or, classically, the eye, being a product of rapid and chance occurrence is vanishingly small; and the greater the complexity, the more vanishingly small does that probability become. Complexity of high order can only be understood as the product of a step-by-step, cumulative process occurring over many generations. So if a trait is complex, then it likely is an adaptation because only adaptations have the features which ensure their continued existence within a population over long periods of time. If chance complexity were to arise suddenly and be without function it would quickly disappear.

The second indicator that one is looking at an adaptation is an intuitively obvious case of goodness-of-fit in the relationship between a trait and some aspect of the environment. Wing markings on a moth that serve to camouflage the animal, making it hard, if not impossible, to detect against the tree trunk on which it is perched are, again, statistically extremely unlikely to have occurred just by chance. To argue that concealing coloration in *all* species of animal is in every case due to chance is simply unacceptable to any scientist, especially given the existence of a coherent alternative explanation in terms of the evolution of adaptative traits which enhance fitness.

The third indicator is the existence of powerful and pervasive selection pressures. For example, if a mobile animal lives in water, then the selection forces deriving from the relatively dense medium through which they have to move will result in creatures with highly streamlined body shapes. It is no coincidence that water-dwelling mammals like seals and dolphins and most species of fish have in common general body shapes that have reduced drag to a minimum. The streamlining, and the existence of other common features such as fins and tails that steer or generate thrust in water, are adaptations which have evolved independently in remotely related animals because of the effects of identical and strong selection pressures.

Now, given these three indicators and being evolutionists armed with the powerful explanatory notion of adaptation, which are the features of the human mind that we would want to look at in the light of the hypothesis that this or that is an adaptation, and hence must have those characteristics that all adaptations must have, in other words, is goal-directed, part-genetically caused and contributes to individual fitness? Language is an obvious choice and has been considered in this context in Chapter 4. The intricacies of emotion with their close connection to survival and reproduction are another clear candidate, or more likely a set of candidates because it is probable that human emotion and its related characteristics of mind such as attachment and self-esteem, are a whole suite of adaptations. Another possibility (and this is not meant as an exhaustive listing) is cognitive capacity – or more likely, as in the case of emotion, cognitive capacities because there is every indication that our ability to know about the world comes from a number of separate cognitive devices. Well, using the third indicator, high on my list of 'vital things one has to know about in order to survive' would be knowledge about, a sensitivity to detect if you prefer, cause–effect relations.

This brings us back to the main line of argument. How does one square this with the philosophers, and especially with Hume? Hume taught us how hazardous induction could be and how uncertain is the inference that effects have causes. Well, yes, human knowledge is fallible, but that is an epistemological argument – a bit of philosophical 'make work', if I might put it that way. And the argument from quantum theory that the conception of cause and effect is either wrong or irrelevant is a view from theoretical physics which quite simply does not apply to the biological and psychological realm. Experientially, that is, in the terms of the kinds of sensitivities that we humans (and most animals with complex nervous systems) have and hence the ways in which we partition and perceive the world, push–pull cause–effect inferences based upon inductive assumptions are central and essential features of our understanding and negotiating the world. And this is not a triumph for folk psychological theorizing, more of which later in this chapter. It is simply the case that our minds have been honed by evolution to a sensitivity to those features of the world that have a particular scale of size and energy that is outside the quantum physical realm yet within the realm that most scientists understand is the key to understanding that world. This is not some optional extra to our knowledge, some evolutionary extravagance, or some chance acquisition by the knowing parts of our minds. Our literal survival depends upon a finely tuned knowledge of the causal texture of the world. If we could not generate the understanding that a lack of ground underneath our feet will result in, that is cause, an invariable falling until such time as there is ground under our feet, we would constantly walk off cliffs and probably die of it. If we could not appreciate that we cannot pass through large opaque objects, we would be forever walking into trees, rocks and walls. If we could not learn that flames lead to pain and injury, we would never learn not to play with fire. And if we could not acquire knowledge about which members of our social group are reliable friends, which are unreliable friends, and which are reliable enemies, we could never successfully establish social relationships and supportive networks. Not only would we expose ourselves to serious threat from those who would harm us if they could, but we could not know who would nurture us and who we should be nurturing. In every one of these cases – cliffs, fires, friends and enemies – our survival is threatened. And in every one of these cases – and there are many, many more – the general context of understanding and knowledge is one of cause–effect relations. Lack of support causes falling. Being too close to flames causes tissue damage. People can and do cause each other harm. In this sense, philosophy is just words and thoughts – entertaining, interesting, but not important. In the real world, cause–effect relations are matters of life and death. In the world of evolutionary biology, cause–effect relations are both the source of the pervasive and powerful selection pressures which all living things have to adapt to, and they are the end or goal of the psychological sensitivity to such relations which has evolved in animals that can move about in, and act on, the world. So Hume was wrong on this count too. Understanding cause–effect relations is an absolute biological necessity, though he was right in ascribing our belief in such relations as being the product of psychological processes and a psychological compulsion to have such beliefs.

So let us examine some of the evidence and argument for these contemporary assertions about causes and their effects and our understanding of the connections between them. There is increasing, and increasingly conclusive, evidence that within the first year or two after birth, the mind of the infant differentiates into a number of primary or first-order cognitive modules which are evolved structures of mind present in all humans irrespective of culture. Two of them are concerned with learning about and understanding cause–effect relations and they will be considered separately. These are modules for knowing about physical causation and modules for knowing about social causation. It is also probably the case that the latter evolved out of the former, but it is convenient to think of them as quite separate faculties.

Physical causation

There is a useful distinction drawn by the psychologist David Premack between arbitrary and natural causal relationships. The former are relatively unspecific as to what events enter into the relationship – which is another way of saying that the nature of the generative link between cause and effect is unspecified. This is very close to Hume's conception of a psychological compulsion to 'believe' in cause–effect relationships even if the belief is unfounded. Establishing such arbitrary relationships may involve rather lengthy learning and is present in a wide range of species. Natural causal relations, on the other hand, are confined to more restricted events. Because of this an appreciation of natural causal relations may appear to be innate or *a priori*, or at least to be very rapidly learned because of the existence of a learning predisposition. The ethologist Hans Kummer suggests that the ability to acquire natural causal relations is much less widely distributed across species than is the capacity for acquiring arbitrary relationships, being confined perhaps to a restricted group of birds and mammals and concentrated in certain primates, especially humans. We will consider the human case of such putative natural causal relations first, and then the wider issue of arbitrary causal relations.

In recent decades, developmental psychologists have cleverly exploited an experimental arrangement with human infants known as the looking-time procedure. A good example of this is to be found in the work of the British psychologist Alan Leslie and his colleagues, who have studied the perception of 'launching' in infants. Launching is what happens when one object strikes another and causes the second object to move. The archetypal example, Hume's own example, is what happens on a billiards or snooker table, where a moving ball strikes a stationary ball and causes the stationary ball to move in the direction of movement of the first ball. In the looking-time experiments, more technically known as habituation–dishabituation studies, the infant sits on the lap of a parent about a metre from a screen on which is projected a sequence of movements of objects, one of which, for example, appears to strike another. How long the infant looks at the screen on the first, and subsequent, trials is recorded. After repeated exposures to the same display the looking-time declines due to the process of habituation – the infant ceases to find the display interesting. Then some feature of the display is changed, and if the alteration 'surprises' the infant, its looking-time increases. Now, many kinds of change in the display will lead to increased looking-times, for instance, just an additional and irrelevant object on the screen. But by controlling the changes, and by comparing different kinds of change and the accompanying differences in length of looking-time, one can infer that some events 'surprise' infants more than others. Leslie was able to show that twenty-seven-week-old infants are more surprised by the reversal of a previously habituated causal sequence (ball A strikes ball B which then moves, which on reversal becomes ball B moving in the opposite direction and striking ball A which then moves) than they are by the reversal of a non-causal sequence in which the film shows a delay in the movement of the ball that has been struck. Leslie argues that since launching with delay does not comprise a causal sequence in the world of normal human physical experience, and since the reversal component is common to both sequences, the reason why the infants are more surprised by the reversal of the causal sequence is because they have an understanding of such causal launching, hence they do not expect a reversal in which effects become causes: for infants, as for adults, causes precede effects and under normal circumstances there is always this asymmetry in temporal order.

There are two important points to note. The first is the age of the infants. At six months most children do not yet have language, though they may show some understanding of reference to single words (like mamma). They are crawling and manipulating objects but not yet walking. They recognize their carers and are certainly capable of relatively simple associative learning. However, it is not credible that they are capable of the abstract reasoning that is necessary for you or I to have an understanding of what a cause–effect relation is, and what is a violation of such a relationship. If they have not come to such understanding through reasoning then either they were born with it, or, more likely, were born with brain circuits sensitive to the physical causal texture of the world experienced through their own observations, including their manipulations of objects, such that within a few months after birth the human infant has incorporated an unreasoned understanding of launching causality and is surprised when it sees it reversed. Leslie believes that the ability to appreciate physical causal structure 'without having to know what a cause "really" is' is the result not of gradual development, as posited by Piaget, nor of the prolonged experience expected by Hume, but of the operation of a low-level perceptual process which feeds its descriptions of the world, including features such as causal structure, to more central cognitive domains like those that deal with the behaviour of the objects of the physical world.

The second point which Leslie makes is that adults, when shown visual displays like launching, which are in effect causal illusions, and even after they have had explained to them that this is an illusion and not a real case of cause and effect, none the less retain the strong sense that what they are observing is indeed a cause–effect relation. Just like other visual illusions, causal illusions are impervious to reasoning and knowledge. This kind of informational encapsulation or cognitive impenetrability is what Fodor (see the previous chapter) argued is characteristic of the modular structures of our minds. And modularity, remember, reflects the influence of an evolutionary history which has selected for a particular structure of mind which gets the job of understanding something of the world done reasonably quickly and efficiently, which has been encoded in our genes, and which finds expression in each and every one of us provided an appropriate environment for development is encountered. In short, along with many other features of mind, we humans come into the world primed or predisposed to learn certain features of the causal structure of that world. The features that will enter into such 'natural' causal relations will likely be species-specific. They correspond to Lorenz's innate teaching mechanisms (Chapter 2). Kummer suggests that the sensitivity to launching causality in human infants is the result of our being a tool-using species. Perhaps the argument should be run the other way around; it is the sensitivity to launching causality that has allowed us to become such an intensive tool-using species which no other species of primate can begin to match.

In this regard Kummer tells an interesting story about two macaque monkeys. It should be remembered that monkeys are not apes; their common ancestry with humans and other living apes is many millions of years further back in time than is the human–chimp common ancestor. These monkeys were kept in a fenced enclosure, and apples would fall to the ground from a tree and often land outside the fence and beyond the reach of the monkeys. When this happened the monkeys would try to reach the fruit, trying at first with just their hands. But when their own arms were not long enough they would make various futile attempts, including throwing stones or sticks at the fruit. Eventually sticks long enough to reach the apples were found and extended towards the apples, but the monkeys, lacking the launching causal concept, would as often push the fruit away from themselves with the sticks as pull them in towards them so that they could then retrieve them with their hands. The human module for dealing with launching causality would lead a one-year-old, or younger, to orient the stick relative to themselves and the apples such that they quickly rake them in, launch them, in effect, in the right direction. Observed through some fifty sessions totalling almost twenty-five hours, the monkeys were not able to do this because they were using a much more general, but less efficient, causal rule of 'get a tool close to the apple and then the apple may come within reach of my hand'. The crude causal rule of the macaques is a striking contrast with the much finer-resolution causal rule that humans have.

Several other groups of investigator have used the looking-time procedure to great effect in providing insights into the development of the child's understanding of the causal texture of the physical world. Renee Baillargeon and her colleagues have systematically mined this rich seam of research using children of differing ages and presenting to them wonderfully clever displays which have begun to tease apart just what kinds of causal understanding very young humans have. Take the example of the way objects support one another, as on the surface of the desk at which I am working. It has several piles of books and files on it, and a lap-top computer perched precariously on top of a smaller dictionary. In creating these piles I used some combination of my understanding of the way gravity works, of the effects of the shapes and sizes of objects acting under gravity on the behaviour of these objects, and of their tendency to topple, in order to produce a reasonably stable, if cluttered, desktop. All of us are even more clever when we use our understanding of support to move objects about in space, for example when carrying a stack of parcels or plates. Now, the important point to note is that when I create a stable pile of disparate objects, I do not consciously invoke my understanding of gravity and the relative positioning of objects – indeed, most of us have only the haziest notions about gravity and would find it difficult to speak clearly about why the shapes of objects might render one unsuitable in supplying stable support for another placed on top of it. None the less, through the highly practised skill of supporting objects we are all of us able effortlessly and rapidly to compute what will provide stable support and what will not. We act as though we are physicists, but without the conscious knowledge of the laws of physics. How do we do this? Where does this unreasoned knowledge come from?

Baillargeon and others have shown that if one presents to eighteen-week-old infants a physically possible event (the display shows a hand depositing one block squarely on top of another, the hand then withdrawing leaving the second block resting on the one underneath) and a physically impossible event (the display shows the hand releasing the block next to the resting block, not on top of it, and then the released block remains suspended in air), the infants reliably spend significantly more time looking at the impossible event. In other words, they show more surprise when looking at an event that physically could not occur in the real world. In another version of the experiment twelve-week-old infants watched two different displays. In the one a hand was seen to push an object along a surface, but the object always remained on the surface. In the other the hand pushed the same object through the same distance, but because of a different starting position the object was pushed off the surface, but remained suspended in mid-air. Once again, these very young infants, and they were only three months old, showed significant surprise at the impossible event, but none at the possible event.

So by a really quite young age infants understand that one object must be in contact with another if it is to be supported by it. In order further to tease apart quite what this understanding is, more experiments were carried out in which the possible event depicted was of a block in contact with two others, one being the surface on which the block rested and the other a sideways contact with a larger block, and the impossible event was where the sideways contact was identical but the block was suspended in mid-air some way above the upper surface of the block underneath it. Male infants eighteen weeks old, whose rates of maturation are slower than females, showed no surprise at the impossible event, that is, they had not yet come to understand what kind of contact is needed for support, merely that contact of some kind is necessary. However, more rapidly developing eighteen-week-old female infants did show reliable and significant surprise at the impossible event, having cognitively differentiated a more specific understanding as to the difference between 'support next to' and 'support under'. Furthermore, though at twenty-two weeks infants are not surprised when shown a display where the condition of 'support under' is of an amount too little to comprise adequate physical support (adults would say that the object would slip off the edge if left unsupported in that position), by twenty-six weeks they do show an understanding that amount of contact is crucial to stable support, not just any 'support under'.

In summary, then, what Baillargeon has demonstrated is that by twelve weeks infants understand that contact, any contact, is necessary for support; thereafter they pass through a nicely defined developmental sequence in which first the nature of the support that is necessary, and then the amount, comes to be appreciated. Baillargeon is of the view that all physical causal understanding follows a similar sequence of an initially undifferentiated causal concept, which then becomes elaborated into more precise understanding. Again, it is worth emphasizing that twelve-week-old infants are quite unskilled in manipulating objects and it would be a matter of chance whether they could balance one object on top of another. So their causal understanding runs ahead of their manual skills. Indeed, these remarkable findings are at odds with the predictions of Piagetian developmental theory precisely because Piaget's thinking was based on what infants do manually. Piaget did not have available to him this looking-time methodology.

Using rather more life-like representations of real events than did Leslie, Baillargeon and others have shown the same general sequence in the unfolding of causal cognition of launching from as early as ten weeks after birth. Within a couple of months after birth, when infants are still helpless and unco-ordinated in their manual control, the looking-time method shows that they already expect a launching effect when a moving object hits one that is stationary, but only months later do they identify variables, such as the relative sizes of the colliding objects, that influence the outcomes of these kinds of causal event. Similar sequences of causal understanding have now been documented with regard to veiling and protuberance (where an object is covered by some form of material which bulges and hence indicates the presence of the object – the veiled object causes the protuberance), occlusion (where one object causes another to be hidden from view) and containment (one object is placed inside of another). In each case, an initial causal concept appears to be acquired, or to develop, soon after birth, and then subsequently elaborated by the incorporation of variables that make the causal understanding increasingly refined.

The development of the causal understanding of phenomena such as launching and containment were meat and drink to Piaget, but as already pointed out, he investigated them in a very different manner. Even more different was the interpretation that he placed on them. As in the case of language (see previous chapter), Piaget interpreted such causal cognitive development as due to the operation of general processes of intelligence gradually embracing an increasing range of cognitive skills, and doing so without any vestige of help from innate factors. Baillargeon's interpretation of her findings is very different. She believes that in every case the causal concepts are formed by rapidly occurring and highly constrained learning. As will be remembered from Chapter 4, regular and reliable rapid learning must indicate the presence of constraint because the search space is so large that unconstrained learning alone is extremely unlikely to succeed in finding the right things to learn in the short time available to the conscious experience of a newborn child. For unconstrained learning to find the right place in search space by chance alone in such a short time in all infants is an event statistically so unlikely to occur that no scientist would accept it as an explanation for fast learning in all the members of a species. The search space must be being narrowed by something that aims the learning into a relatively tiny corner of all possible search space. This direction or aiming must be coming from genetic instructions which are found in every member of the species *Homo sapiens*. Just as every human has genes that lead to the differentiation of structures such as the pancreas or the knee joint, so every human has genes that lead to the differentiation of specific learning mechanisms in the brain that are aimed at acquiring particular kinds of understanding of the causal texture of the world. Such genes can only be the product of evolution.

Other developmentalists, like Alan Leslie and the American psychologist Elizabeth Spelke, adopt the view that causal understanding is rather more directly linked to innate factors. Yes, learning does elaborate such understanding, and makes it more precise. But the infant is born with neural structures already in place which give it *a priori* knowledge of the causal texture of the world, in this case specifically the mechanical world of experienced physical causation. Such neural structures, of course, are genetically part-caused and, again, the genes are products of evolution.

Well, whichever position eventually prevails, all are agreed that the human child has a mind that is structured by our evolutionary history to allow early understanding of mechanical causation. It is the process of evolution, that giant statistical machine that crunches vast numbers over deep evolutionary time, that has put in place in the human genome a literal knowledge of the kind of physical cause–effect relations, like launching and support, that are the physical causal warp and weft of daily life. Such innate knowledge has been phylogenetically acquired and hence is 'natural' in Premack's terminology. The number-crunching has been remorsely accurate in narrowing the search space. However, nature can never be absolutely prescient. In *Darwin Machines* I spelled out what Waddington, the British biologist, called the uncertain futures problem which refers to the essential and unavoidable uncertainty of all existence. There is not enough room to present that whole argument again. Suffice it to say that the uncertain futures problem means that the search space is not only huge but continually changing in detail. Nature, no matter how big the evolutionary machine, can never narrow the search space sufficiently so as to home in on everything that is ever to be known – which would be true prescience. Lacking that ability, evolution learns, so to speak, of its own limitations. It learns that uncertainty can never be entirely eliminated; that the chance, the contingent, the arbitrary, have always to be reckoned with. In short, that not everything can be phylogenetically acquired and doled out to individuals by way of their genes as *a priori* knowledge, either complete in the form of instincts or partial as in the case of constrained learning. Some relatively open learning ability is necessary which will operate on the circumstances local to, and perhaps unique to, each individual learner. Such relatively open learning ability will 'mop up' the local uncertainties that the evolutionary process could not foresee. This is likely to have been the principal selection pressure leading to the initial evolution of learning and intelligence 500 million or more years ago. Such early intelligence is still with us and it corresponds to what Premack termed arbitrary causal relations.

This earliest of learning abilities almost certainly revolved around establishing local cause–effect relations. Now, cause–effect relations are, in effect, relations of association. Causes and effects go together, so if a relatively unspecified causality detector and learner were to evolve, it should take the form of an associative learning mechanism that is sensitive to either the general conditions that hold between causes and effects, or the learner's own behaviour as a cause of certain events. Well, it has been known since the turn of the century that humans and quite a large number of other species of animal, especially vertebrates, do show associative learning. Furthermore, most psychologists who work on associative learning consider that it comes in two general forms. In one the events that are associated are stimuli, things happening out there in the world, which may reflect significant causal chains that the learner needs to know about. In the other, the behaviour of the learner stands as cause to the consequences of that behaviour, the effect. The former has been variously labelled Pavlovian (after its discoverer), classical, respondent or stimulus–stimulus conditioning. The latter is known as trial-and-error learning, instrumental learning, operant or response-reinforcer conditioning.

In classical conditioning, what the learner comes to associate is a relationship between events in the world over which the learner does not necessarily have any control. For example, in Pavlov's original experiments the sound of a metronome (the conditional stimulus or CS) regularly preceded the squirting of a food powder (the unconditional stimulus) into the mouth of a dog. The dog had no control over either event, but that the animal had formed an association between them was shown by the dog coming to salivate to the metronome, to which it previously had not salivated, prior to the delivery of food powder into its mouth. Whether salivation in this particular case was instrumental in changing the receptivity of the dog's mouth to the food powder is an old and technical argument that need not concern us. The point is that the dog, in associating two events, was able, in effect, to predict the occurrence of the second by the appearance of the first. The word predict is used loosely here. No one suggests that Pavlov's dogs were making conscious predictions, but their behaviour indicates that the learning of an association allowed them to anticipate a future event. They behaved as if they were predicting an event. In the laboratory case, of course, the metronome did not cause the food powder to be squirted into the animal's mouth and so their pairing was really a causal illusion set up by Pavlov. And often in normal free-living environments animals and humans will observe regular sequences of events that are correlative rather than causal. However, that does not negate the possible value of predicting future events. The sight or sound of mother is not directly the cause of the good nurturant events that frequently follow her appearance, but that does not reduce the value for an infant of learning that mother, as a set of sensory impressions, is associated with satisfying events. The correlation, not causal relation, of mother as sense impression and mother as nurturer is one of the seminal events in the survival and future behaviour of every human child. In effect, much of classical conditioning places the learner in the position of being Hume's ideal judge of, and believer in, cause–effect relations. It is also the case, though, that sometimes what the classical conditioner observes are true cause–effect relations, and conditioning allows the learner to insert itself to its own advantage into that causal chain of events. To do this, of course, the learner must act in order to place itself within the observed causal chain, and we will pick up on the theme of action and associative learning shortly.

Almost a century of experimentation has demonstrated that classical conditioning is a learning mechanism that is indeed sensitive to just those variables that one would expect if conditioning had evolved as a device for detecting physical causal relations. Temporal and spatial contiguity are important indicators of a causal relationship. Learners should be significantly affected by such contiguity between putative causes and their effects, as indeed they are. It has been clearly and repeatedly shown that delaying the appearance of the second event after the occurrence of the first results in the marked deterioration in the rate and strength of conditioning; and that conditioning is greatly enhanced if the two events are close together in space. However, contiguity is not everything.

In the 1960s, the American psychologist Robert Rescorla showed in a classic series of experiments that contingency is also a critical variable in determining whether conditioning occurs. Contingency is defined as the condition in which the probability that event B is preceded by event A is greater than the probability that event B occurs when it is not preceded by event A. What this means is that in a complex and less than certain world of experience, invariant pairing of events, even if they are generatively linked causes and effects, may not always occur. The second event may actually sometimes occur without its normal cause, or the cause may not always be detected. At some point the linkage between events becomes so loose that uncertainty makes it unprofitable to acquire that association, and contingency provides an objective and quantifiable measure of where that point is. Implicit in the notion of contingency is the extent to which the first event of an association predicts the second event. In recent years a strong cognitive flavour has crept into associative learning theory and words like prediction, expectation and surprise have become commonplace. It is now acceptable to say that initially Pavlov's dogs were surprised by the metronome, and that once an association between metronome and powder had been established, little learning occurs when a light is paired with the metronome because the metronome alone adequately predicts the food powder. The most influential account of conditioning of the last half century, the Rescorla–Wagner model, is remarkably simple and postulates that the mismatch between past and presently experienced second event (the effect) is the crucial variable determining conditioning.

The other factor that has been shown to be important in classical conditioning is relevance, salience or preparedness. Relevance brings us back from space, time and probability to biology in the form of ecology and the selection pressures that animals experience in real environments. It is an expression of the principle that even 'arbitrary' causal relation detectors cannot escape the biasing effects of the evolutionary history of the species to which the learner belongs, such that certain events are more readily associated than certain others either because they have been more prominent a part of the environments in which selection for such learning ability has occurred, or because such events were and perhaps still are more central to the fitness of these animals than others. However, it is clear that contiguity and contingency are at the heart of the associative laws of learning; and contiguity and predictability are at the centre of the laws of physical causality. This is not a coincidence wrought by chance but an example of the goal-directed nature of adaptations: associative learning is the adaptation to physical cause–effect relations.

Unlike classical conditioning, instrumental learning involves the learner much more directly in that it is the behaviour of the learner that constitutes the one element (the cause) and the consequence of that behaviour that is the other element (the possible effect). In the jargon of learning theory, what is being learned is an association between a response and a reinforcer, which is an event of significance to the learner. The archetypal experimental arrangement for studying instrumental learning was established by Skinner in the 1930s in the learning chamber now known as the Skinner Box and described in the previous chapter. Because of the way the apparatus is wired, the behaviour of the rat in pressing the lever causes the food pellet to be delivered into the food tray. Instrumental learning has occurred when an initially naive rat, placed hungry into the chamber, will go straight to the lever, press it, and then wheel around to the tray and retrieve and eat the food pellet. The animal has learned the connection between its action and the outcome of that action. But can one assert that rats, or even humans, placed in comparable situations, acquire through instrumental learning knowledge about cause–effect relations? Tony Dickenson and his colleagues at Cambridge University say that the answer is yes. Through a complex and elegant series of studies they have shown first that one set of human subjects make judgements about causal relationships and another set of subjects act instrumentally to maximize payoffs (rewards) to them in a manner that shows virtual identity of sensitivity to both contiguity and contingency; second, that instrumentally acquired behaviour in non-humans is based upon the formation of a representation of action-outcome relations (that is, the animal learns that its behaviour has a specific consequence, rather than simply learning the automatic performance of a particular act); and third, that causal judgements in humans and instrumental behaviour in animals are affected in the same way by manipulating the same parameters. What is especially interesting is that these experiments demonstrate that illusions of causality can be induced in exactly the same ways in both humans and rats. It really does look as if human judgements of causality are based upon the same mechanisms that induce instrumental learning in non-humans.

Piaget liked to say that 'in the beginning was the response'. One interpretation of this gnomic assertion is that behaviour, action, is central to the ability of non-autotrophs to earn their living in the world. Autotrophs like plants are living things that are able to make the complex chemicals of life from simple inorganic ingredients and the energy from the sun. Because these essential ingredients are relatively evenly distributed within a few metres either side of ground surface, plants do not have to move about much. Animals are non-autotrophs who can only break into the system of access to chemically usable solar power which is trapped into a chemical web by autotrophs either by consuming autotrophs (eating plants, to put it plainly) or consuming animals that have themselves consumed autotrophs (eating other animals). However, unlike air and sunlight, the energy-rich chemical packages, which is what plants and animals are, are not more or less evenly distributed. They are clumped, localized in particular places, and so non-autotrophs have to move about in space in order to contact the energy sources by which they survive. This is why 'in the beginning was the response'. This need for locomotion and its derivatives is the action, the response, that stands at the beginning of the need to evolve an appreciation of cause–effect relations. So, in the beginning was instrumental action, the cause, whose effect is to bring us consequences in the form of sources of energy. In the words of Tony Dickenson and David Shanks, it was 'the capacity to control rather than just react to the environment that provided the . . . impetus for the evolution of a mind and a nervous system capable of representing causality'. The only way for animals, including humans, to control the environment and extract life-giving resources from it, is to act upon it and to be sensitive to the consequences of those actions.

There are, of course, many kinds of action and different sorts of object on which to act. One of the fascinating findings from the looking-time experiments of Spelke and others is that infants are surprised when they see violations of the launching effect (one object approaches another, then stops at a distance from the second which begins to move though no physical contact between them occurs) involving objects whose appearance is inanimate. However, when the inanimate objects are replaced by human figures they show no surprise at such violation (one figure approaches another, stops at a distance, and then the second figure moves away). Action at a distance, which is contrary to normal mechanical causation with non-living objects, is considered normal when the objects being observed by young infants are humans. This is because cause–effect relations involving humans are another part of Premack's natural category. Humans are self-propelled, socially responsive, communicating at a distance, perceiving, thinking, goal-directed entities. The child's understanding of cause and effect when human agency is involved has to take these characteristics into account.

Social causation

There are, roughly speaking, two ways in which my perception of others will affect my understanding that they are causal agents. The one is to think of people, unlike inanimate objects, as rather complicated machines, robot-like in that they are entirely physical in nature; but complicated none the less because they have goals that extend into the future (impelling action at a time-distance) and can react to and communicate with others spatially removed (action at a space-distance). The second is to grant to others the interior experiences, the same or similar mental states that I know that I have; in other words, that they have minds, and that their minds cause them to behave in certain ways. As we will see, most contemporary psychologists, especially developmentalists, consider that we think of other people as causal agents in both these ways, and that the infant and young child pass through distinctive phases in which they move from one kind of causal attribution to the other. But first we had better deal briefly with the problem of what status to accord mental states, and how these issues are dealt with by folk psychological theory.

Anyone who takes psychology as a science seriously must adopt for themselves a position on mental states. Here is as appropriate a place as any in this book briefly to dwell on this issue because the psychological literature on social causation is now littered with the concept of mind and mental states. This is because here, more than anywhere else in psychology, mental states do powerful explanatory work. Let's return for a moment to physical causation. As we have seen, each and every one of us is a natural physicist to the extent that we successfully operate in a world according to the laws of physics as they apply to the human scale of perceived magnitude and sensitivity to energy. By and large we do this unconsciously, and while most of us would have difficulty saying exactly what a lever is or what is kinetic energy, we have no problem prising open a nut or catching a thrown object without hurting ourselves. So we negotiate the physical world with a good deal of intuitive knowledge of physics.

However, our ordinary, everyday, 'folk' theories of physics are underdeveloped in comparison with our working knowledge. To repeat what was pointed out at the start of this chapter, there is a marked contrast here with social interactions and causation, where this is not the case. It was noted in Chapter 4 that we are skilled natural psychologists in the sense that when it comes to dealing with other human beings we have the sense of a highly developed understanding of 'what makes others tick'. Whatever the source of this knowledge, and as we will see this is a mix of inference and generalization from one's own thoughts and feelings to those of others combined with close observation of the behaviour of others, it comprises a quite comprehensive account of people's psychological characteristics and how these are cashed out into behaviour. How well such folk theories map into scientific theories of social behaviour is an interesting and contentious issue that will not be pursued here, although as pointed out in the previous chapter, to the extent that psychological science does not go beyond folk theory we legitimately stand accused of articulating the known and the obvious. Be that as it may, what is apparent to anyone who thinks about it, and that requires a bit of introspection, is that such theories are quite extensive and detailed when compared with our folk physics, and they are rooted in a conception of mental life that drives behaviour. As natural psychologists we are not behaviourists. Maxims such as 'You reap as you sow' are not the behaviourist exhortations that they seem;

they are based on complex notions of psychological processes (like memory), mental states (like seeking after gain or revenge), and social principles (such as reciprocity and justice). Folk psychological theory is awash with mental states like felt emotions and intentions, and these interior states are not just experienced but are held to fuel behaviour. And that is the point that is being made. Folk psychological theory must originate in some function; that function must be to give us some understanding and insight into how each of us should behave in a social context such that we gain benefit from such interactions and are able to predict what others might do; and that understanding is predicated upon the acceptance that we all have mental lives that are in some sense causes of our behaviour.

In itself folk theory may prove very little. It is just one of the many products of our minds and not a scientific account of anything. But it does indicate the social causal powers each of us invests in our mental states. Whatever the scientific status of folk theory, and however science eventually resolves the problem of mental states, it is in mental state terms that ordinary people think when they are thinking about social causation. In that sense, mental states matter because to a social species social causation is literally life and death. This is one of those issues where we can't duck mental states. And mental states, and the language of mental states, present serious conceptual challenges the resolution of which, like the structure of mind and its relationship to genes, lies at the heart of psychology as science. Here are some of those difficulties.

For one thing, mental states are private states to which only the possessor of the mental state has direct access. This curious, 'privileged', status of mental states presents, perhaps, no greater problem than do other non-observables in science, such has quarks or chemical bonds. However, quarks are things, entities, which we could touch if our hands were small enough, or which we could (and do) eat. But do mental states have the same entitivity that other postulated but unobserved causes in science have? Indeed, do mental states like wanting or feeling even have the same status as unobserved postulated psychological processes such as episodic memory or attention? The question goes back to the seventeenth century and coincides with the rise of modern science. The French philosopher René Descartes maintained that there are two fundamentally different kinds of sub-stance: extended substance (*res extensa*) that can be physically measured in terms of properties like length or weight, and thinking substance (*res cogitans*) which is indivisible and has no physical extension. It is *res cogitans*, our non-extensive minds, that is our essential selves and that marks us off as different from all other creatures. Our minds are what we really are, and being indivisible, we have direct access to our minds. In this special Cartesian sense we have an awareness of our minds that falls naturally out of *res cogitans* being different from the rest of ourselves, that is, different from our bodies including our brains (and our psychological processes, we would now add). But is this possible? Do mental states have an existence separate from the rest of the world and yet able to influence that world, that is, to be a cause of material events like behaviour? And since only humans have mental substance, how did it evolve? What are its precursors?

The mind–body problem, to give it its proper name, and Descartes' dualism, has sat unresolved at the centre of the philosophy of mind for over 300 years. Even modern theoretical physics with its many dimensions, the possibility of time flowing backwards, and inherent uncertainty, cannot help us deal with a concept divorced from the physical world. Part of the problem is that no one denies the existence of mental states since we all have them. The real difficulty is adopting a stance which allows us to understand and explain them, and even use them by asserting that they have causal force. There are several suggested solutions, all of which have serious problems of one kind or another. Being a thorough-going materialist, this author adopts what is known as an identity position. That is, I assume that mental and brain states are the same thing, and that the language of these are different ways of describing the same thing. The assumption of identity wins (all too easily, some would say) the advantage of being able to play, as it were, in both games – I can talk about mental states as material causes because I can point to brain states when asked to say where these mysterious forces reside. On the other hand, there is a possible price to be paid when considering the comparative question of whether non-human animals have mental states, which we will consider towards the end of this chapter.

Well, as said before, *every* reader with an interest in psychology must adopt for themselves some consistent position on mental states, because when thinking about social causation it cannot be avoided. Indeed, in this specific context, the notion of mental states serves several functions. It extends the social function of intellect hypothesis; it explains social causation; and it explains certain kinds of psychopathology. Let's begin with the social function of intellect hypothesis, first put forward in the 1970s by the British psychologist N. K. Humphrey. Humphrey asked the simple question why intelligence in some animals, like monkeys and apes, appears to be greater than it is in other animals, like newts and fish. 'Appears' is important to bear in mind, because cross-species comparisons of intelligence are notoriously difficult to make. However, the problem is simply noted here and we will go with the widely held, if poorly supported, assumption that primates are cleverer than newts. (Few doubt that they are different. It is the 'smarter than' that leads to problems.) Humphrey's argument was that there is little in the physical world of the salamander that is so different, so impoverished, when compared to the physical world of the rhesus monkey, that it could be held to be responsible for their differences in intelligence. What are different are the social worlds of these animals. Unlike newts, social primates live in complexly ordered social groups. Group living probably evolved as an anti-predatory device, so there are certainly benefits to being a part of a larger social unit. There are, however, also costs as members of the group compete for limited resources. One has to do well for oneself, yet remain within some acceptable balance relative to the needs of others in the group because the group itself has value to you and one is worse off without it than being in it and dealing with its disadvantages. So sometimes one must help others, which may include sharing, sometimes keep what one has for oneself, and sometimes even take what others have. Social primates, Humphrey asserted, have 'to be calculating beings; they must be able to calculate the consequences of their own behaviour, to calculate the likely behaviours of others, to calculate the balance of advantage and loss'. It isn't clear what calculate means here, but as we saw in Chapter 3 there is ample evidence of reciprocity in many social species. Furthermore, it is well documented that certain social birds and primates form complex and changing patterns of coalitions and alliances depending upon circumstances both within the group and outside of it. Robin Dunbar, in his studies of the gelada baboon in Ethiopia, reported the existence of up to six different levels of alliance within troops numbering several hundred individuals. Perhaps, then, it is the demands of social life that have formed the selection pressures that led to the evolution of the increased intelligence of social species like primates.

Now, as pointed out in Chapter 3, Game Theory studies of the evolution of co-operation do throw some doubt on just how intellectually challenging reciprocity is. However, let's just take the social function of intelligence hypothesis at face value. What is needed at the very least is the ability to tag each member of the social group with some history of their behaviour – something like 'This is X who last time we met shared some of their food with me, but who in general, if I can remember, is not a reliable reciprocator' – and a strategy for turning that memory of how X behaves into an appropriate social interaction, probably taking into account a few conditionals and rules as well (like 'If others are showing signs of ill-humour don't expect any favours' and 'Be good to the strong because they can be useful allies in the future'). With these kinds of social observations, memories and rules, our social animal is a behaviourist since no assumptions about mental states causing behaviour are made. All you need is memory, strategy and conditionals. However, if the animal concerned has mental states (like believing, feeling and wanting, it being *intentional* mental states that are important in this context), and if the animal also has the ability to attribute such mental states to those with whom it is interacting and knows that others are attributing mental states to them, then the 'calculations' that are made as group members compete, co-operate and enter into alliances, do indeed become very much more complicated. Now one has entered a world of social planning and navigation of the 'I want her to believe that I know M so that I can then persuade her of N', or 'Knowing him as I do I think his reaction on being confronted with situation X will be Y so I had better consider doing Z instead' type. The problem space in which friends and competitors have, and attribute, intentional mental states is a much bigger and more complex space than the problem space occupied only by strategies and remembered behaviours, because the former, intentional social space, has all of the latter features, and a great deal more besides.

Whether other non-human animals have intentional mental states and can attribute similar states to others will be taken up shortly. What is obvious, of course, is that we humans do have them and do make the appropriate attributions. The first appearance of early human-like creatures is generally put at around two to two and a half million years ago. Current best evidence puts the origins of *Homo sapiens* about 150,000 to 200,000 years before the present. Over this period of some two million years, the absolute size of the human brain almost doubled. Over this same period there was little or no increase in the brain size of any other species of primate; indeed there is no known comparably rapid increase in brain size over so short a period of evolutionary time in any other species at any time in the history of life on Earth. We have no clear understanding as to why the size of brains of members of the genus *Homo* increased in this way. It might be, and probably is the case, that several factors combined to have this effect. These might include changes in physical habitat, in patterns of sociality, possibly alterations in group size, and discoveries such as the control of fire which had, according to the physical anthropologist Leslie Aiello, potentially very significant effects in allowing humans to evolve larger quantities of energetically costly nervous tissue. It may also be the case that the evolution of the capacity to be aware of one's own mental states and, perhaps as a separate trait, the capacity to attribute mental states to others, and the accompanying requirements for increased thought and planning that this entailed, were additional factors that racked up the size of the brains of our ancestors.

Well, while one can speculate on the evolution of intentional mental states and their attribution, what we do know with increasing certainty is something about the development of these states in individual modern humans. It is known that by eighteen to twenty-four months of age, infants begin to understand fictional (that is, pretend) states of mind in others, and can share such attitudes by entering into pretend play. The famous and much quoted example is mother and infant both pretending that a banana is a telephone. The mother sings out, 'The telephone is ringing . . . (places banana in appropriate position

relating to her mouth and ear) . . . hello . . . yes, she is here, hold on
. . . (puts banana-phone down) . . . it's for you,' hands the banana to
child, who says 'Hello' into the banana. This is a commonplace kind
of episode of pretend play, and is generally taken as evidence for the
existence in the child of some understanding of the intentional mental
state of the mother. That is, the infant recognizes a particular mental
state, one of pretence, in another person, that does not relate to the
physical world. Words alone cannot explain the child's understanding
of the mother's speech or behaviour – the banana is neither a telephone
nor does it ring. So the pretence is doubled – pretend telephone and
pretend ringing – but the child clearly understands that both are
fictions of the mother's mind and is even able to adopt them for herself
as well.

At about the same period of development infants also make extensive and appropriate use of mental state terms in their language such
as experiencing (feeling) and wanting. By three years of age the child
is using a much wider range of mental state terms, like think, know,
believe and dream. Ask a three-year-old why, in a picture, Peter is
looking under the table, and the answer may well be 'Because Peter
wants the doll' (showing attribution of desire in another), or 'Because
Peter thinks it is there' (thus attributing a mental state of knowing).
However, if that same three-year-old is tested on what is known as
the Sally–Anne task, it will fail it.

In this task, through a mixture of pictures and narrative, children
are shown Sally putting a marble in a box, and then going off for a
walk; Anne comes in, finds the marble and relocates it in a basket,
and then she too goes off; Sally returns and the child is asked where
Sally will look for the marble. Most three-year-olds will reply that
Sally will look in the basket. Most four-year-olds, understanding that
Sally has a false belief and hence showing an appreciation that more
than a single representation of the world is possible, will say that
Sally will look in the box. In other words, the three-year-old thinks
that what it knows is what all others know, whereas the four-year-old
understands that others can hold intentional mental states different
from their own. There are many variants on these tasks. For instance,
show a three-year-old a box or tube of some well-known confectionery
and ask what they think is in it. They will invariably respond with

'Chocolates'. The box is then opened to reveal some other object, say a pencil, not a chocolate. Then ask the child what others will think is in the box, and the child will reply, 'A pencil'. Four-year-olds, conceptually equipped with the notion that others can harbour false beliefs, knowingly reply 'Chocolates'. This is a rock-solid finding, now being one of the most easily replicated experiments in all of psychology.

What we see in this developmental sequence is the gradual appearance of the concept that the child, and others, have intentional mental states – that they and others have minds. This is increasingly referred to as the development of a theory of mind. Quite how this occurs, and what exactly precedes the appearance of pretend play at about eighteen months, is not yet clear. Simon Baron-Cohen, an English psychologist, has an ingenious theory involving a complex of cognitive devices that leads to the fully fledged theory of mind of the five-year-old. Based upon Premack's idea that the human infant is born with the innate tendency to perceive intention in any self-propelled object that changes its motion unaided by another object, Baron-Cohen postulates the existence of an 'intentionality detector' that acts in concert with another perceptual device for detecting the direction of gaze (an eye-direction detector), to result in what he calls simple dyadic representations such as 'Mother sees me' or 'Kitty wants food', but which themselves do not allow for understanding of shared attention or understanding. The notion of an eye-direction detector is based on data showing that within weeks of birth, infants are very sensitive to the presence of eyes and look at them long and hard when they see them. Somewhere around nine months of age a 'shared attentional mechanism' comes into action. Its presence is signalled by the appearance of protodeclarative pointing, the twelve- to fourteen-month-old extending an index finger towards an object and checking the direction of gaze of the person for whom the infant is pointing, as if making sure that both are attending to the same event and hence registering shared attention. When this occurs a triadic representation is formed, involving an object and two perceivers: something like 'I see kitty; Mummy sees kitty; Mummy and I both see kitty.' In Baron-Cohen's words, shared attention fuses 'dyadic representations about another's perceptual state and dyadic representations about the self's current perceptual state into a triadic representation'. These triadic representations of shared perception then lay the ground for the subsequent development of a full-blown theory of mind involving the appreciation that others also have epistemic mental states of knowing, believing and imagining, and that these can form the basis for deceiving mental states. Deception, like pretence, is important because it demonstrates the understanding that one can have mental states about mental states that are false.

Alan Leslie's theory of agency, which is not at odds with that of Baron-Cohen, is a rather more spare account of the development of a theory of mind. It is based on the essentially adaptationist view that evolution has resulted in the human infant being a specialized information processor with mental and brain structures that reflect the properties of the infant's world. Agency for Leslie can be divided into three properties of the world, the child's mind comprising three subsystems each specialized for detecting information relevant to these properties. These are, in order of development by the child, a theory of body mechanism which is tuned to mechanical properties of inanimate objects (considered in the previous section of this chapter) and which results in an understanding of 'agents and objects'; a theory of mind mechanism (system$_1$) which is sensitive to goal-directed actions and which leads to an understanding of 'agents and actions'; and a theory of mind mechanism (system$_2$) which is tuned to cognitive properties in the world and which results in an understanding of 'agents and attitudes'. As we have already seen from Spelke's work, the infant thinks about people differently from how it thinks about inanimate objects, because it is not at all surprised that people constantly violate the theory of body principles based on physical contact. The theory of mind mechanisms have the job of dealing with understanding how agents can have distant goals and the perception of distant objects, and behave accordingly. But the real problem for the theory of mind mechanisms is, as Leslie sees it, what he calls 'the fictional causes problem'. When dealing with physical objects, the only relevant facts are what are out there in the world, which he captures with the phrase 'only real causes real'. However, because human agents have cognitive properties in the form of mental states, which while real in themselves may have fictional content, what the theory of mind mechanisms solves is 'how to describe the relation that holds between the actual behaviour of agents and fictional circumstances while maintaining a causal, that is, rational framework . . . [the] theory of mind mechanism's job is to square this circle'. Put another way, when mental states are involved, real fictions can cause behaviour; mental states are real properties of the world, but their contents can be false. The product of theory of mind mechanisms is what Leslie calls M-representations, which take the form of 'agent-intention-proposition' structures such as 'Joss wants a chocolate' or 'Sally thinks the marble is in the box.'

Well, the function of theory of mind mechanism is clear enough. People have mental states which cause behaviour. Theory of mind mechanisms are, in Baron-Cohen's words, a device or set of devices for mind-reading, and mind-reading is essential for understanding why people do the things that they do. And the general sequence of stages in the development of a theory of mind is now reasonably well established. However, we are still a long way from knowing much of the detailed psychological mechanisms from which our theories of mind are built. Most contemporary psychologists consider the theory of mind mechanism to be an evolved, specialist and innate structure or set of structures. As always, though, this only buys us a limited understanding. One of the big questions is how the child ever comes to have an understanding of, even just makes contact with, their own private mental events. How do we know what they are? How do I know that my mental events and states bear any relationship to those of others? Alison Gopnik of Berkeley University neatly divides the answers on offer into three broad kinds. The first is quite close to the answer that Descartes might have approved of. We understand that we have mental states like wants and feelings because *res cogitans*, the substance of mind, is indivisible and able to know itself – it simply gives rise to knowable mental states. The American philosopher John Searle refers to this as 'intrinsic intentionality'. Having such direct access to mental states allows us to compare how we feel in particular situations, and then observing others in similar circumstances we make inferences about what they must be experiencing. This is sometimes known as simulation theory.

The second approach, referred to by the philosopher Daniel Dennett as 'the intentional stance', asserts that all that we can know *with certainty* about intentional mental states is that they are enculturated conventions of thought and meaning requiring what Wittgenstein wrote of as 'preservation by public criteria'. The existence of mental states is not denied, nor that we all experience them. The claim is that their meaning is only ever achieved by public application. In some ways this is a form of behaviourist or culturally determined approach to theory of mind.

The third approach has come to be called, rather confusingly, 'theory theory' because the central claim is that our theory of mind is literally a theory, or rather a succession of theories as we grow through infancy and childhood. The argument, briefly, is that we have interior experiences, perhaps innately given access to them, and these are probably innately geared to some sense of perceived intentionality from early in our lives. Initially, however, the infant's theory of mind is not representational or causal in the way that the adult mind is. What the child does, on the basis of the evidence available to it and given its cognitive resources, is to generate a sequence of theories which culminate in the understanding that it is mental states, what people think, that determines what they do rather than the state of the world itself. In short, we come to understand that much of human action, including our own, derives from the way we represent the world in our minds. Some proponents of 'theory theory', like Gopnik, assert that intentionality is a product first of inference and only later comes to be labelled as a mental state. That is, quite unlike the Cartesian view, our knowledge of intentional mental states is indirect. In Gopnik's words:

First we have psychological states, observe the behaviours and the experiences they lead to in ourselves and others, construct a theory about the causes of those behaviours and experiences that postulates intentionality, and then, in consequence, we have the intentionality of those states.

The preoccupation of developmentalists with the child's mind, with certain notable exceptions like Piaget and Piagetians in general, is a relatively recent one. Other theories will almost certainly be offered in the future, and those that we now have will doubtless be extended, blended with one another, and transformed as more clever experiments and observations of children are made. Right now there simply is not good enough evidence on which to judge the explanatory power of the available theories. However, the behaviourist or intentional stance view is, as always, the least interesting psychologically, and the one that seems least compatible with what might be one of the most conceptually important applications of theory of mind, which is the possible explanation of autism.

Autism was first described by Leo Kanner in 1943, though there is now reason to believe that it has existed as a childhood disorder since the beginning of time. Before 1943 it had, presumably, been lumped together with other kinds of impairment, especially generalized mental retardation. Kanner's description emphasized 'extreme aloneness', an obsessive desire for sameness and routine, and, sometimes, 'islands' of astonishing talents that seem to co-exist with frequent general retardation, as the features that mark autism off as a specific form of disorder. Although most autistics are mentally retarded in some way, about 15 per cent fall within the normal range of intelligence; thus suggesting that retardation is an additional burden carried by these children and not a trait characterizing the illness. It is impairments specifically in social, communicative and imaginative functioning that really mark out the autistic child, and these only become apparent in the second and third years after birth. Because autistic children usually appear physically normal, initial theories of the cause focussed on the extreme withdrawal of these children. It was suggested, and for many years seriously believed, that autistic children had suffered some form of catastrophic rejection by their caretakers which led them to wall themselves off from the social world. There is absolutely no evidence to support this. Through the 1950s and 1970s, as the existence of autism became widely known within the clinical community, and so more and more children were recognized as suffering from the condition, figures began to accumulate suggesting a specific biological cause. Although a relatively rare condition occurring in about two to three per 10,000 children, autism is some three to four times more prevalent in boys than girls. It is also the case that if one of a pair of monozygotic (identical) twins is autistic, it is much more likely that the other twin will be autistic than is the case when the autistic child is one of a pair of dizygotic (non-identical) twins. Finally, the occurrence of more than one autistic child in a family is an order of magnitude greater than would be expected to occur by chance. These facts indicate a genetic, possibly sex-linked, cause.

The real breakthrough in understanding the cause of autism came in the late 1970s and early 1980s when it became clear that the age at which the condition was being diagnosed coincided with the onset of metarepresentational skills, that is, the ability to represent for oneself the representations of others. Could it be that autists cannot think about the thoughts of others? Devised initially by Austrian psychologists, the Sally–Anne task described earlier is a way of seeing whether young children can understand that others are able to have false beliefs which may govern their behaviour. When autistic children were tested on the false belief task by Simon Baron-Cohen, Uta Frith and Alan Leslie, it was found that when compared to age-matched normal children and children suffering from Down's syndrome, all of whom pass the Sally–Anne test, the great majority of autistic children fail it. They do not have a properly developed theory of mind. This is now a well-replicated finding, and it is buttressed by other data. Autistic children usually do not show protodeclarative pointing, and usually do not indulge in pretend play. In terms of Baron-Cohen's model of normal theory of mind development, autists appear to have relatively intact intentionality and eye-direction detectors. However, their shared attentional mechanism seems to be grossly impaired or entirely absent and as a result autists have dysfunctional theory of mind mechanisms. Recent research from Baron-Cohen and his colleagues, based on prospective studies (that is, screening large numbers of children before the usual diagnosis of autism is made), shows that eighteen-month-old toddlers who fail tests on pretend play, joint attention and social interest (empathy) will be diagnosed as autistic around thirty to thirty-six months. There is also some indication from functional imaging studies that a specific region of the frontal lobes of the neocortex is involved in theory of mind mechanisms.

The patterns of deficits in autistic children are probabilistic and not absolute. Some small number do show signs of theory of mind, and some seem to mature very late, in their teens and beyond, into some kind of functional theory of mind. Some are of normal intelligence though usually showing a characteristic profile of performance on the sub-items of intelligence tests. Many are grossly impaired. This variable pattern is best understood as being the result of damage limited to a specific brain mechanism, which in some may only be partial, hence allows a degree of normal function in those in whom the damage is not total; in others, the condition may arise from more widespread damage to the brain, perhaps through an infection or some other non-specific cause, which includes both areas functionally dedicated to theory of mind mechanisms and also regions not involved in theory of mind, which is why the core loss of theory of mind is so often accompanied by other psychological abnormalities. The general picture that is forming, none the less, is tending to confirm that whatever the precise nature of the theory of mind mechanism, it is, like language, face recognition, visual scene construction and so many other cognitive faculties, an innate organ of mind – a module sensitive to and specialized for computing specific kinds of information in particular ways and in fixed brain regions.

It remains possible that theory of mind, and its failure to appear in a small number of people, is the result of an even more fundamental mechanism upon which theory of mind and certain other capacities are crucially dependent. Uta Frith has speculated that autistic children have weak central coherence processing. By this is meant that normal children place information within a rich and complex context, hence understand the significance of events within the wider enmeshing characteristics of normal experience. What is right and wrong behaviour is understood within a broader framework of fairness and oiling social wheels, nor just the immediacy of praise or punishment. The autistic child may not be able to do this and so lives in a fractionated world where understanding is fragmented and isolated. There is some experimental evidence that allows this interpretation, but as yet no one has shown a good way of constructing theory of mind mechanisms from such a general process. At present the weight of evidence and argument favours an innatist, modular, domain-specific view of our understanding social causation, akin to Premack's category of natural causal relationships. This, of course, is the view with which evolutionists would be most comfortable.

The developmental story of the child's theory of mind is as good an example as can be found of how the nature–nurture problem described in Chapter 2 is resolved by developmental studies that bring together the way in which genetic information becomes embodied in specific brain mechanisms and psychological processes through the complex construction of development. Right now we might only have the barest outlines of how this all happens. None the less, such studies constitute evolutionary psychology at its best. However, there is no one single method that must be pursued by those interested in making connections between psychology and evolution. It will be remembered from Chapter 1 that part of the Darwinian revolution was the understanding that historical causation is essential to evolutionary explanation, and from Chapter 2 that the nature—nurture problem is one of understanding the ways in which historical cause places constraint on processes and structures operating within contemporary ecological theatres. Well, the oldest methodology pursued by evolutionists in realizing these aims has been comparison between species because knowing the phylogenetic distribution of a trait tells us something about its origins.

Now, psychological processes and mechanisms do not fossilize. The only kind of comparative data available in psychology is that from present-day species. But even with these limits one can tell quite a good story provided that the phylogenetic evidence is extensive enough. It will be remembered from Chapter 3 that altruistic behaviour has evolved many times, *independently*, in certain groups of social insect. This is certain knowledge because there are large numbers of species of these social insects, and the phylogenetic pattern depicted by a sufficiently complex tree of relationships allows one to deduce with certainty that the origins of a characteristic is the result of the independent operation of forces, like Hamilton's Rule, and not due to common descent. In the jargon of evolutionary theory, we can ask the question about altruism in terms of its presence in a species because of convergent or divergent evolution. Well, we can ask the same question about mental state attribution. Is it a uniquely human trait or can it be shown to be present in other animals? And if it is present in other animals, what does its phylogenetic distribution tell us about its origin in terms of convergent (independent) or divergent (common descent) evolution? Could it be that the advantages of having intentional mental states, and of attributing such states to fellow species members, is so great that theory of mind has evolved repeatedly in different species? It is in the light of these kinds of question that we should understand why David Premack and Guy Woodruff asked in 1978, 'Does the chimpanzee have a theory of mind?'

Since then a number of different lines of research have developed. But the comparisons that have been made have not involved sufficient numbers of species, most of the work having concentrated on chimpanzees and a small number of monkey species. As a result we cannot draw any firm conclusions on the convergent evolution of a theory of mind mechanism in social primates. Well, failing evidence on this wider issue, is there, in the findings on chimpanzees, enough to answer the more restricted question as to whether it is possible that a theory of mind was present in the ape that was ancestral to both chimpanzees and humans? That is, do contemporary chimpanzees show evidence of having the ability to attribute mental states to others? If the common ancestor had a theory of mind mechanism which was inherited down successive species of hominids (the name given to the apes that led to contemporary humans), and assuming that theory of mind does good adaptive work for its possessor, then it is unlikely to have been lost in the evolutionary line that resulted in contemporary chimpanzees. So, if chimpanzees can attribute mental states to others, that would tell us at the very least that theory of mind is likely not a human-specific trait but a feature of the larger taxonomic group which includes humans past and present, the two species of chimp alive today, and the ancestral lines about which little is known, that link us to chimpanzees. It would also tell us that theory of mind is present in all humans. However, if chimpanzees do not have the capacity to attribute mental states to others, then the evolutionary story of theory of mind becomes much less certain. It might even be the case that it is not a species-wide attribute of contemporary humans. This strikes me as extremely unlikely given the evidence for its innate origins in the children that psychologists normally observe. However, until anthropologists tell us about theory of mind in cultures very different from our own, if chimpanzees don't have theory of mind it opens up the possibility that theory of mind is even more restricted than is presently believed.

So what does the evidence look like? It comes from a variety of sources, and right now it is far from conclusive. The technical literature uses a number of different phrases (metacognition, Machiavellian intelligence and perspective-taking, to name some), all referring to the same question: are non-humans, especially chimpanzees, capable of attributing intentional mental states to others? Let's consider deception which, as indicated earlier in this chapter, requires a capacity for understanding that not only do others have mental states, but these can be manipulated into representing a false state of the world to further one's own ends. Andy Whiten and Richard Byrne, both of St Andrews University in Scotland, have gathered together an extensive collection of anecdotes from primatologists who have observed incidents amongst free-living monkeys and apes which might bear the interpretation of being acts of deception. For example, not uncommon variations on a theme are observed instances where an animal, animal$_a$, who is being threatened by animal$_b$, adopts a posture or puts out some other signal indicative of the approach of a predator, which distracts animal$_b$ and leads to animal$_a$ escaping punishment. Such cases, it could be argued, are occasions when one animal deliberately changes the belief state of another knowing that if the other animal believes that a predator is present it will alter its behavioural priorities.

Many other types of deception anecdote are available, but whilst suggestive, such stories are not acceptable as evidence that one animal intends to alter the mental state of another. Lacking proper control procedures, there are always other interpretations possible of what is going on. For example, in the case of the purportedly false alarm signal, we do not know how often animals give out false alarm signals when not under threat from another animal, hence we cannot judge the likelihood that purely chance occurrence is responsible for the observed events. That might be thought to be stretching scientific caution too far. Perhaps. But there is another, more plausible, explanation. Animals may learn that when confronted with a threatening conspecific, the giving of a predatory warning signal lessens the likelihood of attack. No mental state attribution need be involved, simple instrumental learning supplying a killjoy explanation. Such alternatives must be taken seriously because the anecdotal method can be extended to many species (why restrict the observations to monkeys and apes?) where associative learning explanations of behaviour might be deemed more appropriate. And since we can all play the anecdotal game, let me give you one of my own.

I grew up in a house full of animals, including two dogs. One was a small and rather unpleasant poodle, the other was a large and ferocious boxer. It not uncommonly happened that the boxer was in possession of a tasty morsel whereas the poodle was empty-pawed, so to speak. On such occasions the poodle would rush to the front door of the house, barking furiously. The boxer would abandon the delicacy and bound after the poodle, intent (well, perhaps – it depends on how far you want to take the interpretative art on these kinds of stories) on defending us all. While the boxer was still thundering forward to attack the supposed intruder, the poodle would turn and dart back to where it had all begun and grab the boxer-abandoned morsel. On the occasions that I witnessed this, there never was an intruder. I observed this kind of episode many times and pondered both on the stupidity and magnanimity of the boxer who never punished the poodle for its seeming duplicity and never learned its lesson, and also on exactly what was happening. Perhaps there was deception. Or perhaps on one or a few occasions someone had come to the door and set off a similar train of events in similar circumstances of poodle not having and boxer having, and the poodle learned that rushing to the front door barking and then doubling back to the starting positions led to it having and the boxer not having. Pet owners the world over can doubtless tell similar stories.

So uncontrolled observations of apparent deception tell us nothing. Experimental approaches with the potential for control procedures should be much more promising. For example, the American psychologist D. Povinelli and his colleagues have used a procedure that tests 'perspective-taking', which is based on the assumption that the attribution of the mental state 'knows that' will only be made if the one making the attribution has evidence that the supposed possessor of the knowledge state has indeed had access to information that is the source of that mental state. In the actual experiments, chimpanzees were able to observe a general scene of one person (the 'knower') placing food in one of several possible containers, but the animal was not able to see precisely which, and then another person (known as 'the guesser') entered the room, a screen was lifted, allowing the animal to see all the containers clearly, and both 'knower' and 'guesser' then pointed to different individual containers indicating where they thought the food was. Of course, the 'knower' is always correct whereas the 'guesser' is only correct by chance. If the chimpanzee attributes a knowledge state to the 'knower' but not to the 'guesser', then this would be good evidence of mental state attribution. In fact the experiment is more complicated than that described, but the details are not important because they have so far not been properly designed, and so presently no conclusions can be drawn from them. In general the experiments on mental state attribution are so poorly conceived and designed that they constitute evidence only of the experimental ineptitude of primatologists. It isn't as if it isn't possible to design and run the experiments that will differentiate between mental state attribution and other explanations of the behaviour on non-human animals, asserts Cecilia Heyes, so presumably in time sound evidence will become available. But right now there is no good empirical evidence that apes mind-read.

Many will wonder why empirical reasons are needed at all. In many ways the great apes, and especially the chimpanzees, seem so like us. Why not assume that chimpanzees have mental states in the same way that we assume, for instance, they acquire information associatively? Why not just assume mental states and mental state attribution for them in the same way that we do for other humans? And, if mental states and brain states are just different ways of describing the same thing, then does not an identity position on the mind–body problem commit one to accepting that any animal with a brain may have mental states, and the more similar the brain, the more similar the mental states? These are important questions, and so to end this chapter let's consider the answers to each in turn.

If we take an animal and subject it to a particular set of events that defines classical conditioning as a method, and the animal shows a learned association between those events, then associative learning has been demonstrated, and one does not assume anything. The precise mechanisms of classical conditioning remain unknown, and may vary across species. But a repeatable methodology and replicable effects of the method leave no room for doubting that an animal can acquire information associatively through some as yet to be specified mechanisms. By contrast, mental state attribution simply doesn't have a tried and trusted methodology comparable to classical conditioning. Furthermore, associative learning does not require mental states in the way that mind-reading does, central to which is familiarity with one's own, mysterious, interior mental states and the ability to project them on to others. Private experience is of the essence for mental state attribution, whereas no interior experience at all is necessary for the occurrence of conditioning.

As for just thinking that apes can do something because they seem like ourselves and so why not consider them to have human-like psychological traits, the response has to be that they are not human. Our close cousins chimpanzees might be in terms of general biology, but their psychology embraces neither language nor culture. Why then make the assumption that they have mental states of the kind that we do? Strictly speaking, I cannot be absolutely certain that my children have minds precisely because of the curious, isolated, private nature of mental states. I can only be certain of my own. However, I am a member of the same species as other humans; my children are products of the same immediate physical environment that influences me; they were raised with similar experiences to my own; and we share a culture. Same genes, same culture and ready communication mean that I concede the likelihood that my children too have minds. And I then extend the argument to all other humans, even if their language and culture are a little different from my own. What others will have in their minds, the contents of their mental states, may be different from mine, but I have no reason to doubt their existence. But with chimpanzees the brute similarity is biological alone. I share no cultural or developmental experiences with them and am unable to communicate with them via language. This argument for accepting the presence of minds in others only because of similarity along many dimensions of structure and experience leads me to be profoundly sceptical of the proposition that chimpanzees, much less dogs and birds, have minds made up of mental states like consciously knowing, wanting and believing. To accept *that* I certainly want evidence, and the evidence has to be good.

Finally, could it not be argued that some form of identity position on the mind–body problem forces the acceptance that non-human apes with brains at least superficially similar to ours will have minds similar to ours? Well, perhaps. It certainly leads us to that possibility. However, our brains are several times larger than those of our fellow apes, and we have no knowledge at all of the massively complex microstructural details of brain structure and function that correlate with human mental states. One day we may have such knowledge, and if it should then be shown that chimpanzees have the same microstructural architecture working the same way in the same parts of their brain, then I would concede the strong likelihood that they too have mental states which are similar to that of humans. We are decades, at least, from having this kind of knowledge. By then it is likely that some clinching psychological studies will also have been carried out. In the meantime, my guess, and it is no more than that, is that if our ape cousins do have interior mental states, they are very different from that of humans.

Suggested Readings

Baron-Cohen, S. (1995) *Mindblindness: An Essay on Autism and Theory of Mind*. Cambridge, Mass., MIT Press. (An easy-to-read review that goes somewhat beyond autism.)

Frith, U. (1993) 'Autism.' *Scientific American*, vol. 268, 78–84. (A simple review by a world authority.)

Heyes, C. M. (1993) 'Anecdotes, training, trapping and triangulating: do animals attribute mental states?' *Animal Behaviour*, vol. 46, 177–88. (A very hard look at the adequacy and inadequacy of the evidence for mindreading in non-humans.)

Premack, D. and Woodruff, G. (1978) 'Does the chimpanzee have a theory of mind?' *Behavioural and Brain Sciences*, vol. 1, 515–26. (Seminal paper on whether chimps can attribute mental states to others.)

Sperber, D., Premack, D. and Premack, A. J. (Editors) (1995) *Causal Cognition*. Oxford, The Clarendon Press. (Superb cross-disciplinary anthology of recent essays on both physical and social causation.)

6

Culture: One of the Last Great Frontiers of Science

It is often said that the human brain is the most complicated thing in the universe. Not so, say I. The most complicated thing in the universe is the collective of human brains and their psychological processes that make up human culture, which is defined here as shared knowledge and beliefs. In part this complexity arises from the extragenetic transmission of information that lies at the heart of culture. There are, of course, other species that are able to communicate to some degree with one another in ways that bypass the genes. However, the quantity and precision of information that humans can pass to one another extragenetically are so unlike that which occurs in any other animal that human culture has to be seen, in the words of the biologists Szathmary and Maynard Smith, as one of the major evolutionary transitions in the history of life on Earth – an event equivalent to, say, the transition from asexual to sexual reproduction or the evolution of multicellularity. Following on from the argument presented in Chapter 1, while one may often reasonably choose to understand something in psychology solely in terms of the proximate causes of brains and minds, the importance and sheer magnitude of culture as a phenomenon provides compelling reason for wanting to understand it in as large a context as possible, and that must include evolution if a complete understanding is what one wants.

Another source of the complexity of culture lies in a curious feature that is exceedingly difficult to nail down. It has something to do with a collective of humans seeming to be more than the sum of the individual minds and brains making up that culture. To illustrate this, consider a commonplace event. Needing to get from one place to another quickly and comfortably, I flag down a taxi. At the end of my journey I give to the driver a piece of paper. The intrinsic value of that paper in negligible. Yet because both driver and I (and others) all agree that a £10 note has a certain value and hence will buy a good pub lunch, a cheap theatre ticket or a paperback novel, the taxi driver is happy to exchange his time and effort for this piece of paper. Only human culture allows this exchange to occur whereby an essentially useless entity becomes something to be valued and sought after simply because we *agree* that that something has value. This needs explanation. The ramifications of social constructions like money are even more extraordinary. When the pound crashed out of the European exchange rate mechanism in September 1992, it was because confidence in the value of that £10 note was lost, not by the taxi driver or me, but by nervous money markets. Financial crises in the past have triggered large-scale and sometimes cataclysmic events in human history. Whatever a money market is, it is something with causal power. That is indisputable. Yet how do we explain what a money market is, and especially how such a thing can be nervous or lacking in confidence? Is a money market something more than the sum total of psychological processes of all the individuals participating in that institution? And if it isn't, if the whole really is no more than the sum of its individual human parts, so that a money market simply comprises everyone who participates in that market, none the less the cohesiveness of the thing that we call a money market is remarkable and that too needs to be explained. The problem is reminiscent of the great social scientist Herbert Simon's comment about how complexity can turn an in-principle reductionist into a pragmatic holist. So it isn't just complexity that marks off culture from all other issues in the biological and social sciences. Culture seems to involve the creation of something whole, something cohesive, and possibly something which seems to be greater than its constituent parts, all of which are properties that are hard to conceptualize within the usual framework of thought characteristic of the biological sciences.

A further aspect of the complexity of culture comes from the sheer 'size' of the phenomenon – what it is that enters into culture, and what the effects of culture are on individuals, on our world, and on the evolution of our own and other species. Culture really is big science, and it needs a great deal of conceptual space for a complete account, which would have to come from many different kinds of scientist.

Within the restrictions of space imposed by just one chapter, and the restriction of knowledge of one author, what follows is a highly selective account of culture through evolutionary eyes. For the sake of simplicity we will first consider how to think of culture in relation to things biological, particularly evolution. Then some room will be given to how culture might relate specifically to psychology, especially in terms of mechanisms. Finally we will try to bring all three, culture, evolution and psychological mechanisms, together. At times we will seem to be a long way from culture, but that is forced by the magnitude of the phenomenon that we seek to understand. There is no simple explanation of culture, and few things in science tax our understanding more.

The challenge of culture to evolutionary theory

Is it possible that culture, or more correctly the human capacity to enter into culture, is not a consequence of human evolution? That it is just an amazing chance outcome of a chance collection of human characteristics? Well, possible it might be, but I would have thought it most unlikely. The question must be asked because one of the oddities of recent human science is that Chomsky, the great proponent of the conception of language as an innate organ of mind, has long been of the view that language is not a product of evolution. However, the problem with Chomsky's argument is that language runs counter to that most general of guidelines on how to tell traits that have evolved from traits that are there for other reasons. That is, the more complex a characteristic, the more likely it is that it has been selected and shaped by evolutionary forces. Quite apart from the host of complex structural adaptations, like the larynx and its innervation, that are needed for spoken language, language qua language is so complex that it seems inconceivable that it could have arisen as a chance consequence of other aspects of human biology or psychology – and, of course, as we have seen in Chapter 4, the claim that language is acquired by general purpose unconstrained cognitive or associative processes finds little support. As we will see, language is not the same thing as culture, though it is undeniably an important part of it. Over and above language, culture requires a number of psychological processes and mechanisms. It is so complex a human trait – really the word 'supertrait' is more appropriate – that the argument against culture having evolved, whether or not it has adaptive advantages for us as the members of a very peculiar species, is even weaker than in the case of language. Given that culture is complicated and comprises a number of psychological mechanisms, it might be conceded that perhaps not all of them evolved, though since each is in turn complex, even this concession is unlikely. But maybe only some number, say one-third or one-half, are products of evolution. Well, in that case our capacity for culture remains an evolved supertrait because without all the component psychological mechanisms, human culture would not exist as we know it. And to assert that none of them are evolved mechanisms strikes this writer as simply ludicrous. To deny that our most unique, complex and characteristic trait is a product of evolution and maintain the view that none of its component processes must have evolved is, in essence, to deny the force of evolution in human history. In other words, it is to adopt an anti-evolutionary stance. We are coming to the end of a century marked by extraordinary achievements in science. One of these has been the growth of evolutionary theory. It would be oddly regressive to think of our most distinctive characteristics as somehow having arisen for non-evolutionary reasons. There is not much intellectual risk, it seems to me, in making the assumption that human culture is a product of human evolution, and that is the assumption that we will make here.

Now, it is precisely because human culture is such a complicated thing that so too is everything to do with it, and that includes the evolutionary theory that is applied in order better to understand it. Darwin's theory of evolution was originally aimed at that 'mystery of mysteries', the origins of species. The rise of twentieth-century genetics accentuated the two-stage nature of the theory in which genetic information, embedded within a mechanism that generates prodigious variation, becomes transformed by the processes of development into a phenotype (a plant or animal, say) on which selection acts. If the phenotype is sufficiently fit, it will transmit the information in its own genes on to its offspring, who in turn develop into phenotypes upon which selection acts. Genes and their transmission are the one stage; phenotypes and selection are the other. They are linked together to form an endlessly repeated cycle. However, whilst clearly a theory that envisages two stages, until well into the second half of this century the theory was largely confined to its original explanatory brief, the origin of species, and it remained a flat, unilevel, conception. This began to change in the late 1950s and 1960s. Evolutionary theory's success in explaining the species problem also involved explanations of adaptations and of the distributions of living things in time and space, and it was so great a success as a scientific theory that it led people to think about how such a powerful theory might contribute to understanding other pressing and complex issues in biology such as ecology and development. At the same time, the conception of hierarchical structure began to have a significant impact on the way people were beginning to think about complex systems. It was inevitable that some of the attempts to expand evolutionary theory should have used the conception of hierarchies because the general idea had the specific aim of somehow elaborating evolutionary theory in ways that would allow it to encompass complex structures. Two kinds of approach began to appear. In the one a hierarchical structure is envisaged in which all the component parts of the evolutionary process are postulated to be operating at every level of that hierarchy; in the other, the processes making up evolution are considered to be distributed in some way across the levels of a hierarchical structure. In order to see how evolutionary theory can be used to understand culture, each of these will be considered separately, although, of course, it is possible that both actually operate simultaneously. Culture, remember, is no simple matter. First, however, it is necessary to consider a particular way of depicting the essential component processes and entities of any system that is evolving because these are the things that are distributed across these hierarchical systems.

Until relatively recently most people were content to think of evolution in terms of the processes and mechanisms of variation, selection and transmission. Following the publication in the 1960s and 1970s of the work described in Chapter 3 which led to the concept of the selfish gene, two terms of Dawkins, 'replicator' and 'vehicle', assumed significance. A replicator is an entity that can copy itself, and genes are the archetypal replicators. Replicators are key entities in evolving systems because accurate replication means that whatever they are, they can, by the process of copying, be preserved across time and moved about in space. In creatures like ourselves, when the replicators are genes, they are transmitted between individuals by sexual reproduction and serve as the repositories of information out of which are constructed individual organisms of varying characteristics and degrees of fitness. Once replicators are combined together in a fertilized egg and the processes of development lead to the actual 'flesh and blood' organism, the phenotype, the replicators are now contained within most of the cells of that organism, including the sex cells, upon which selection is acting. Dawkins called the organism the vehicle, and it is the differential survival and reproduction of vehicles that results in the differential spread of replicators, genes, and their preservation across time. The important distinction to note is that replicators, through the unique property of copying themselves, are for ever, and what is being conserved and transmitted is information. How good that information is is tested by selection pressures on vehicles. Vehicles are not long-lived entities when compared with replicators precisely because vehicles do not faithfully copy themselves. In sexually reproducing species like ourselves, only half our genes are passed on to our offspring, and because of the ways genes, and the forms of individual genes called alleles, interact, this means that our offspring are often not like either parent.

This simple but powerful formulation quickly becomes complicated when one tries to fit it to real living creatures and evolving complexes of creatures because it is not only genes and individual organisms that can be identified as replicators and vehicles respectively, and sometimes a single entity, like a gene, can be both. A pertinent example of how things can become complicated comes with thinking about an individual human, who is made up of a vast number of cells which in turn make up all the complicated organs whose collective functioning is necessary for life to be sustained. The individual person, as a vehicle, is a whole made up of many collaborating parts. It is in the interests, so to speak, of the genes riding about in the individual that those many parts work together as well as possible to ensure the survival and reproduction of the individual, because that is what ensures the propagation of the genes. Now no one questions the status of the individual person as a vehicle, albeit a complex vehicle of many parts; and no one questions the importance of genes. But what about social groups, that is, groups made up of a number of collaborating individuals? If an individual made up of collaborating organs is a vehicle, is it possible to think of a group of collaborating individuals as a vehicle?

The answer to this question is important to us for two reasons. The first is that culture is, by definition, a group-level phenomenon. Individuals form a part of culture, and indisputably possess properties without which culture would not exist. But culture is a collective attribute of numbers of participating individuals. If the social group can be a vehicle, then whatever advantages culture has for the survival of the group may have been instrumental in the evolution of the traits that allow for the human capacity for culture. Second, whilst there is much speculation about our ancestors in terms of what they did and how they lived, one thing is fairly certain from both archaeological and anthropological evidence. This is that human evolution has occurred within a lineage of species, the individual members of which lived in small groups. Humans are not solitary animals, and the appearance of large concentrations of individuals living in massive groups is a recent phenomenon. It is likely that the small social group, numbering perhaps tens or at most a few hundred people, has been one of the few constants in our evolution.

Let's return then to the question of whether a social group can be like an individual in the sense of the group being a complex of collaborating parts which might act as a vehicle for the gene replicators riding about in the bodies of the people making up the group. Until recently the consensus has been that while it is possible, it is also unlikely. However, largely through the work of a small number of biologists and philosophers, notably D. S. Wilson, the American evolutionist, which leans heavily on the notion of a structural hierarchy in which one thing is contained within another which may in turn be part of another (like a Russian doll again – see Chapter 2), there is now a good theoretical argument for the existence of group selection as a relatively common phenomenon in species like ourselves, who evolved as co-operating members of small communities of individuals. The argument goes as follows. First, groups are not replicators and should not be thought of as such. The concept of the group as a vehicle, equivalent to the single organism, does not impinge in any way on the importance of genes as replicators in biological evolution. Second, contrary to the generally held assumption (outlined in Chapter 3) that traits like collective defence that increase the fitness value of the group are invariably unstable and vulnerable to selfish mutations that favour the individual over the group, it is perfectly possible, especially in species like hominids where individual survival may be (and likely was) closely bound up with living in a group, for traits that favour the group to have higher fitness value for the ultimate survival of individuals in the group than do traits that favour the individual at the expense of the group. This is particularly the case in species like our own with sufficiently advanced cognitive skills that calculations of alternative strategies in terms of group and individual advantage, and the advantages of the group for individual survival, can be consciously reasoned through. Humans have these cognitive skills which serve as the basis for the formulation of moral-behavioural codes. (There is another way of putting this. If individual brains are themselves capable of selecting from alternative behaviours and social strategies, then these additional selection mechanisms, operating within sufficiently powerful computational devices, may shift the balance in the tension between individual versus group selection.) Third, vehicles should be thought of not as some single entity, but as a complex structural hierarchy of entities: the vehicle might be the individual, the group, a metapopulation (a group of groups, for example all the villages in a valley), or entities at lower or even higher levels. There is no single vehicle for a species like ourselves, and so traits might be selected which will be adaptive at one level of this hierarchy of vehicles but which are less adaptive or even maladaptive for other vehicles. Which level of selection prevails depends upon the relative contribution to gene propagation. The result of there being multiple vehicles on which selection is acting is a host of well-known human social dilemmas (should I act in ways that are good for me, or for my family, or for my community?). The difference between ourselves and other species which are also subject to such dilemmas is that we are consciously or reflectively aware of their existence. The members of no other species agonize over whether they should cheat on a social obligation of, say, mutual defence, in order to pursue individual gain.

In summary, the group *can* be considered a unitary vehicle on which selection acts. It is not just theoretically possible but, in a species in which small groups were a consistent feature of its evolutionary history, it almost certainly has been a significant part of the evolution of *Homo sapiens*. Human evolution, therefore, will have favoured behavioural traits that enhance the fitness of individuals, but some of these will do so because they operate at the group level. Since culture only has meaning within the context of a social group, developments in contemporary evolutionary theory that sanction the idea of group selection give us the conceptual firepower that allows us to think of the human capacity for culture as being a product of evolutionary forces. In other words, it is both possible and theoretically respectable to think of culture as something, or more likely a set of traits that results in something, that is indeed specifically a product of evolution. This invocation of hierarchies in which the component parts of the evolutionary process, in the form of replicators and vehicles, are thought of as being spread across different levels of a structural hierarchy gives us the theoretical authority that allows us to think about culture as an evolved supertrait.

In contrast with a conception that has the component processes of evolution spread across the levels of a hierarchy, let's now consider the notion of a hierarchy in which all the processes of evolution are present at every level of that hierarchy. This is important because it helps us to understand one of the things about culture that no one disputes but which is poorly understood. This is that it has significantly affected the evolution of our species. If gene frequencies are one of the metrics of evolution, then manifestations of culture like tool use and artifacts across the ages from stone axes to weapons of mass destruction, the gradual control of food resources that constituted the agricultural revolution, the rise of medical science with its increasing control of diseases of almost every kind, and injunctions about sex-roles, marriage and participation in wars (and probably instances of genocide too), all have had an effect on the constitution of the human gene pool. Current doomsday scenarios about the death of humankind through greenhouse effects, holes in the ozone layer or nuclear winters, if correct, will be final proof to an alien intelligence observing our planet that culture has this power over our biology.

But how can this be? Culture has to be either a direct product of evolution, that is, the traits that cause culture have been selected for (which is the view favoured here), or it is the consequence of a number of processes and mechanisms at least some of which evolved for other reasons. How can something have evolved, even if indirectly and only partially, which can sometimes adversely affect our biological fitness? Celibacy, often of socially high-ranking individuals, is demanded in many different cultures. So too is risking life and limb in distant wars. How is this to be understood? The only explanation is that culture entails causal mechanisms that are somehow decoupled, not necessarily completely, but some partial decoupling is necessary, from the causal mechanisms of our biological evolution. It certainly cannot be that culture is tightly held on some biological 'leash'.

Well, one possible conception of the relationship between biological evolution and culture is that the latter is something whose transformation in time comes about through the operation of processes of evolution identical to those of biological evolution, but embodied, of course, in entirely different mechanisms. Variation, selection and transmission of selected variants (or replicators and vehicles in Dawkins' terms) exist at the level of culture, just as they exist at the level of biological evolution. Such mechanisms did not appear just by chance. The cognitive features of humans that are the basis of culture must have, as just said, at least in part evolved. And so whatever these cognitive features are, if they have evolved they must be part-caused genetically. However, if the capacity for generating and selecting cultural variants has evolved, the outcome of the operation of these mechanisms must be independent in some way of the genes that code for these mechanisms. This must be so otherwise culture could not result in behaviour that undermines individual survival. Put another way, if cultural change is wrought by the actions of cultural replicators and cultural vehicles, then those replicators copy and propagate themselves sometimes without regard to biological replicator survival.

Almost all attempts by biologists to understand culture have made similar kinds of assumption. That is, some kind of non-structural or control hierarchy exists, two of whose levels are biological evolution and cultural evolution. At each level all the processes of evolution are present, and as with all control hierarchies, the levels may affect one another in significant ways. Our biology can influence our culture, and our culture can influence our biology. This two-way interaction involving both upward and downward causation, to use 'hierarchy speak', means that reductionist explanations of culture are ruled out, but neither can culture be seen as isolated from our biology. The net result is a system of complex interactions both upward and downward in direction, and this is exactly what we see when we look at well-known examples of cultural practices that have biological significance.

Take as one example the case of lactose absorption. I am indebted to the writings of the American anthropologists William Durham and F. G. Simoons, amongst others, for the detail, but a fraction of which is presented here. Something like two-thirds of the peoples of the world have varying degrees of difficulty in digesting lactose, which is a sugar found in mammalian milk. Prior to weaning, the enzymes that allow lactose absorption are present in the small intestine of all people, but these decline in level in most humans around the time of weaning. The illness that can result from drinking milk in those who are lactose-intolerant can be very severe. The extensive data that are available show that the degree of tolerance or intolerance is characteristic of whole populations of people. For instance, almost all Scandinavians (95 per cent plus) and most Central and Western Europeans (80 per cent plus) are lactose-absorbers, whereas most African, South and East Asian peoples are not (the global picture is actually very complicated, but this generalization is more or less accurate). Across Europe there is a marked gradient in lactose absorption, with high levels in the north declining as one moves south and east. Correlating with this gradient are practices of milk and milk product preparation and consumption such that in Northern Europe there is largely a consumption of unprocessed milk and products like cream which are lactose-rich, whereas towards the Levant and Africa processed milk products like yoghurt, kefir and chal, all of which have much reduced lactose concentrations, become common.

It is now widely accepted that the ability to absorb lactose after weaning is the result of a genetic mutation. So what were the selection pressures acting over the approximately 6,000 years during which dairy farming has evolved that led to the high rates of fixation of the mutant gene(s) in only some populations and not others? There are two non-exclusive answers. The first is that persistent nutritional stress, in other words, malnourishment, in some environments would have resulted in strong selection for individuals with genes allowing them to consume and flourish on milk consumption. Such individuals would have survived better and had more offspring, and since the condition is, of course, heritable, their children and their children's children would have had available to them this additional source of nourishment. However, the calorific value of milk to children and adults is not enough to explain the worldwide distribution of lactose tolerance, which has some odd kinks in it. Something else is needed, and that something is now thought to be the facilitating effect lactose has on calcium absorption in the gut. Calcium is essential for many critical bodily functions, and is especially important in people deficient in vitamin D, because this vitamin acts to facilitate calcium absorption. Vitamin D deficiency may be particularly acute in people who live in climates with low levels of sunlight because an important effect of ultraviolet radiation on the skin is the production of vitamin D. And finally vitamin D deficiency has other serious consequences, leading to rickets and osteomalacia which are crippling diseases of the bone. The nutritional value of milk, calcium, vitamin D and sunlight interact in this complicated way to determine physical well-being.

Now agriculture at large, as the very word indicates, is a product of culture. Invented about 10,000 years ago, agriculture comprises knowledge and practices in how to control food resources which gradually spread across large parts of the globe. Accompanying the control of food was its preparation into many different forms suitable for its consumption, and often myths and taboos relating to food and its consumption. Animal husbandry and dairying are specific instances of agricultural invention and propagation. So dairying, the use of animals to produce milk for consumption, the processing of milk in line with whether the population is or is not lactose-tolerant, the accompanying occurrence of myths about its being the food of giants and heroes, and the selection for genes that allow the absorption of lactose with its beneficial nutritional and general physiological effects, is a marvellous example of how biological and cultural forces interact. Culture has been the engine, the driving force, that has resulted in this small instance of human evolutionary change in which the mutant gene responsible for lactose tolerance has become fixated at high levels in some populations. Had agriculture not been invented and then spread, that mutant gene would not have taken hold in those populations.

Durham classifies lactose absorption as an instance of cultural mediation, where a cultural change has an effect on genetic evolution. Other forms of interaction between biological and cultural evolution can be either mutually enhancing or in opposition to one another. The classic case of enhancement is incest avoidance and incest taboos. The deleterious effects of inbreeding are well understood genetically. The closer, in genetic terms, the inbreeding individuals and the greater the number of deleterious recessive genes in the breeding population of which they are a part, the more damaging is inbreeding. All empirical studies support closely the theoretically derived predictions of these deleterious effects. Mortality rates in children who are the products of close incestuous unions are approximately double that of children whose parents are not related; non-fatal congenital malformations are ten times greater than occurs in the general population if the parents are full siblings or a parent and child. There is no arguing with the data. Now there is also some, though not strong, evidence from humans (and interestingly, from animals too) that individuals who are reared together, even if not genetically related, find one another less sexually attractive than they are judged to be by others, such loss of sexual attractiveness seeming not to be related to cultural injunctions and taboos. If this is correct, then what must be operating here is some form of evolved mechanism that switches off sexual attraction under certain circumstances. Both the nuclear and the extended family, of course, involves close contact between parents, children and sibs over long periods of time. Such physical closeness is the trigger that turns on the mechanism that turns off or reduces the attractiveness of family members to one another in matters sexual. And there is good evidence that while cultural taboos on incest are not universal across all cultures at all times, none the less that is almost the case. Incest is very rarely sanctioned in known cultures. This confluence of biological inhibition on close inbreeding and cultural taboos means that both work to individual fitness advantage, and the existence of such confluence is not surprising.

But what of what Durham labels opposition? This is a more difficult issue. The famous example is endocannibalism (eating close kin who have died, and sometimes friends too) amongst the Fore people of Papua New Guinea. Over a relatively brief period, probably less than 100 years, traditionally non-cannibalistic mortuary feasts underwent rapid change with the addition of cannibalism of the dead person, especially by close female relatives. This new custom spread rapidly and had become widespread across Fore territory before it was ended by the government of New Guinea in the 1950s. A little before this time, reports began to appear of a fatal central nervous system degenerative disease called Kuru. It is now known that the incubation time between infection and onset of illness, as with other forms of CNS degenerative disease, can be as long as twenty years. Extensive research suggests that the first case arose around the turn of the century, and that the spread of the disease within the population ran alongside the spread of endocannibalism in the mortuary feasts. (It turns out, oddly, that the oral route for infection is a much less likely transmission route than is the simple handling of brain tissue.) The disease reached its height in the 1950s when in certain areas as many as 10 per cent of the Fore, especially women, died of the disease. The incidence of Kuru then declined sharply as the practice of cannibalism was prohibited.

Here is a clear case of a culturally driven practice having the ultimate effect on reducing biological fitness. However, probably because of the very long incubation period, neither the Fore themselves nor the government that forbade cannibalism had made the causal connection between eating the dead and the disease, despite the Fore having clear understanding in other forms of sickness of the relationship between infection and illness. Also, the period of time during which significant levels of Kuru were present was just a few decades, which is a rather short time even in cultural terms. So it is perfectly conceivable that had more time elapsed before cannibalism was prohibited, the link between cannibalism and Kuru might have been discovered by the

Fore people and the practice eliminated by Fore culture. In other words, whatever nutritional value and spiritual significance endocannibalism had, it seems inconceivable that so dangerous a cultural practice would not have been eliminated when its dangers became known. Surely such opposition between biology and culture cannot last long, and that in such extreme cases some form of 'leash' principle must operate such that biology always wins out and true opposition cannot be maintained over long periods of time?

Well, it is not clear that this is universally true. Nor does one have to look to Papua New Guinea for examples of culturally driven behaviour that reduce biological fitness. In countries like Britain very few people who smoke cigarettes or drive their cars too fast are unaware that they are damaging their health and risking their lives. The causal connections are clear to us all. There are a number of possible explanations for such behaviour which show how complex are the links between our biology and our culture. Risk assessment and decision-making have not, to my knowledge, yet been given much of an evolutionary spin. It is not inconceivable, though, that our perception of risk is biased precisely in order for dangerous behaviour to occur because of possible fitness payoffs. Furthermore, dangerous pastimes may be shaped by culture but fuelled by biological forces such as sexual selection, so a word of explanation is needed as to what sexual selection is.

The individuals of species that reproduce sexually select mates on the basis of heritable traits that may add nothing to their survival, but which, by definition, increase their chances of reproduction. The peacock's tail is the classic example. This trait has evolved to seemingly grotesque proportions given that its only function is to attract mates. Indeed, there is good empirical evidence that the size and splendour of this bird's tail, while positively correlated with sexual success, are negatively correlated with survival. Darwin recognized sexual selection as different from natural selection and wrote a great deal about it. Everyone else dismissed or ignored it. However, in the last decade or so sexual selection has begun to receive increasing attention and recognition as a powerful evolutionary force. The question is, does it operate in our species, and if the answer is yes, how does it show itself?

Human biology, along with that of many other species of mammal, forces a higher investment in offspring from females. This makes females the limiting resource and results in males competing and displaying for the attention and favours of females whilst the females choose between males (see Chapter 3). Humans are moderately sexually dimorphic (that is, there are significant differences between males and females) and this difference is indicative of the existence of sexual selection in humans. It has to be considered at least as a possibility, then, that some of the behaviour of young men, like driving cars too fast or playing dangerous games, is a manifestation of sexual selection. Like the peacock's tail, display and competition between human males indicate that reproduction is the key to evolution, not survival, and this may lead to traits that increase fitness as measured by offspring but might decrease survival fitness. In other words, in at least some instances the apparent opposition between culture and biology may actually be a manifestation of an opposition between natural and sexual selection, and have little at all to do with cultural forces.

Other instances of opposition may indicate a similar nexus of causes so tightly interwoven as to be very difficult to tease apart. Hard-headed sociobiologists might argue that other cases of apparent loss of individual fitness through culturally driven behaviours such as sexual abstinence or risking one's life fighting for a cause or a country are derived from ancient group-level adaptations that indirectly increase inclusive fitness. Thus, fighting for one's country now, in the twentieth century, taps into the psychological mechanisms that led our ancestors to fight in defence of their foraging group or village and hence preserve the lives of genetic relatives. This is a variant on the thesis of ancient provenance discussed in Chapter 3, but one in which selfish genes ensure their propagation by exploiting culture and culturally established institutions. It retains, none the less, much of the feel of improvised argument that characterizes some of human sociobiology.

One way of trying to tease apart the elements that contribute to such complex cases is to construct a model which makes assumptions about the causal forces coming from both biological and cultural directions, and then to run simulations of the model and see what happens, especially whether the results seem to match what is known of real cultural phenomena. Known as gene-culture co-evolutionary or dual-inheritance theories, these mathematical constructions have been offered in several forms for about twenty-five years now. E. O. Wilson (of sociobiology fame) and C. J. Lumsden's theory centres on a cyclical conception of genes leading through strictly determined developmental pathways to biased cognitive processes that determine cultural practice, which then feeds back via natural selection acting on individuals to alter gene frequencies; these then adjust the developmental and cognitive events which in turn alter culture, and so the process cycles through time. Their insistence on non-*tabula rasa* cognition is a strong psychological assumption (see Chapter 4) which combines with the kind of architecture of connectivity between biological evolution and culture that Wilson and Lumsden envisage to result in 'genetic natural selection operat[ing] in such a way as to keep culture on a leash'. In effect, biology always wins out over culture. The leash principle has been severely criticized, precisely because so much of culture, like religious and political beliefs, seems to be entirely removed from the biological realm.

In contrast, other theories offer a very different kind of picture. Their architecture is more like two parallel evolutionary tracks in time; one track is biological (genetic) evolution and the other is cultural, with the kinds of link between the two being the result partly of processes inherent in, and characteristic of, each evolving system. Perhaps the best known of these kinds of theory is that of R. Boyd and P. Richerson, which offers a rich set of assumptions and which takes seriously differences in mechanisms between biological and cultural evolution such as blending (beliefs or motor patterns, for example, can be formed from a rich mix of different forms of observations, whereas genes certainly do not blend) and multiparenting (political persuasion, for instance, is acquired from parents, peers, teachers and the media, whereas our genes come only from our parents). Like Wilson and Lumsden they make strong psychological assumptions, but very different ones. They posit three principal cultural forces, two of which (guided variation and biased transmission) have characteristics which explain how cultural variants can evolve which reduce biological fitness. It must be pointed out that the predictions of these models also rest heavily on assumptions about the homogeneity or heterogeneity of the environments in which such dual-track evolution is occurring.

Simple these theories are not. They are important, though, because they point to essential empirical questions that have to be answered before we will come near to understanding the relationship between our biology and our culture, and many of these questions are psychological. For example, fundamental to Boyd and Richerson's modelling is 'the idea that social learning and individual learning are *alternative* ways of acquiring a particular behavioural variant'. The italics are in the original, and any reasonable interpretation of the meaning of the word 'alternative' and its being thus emphasized is that we are being asked to accept that we have in our heads two *different* kinds of learning device, either of which might be used to effect behavioural change, and different circumstances will determine which gets switched on when and to learn what. So, for example, we can *socially* learn a dietary preference by observing what others eat (or more likely by a mixture of coercion and instruction by caretakers), or one can *individually* learn by sampling various possible objects as food, monitoring the consequences of eating them and then storing the information thus gained using individual learning and memory mechanisms. Boyd and Richerson assume that social and individual learning mechanisms are different things, have different operating costs and different error rates. The latter is especially important and defines the conditions under which cultural transmission becomes more important and effective than individual learning in establishing adaptive responses to events. 'The key assumption in the argument is that individual learning is imperfect,' in their own words. Well, indeed. All learning is imperfect. But why social learning should be less imperfect is not stated. Most psychologists would point out that social learning is subject to two sources of error, that of the original learner and that of the social learner. If I am learning how to construct a stone axe by observing someone else, or am being taught by them, the skills, or lack of them, of the teacher and my own errors will add together in some way. Learning on my own means that I have only one source of error. So it really depends on the skill of the teacher and the complexity of the task, not on some intrinsic difference between social and individual learning mechanisms. Actually most psychologists would question whether social and individual learning differ from one another at all, and many anthropologists would deny that culture is acquired by any kind of copying or imitative process. We will return to this issue shortly.

There are, none the less, many good and important things about Boyd and Richerson. They clearly understand the importance of the characteristic causal forces operating within each level of this control hierarchy which makes cultural evolution different from biological evolution and the former not just a re-run of the latter; they posit credible cultural forces that lead one to expect cultural practices that are biologically maladaptive; and they grasp the nettle of group selection processes to provide an alternative explanation to Hamilton's Rule and Selfish Gene Theory (see Chapter 3) as an explanation of human altruism. Dual-inheritance theory is, I think, a significant pointer as to how successfully to marry the biological and social sciences. However, part of its future success will hinge upon the psychological assumptions that are made about culture, and it is to these that we now turn.

Culture and psychology

There is a long history of people thinking of culture and psychology as being so closely interwoven as not to be separable, or of using the one to investigate and help understand the other. Right at the start of this century the British psychologist W. H. R. Rivers reported on comparisons he had made on the susceptibility to visual illusions of those living in different cultures. He found startling differences between subjects from, for example, Melanesia and Western Europe. Much better known are Freud's works on culture. Freud's lifelong interest in various art forms led him inevitably to the 'culture question', to which he paid much attention in the last decades of his life. It was Freud's view that cultural practices are to be understood as representing the social group's way of dealing with conflict, in much the same way as neurosis is the outcome of conflict within key component parts and needs of the mind of the individual. Cultural phenomena such as taboos relating to food or the dead, and totemism (identifying kinship groups with animals and the strict rules of conduct that are associated with these groups), were all analysed within the same psychodynamic framework, and with the same dominating roles of sex and death, as he had advocated for the understanding of the individual mind. In essence, this is a culture-as-organism approach.

Perhaps best known of all, and considered by some to be one of the great anthropological studies of all time, Margaret Mead's *Coming of Age in Samoa* was an attempt to investigate 'the way in which the personality reacts to culture'. Concepts like 'basic personality structure' and 'modal personality' were used to try to understand how the characteristics of individuals give rise to the characteristics of cultures and their institutions. The Piagetian formulation of stages of cognitive development have been studied cross-culturally. The French anthropologist Claude Lévi-Strauss analysed myths and cultural institutions in an attempt to demonstrate the existence of human cognitive universals. And recently there has been much interest in the way in which psychopathology manifests itself, and is dealt with, in different cultural settings.

Such interweaving of psychology and culture is unsurprising. However one chooses to define culture, it has to be seen at least in part as the outcome of the psychological processes, mechanisms and content of those making up that culture; and since humans have evolved a sensitivity to the environment in which they develop and are proficient acquirers of certain kinds of information, especially that relating to their social environment, many aspects of our psychological function can be expected to vary under the powerful influence of culture. In Chapter 2 it was argued that the nature–nurture issue always was and always will be one of the central questions in psychology. As an amplification and extension of human cognitive processes, culture is at the centre of any nature–nurture question. As a highly salient part of the environment of every human being, it enters as a powerful causal force of nurture. At the same time, because it is a consequence of evolved cognitive processes, it is also, like those processes, a part of our nature. The nested hierarchy introduced in Chapter 2 as one way of resolving this central puzzle of psychology can be extended by thinking of culture as nested within cognition, which in turn is nested within individual development and the evolution of our species. The image is one of wheels within wheels with information flowing between them. So yes, the links between culture and psychology, especially cognition, are very close and tightly spun. And that is why psychologists like Rivers and Freud were drawn to understanding culture, and anthropologists like Mead and Lévi-Strauss were attracted to psychology.

Most of the links between psychology and culture have concentrated on personality dynamics and organization in attempts to explain why culture is the way that it is in particular settings. A much less commonly asked but equally important question is what has made culture possible at all: that is, what it is that we humans have in our minds that is the essential cause of this extraordinary supertrait. Before we begin to speculate along these lines we had better be sure what it is we are talking about. Definitions of culture abound but in general they come in one of two forms. One, which can be thought of as a 'pots and pans' definition, lists cultural achievements. From the last century, Tyler's 'knowledge, belief, art, morals, law, custom, and other capabilities and habits acquired by man as a member of a society including every artifact of cultural behaviour' is typical. Lists, however, reveal little about mechanism or process. Much more interesting and revealing is the second form, one example of which is W. Goodenough's 'whatever it is one has to know or believe in order to operate in a manner acceptable to that society's members'. What this centres on is knowledge, shared knowledge, and how and why it is acquired. The functional nature of Goodenough's definition makes it sound much more like a problem in psychology, and it was for this reason that I began this chapter with a definition of culture as shared knowledge and beliefs, which is compatible with Goodenough. So it is with this definition as a focus that we can briefly explore what psychological processes make culture possible.

Unfortunately for an evolutionary perspective, comparative data give us no clues. This is because while there are reports of cultural, or better called protocultural, traditions in a small number of other species, and not all primates at that but most notably (again) in chimpanzees, no non-human animal demonstrates anything like human culture. Yes, non-human animals do acquire information from each other. This is well documented across a range of species. But no other animal is known in which literally every member of the group shows the *multiple* signs that characterize being a member of a culture. By this is meant that we humans have shared behaviours (linguistic, dietary, dress and many, many others), beliefs (often very abstract beliefs about, for example, deities or justice), and institutions (we all use, or understand the use of, schools, governments and sports clubs, for example) and *all* the members of a culture do the things that others do, have beliefs in common with others and use the institutions that are shared with others. In chimpanzees, by contrast, only a fraction of the social group will share a small number of isolated behaviours – the beliefs of chimpanzees, if they have any, are not accessible to us for scrutiny. And it is almost ludicrous, of course, to point out that they are also lacking in discernible cultural institutions. The sheer staggering richness and scale of human culture are unlike anything in any other species.

Another feature of human culture which is quite different from what is seen in any other species is the incessant and cumulative modification of knowledge and practice over generations. Michael Tomasello, the American behavioural biologist, refers to this as the 'ratchet effect'. The obvious if rather unspectacular example is the history of the conservation and elaboration of stone tools over a period of hundreds of thousands of years of human evolution. The growth in the form and usage of computers in the last forty years is an example *par excellence* of a spectacular ratchet effect. And then there is the amazing quantity and specificity of what it is we know as members of a culture. The detail of constructing a whole range of physical objects, including tools and the subsequent use of tools to construct other objects like weapons and shelters, elaborate recipes for preparing foods, understanding how power works (and being able to manipulate such power) in a social group which encompasses families, peers, policing agencies and democratic governments, doing arithmetic, or having access to literature, art and science – all these and more involve specific detail. It is that detail, and the amount of it, that marks humans cultures off as quite unlike anything else on earth. The message is simple. If we are going to speculate about the psychological processes that drive human culture, then we have to do so using only what we know about human psychological processes. What chimpanzees or song-birds can do is an irrelevance.

The place to start is with the general principle discussed in the final pages of Chapter 4, specifically with the quotation from Chomsky, which is so important that it should be given more fully. Chomsky wrote in 1980 as follows:

Consider again the question whether cognitive functions are both diverse and determined in considerable detail by a rich innate endowment. If the answer is positive, for some organism, that organism is fortunate indeed. It can then live in a rich and complex world of understanding *shared* with others *similarly* endowed, extending far beyond limited and varying experience. Were it not for this endowment, individuals would grow into mental amoeboids, unlike one another, each merely reflecting the limited and impoverished environment in which he or she develops, lacking entirely the finely articulated and refined cognitive organs that make possible the rich and creative mental life that is characteristic of all individuals not seriously impaired by individual or social pathology – though once again, we must bear in mind that the very same intrinsic factors that permit these achievements also impose severe limits on the states that can be attained; to put it differently, *there is an inseparable connection between the scope and limits of human knowledge.* (Italics added.)

In a nutshell, the argument is that in a world where there is so much that could be known, where the search space and the possible pathways through it are so vast, unless human cognition is innately constrained, we could each of us end up knowing different things with little knowledge in common and scant facility for communicating with one another. A principle of cognitive constraint is an absolutely essential starting-point for understanding a phenomenon which is defined by shared knowledge. Culture *is* shared knowledge, and that capacity for sharing is a part of a continuous process that begins at birth (indeed it begins with the genes that constrain cognition), never ceases for any of us, and which firmly delivers us into a small corner of the knowable world, which we occupy along with other members of our culture. So, in this sense, the culture that we end up in is the end-point of a guided journey through an immense space of possible knowledge. And bootstrapping us on our way from birth, and then propelling us along thereafter, are these constrained cognitive processes – constrained in the same way for all of us because they are species-specific traits. That is how we are directed down shared and specific paths and that is how we end up being able to communicate at all and about roughly the same things that we experience as individuals. Somehow the act of sharing knowledge allows us to understand that there are minds and experiences other than our own; and the understanding that there are minds and experiences other than our own is what enables us to share knowledge.

Accepting and then setting aside this fundamental and pervasive notion of constraint as essential to the cognitive processes that cause culture, let's think again of the characteristics of the thing we are trying to explain. It isn't the pots and pans, the temples and music, the space ships and the Internet. These are the material products of culture. As a process, what matters is that culture involves shared knowledge and powerful cohesive forces within a social group, and these together give rise to the immaterial products of social constructions like money, justice and science. Crudely, and crude is what one has to be if one is to get a conceptual toe-hold in this sea of complexity, the equation is *shared knowledge plus cohesion equals social construction*. With equal crudity this translates in terms of psychological processes and mechanisms into *theory of mind* (see Chapter 5) *plus extragenetic transmission of information plus social force equals agreement*. Let's work through each part of this 'equation'.

Why theory of mind? Because what we are aiming at is *agreement*, whether readily entered into through mutual interest, educated into, or coerced into. Agreement is the essence of shared knowledge. We can only share knowledge with one another if we are in rough agreement as to the where, what and how of that which we are sharing. Sharing knowledge means being in a state of agreement. Deviate from agreement and we deviate away from sharing knowledge. If you and I agree that before us (not behind) is a large, brown quadruped with big teeth (and not a medium-sized, grey, semi-biped with a pouch), and we agree that it is what we have both been taught to call a horse (and not a kangaroo), then we can both feel reasonably confident that in some non-trivial sense the nature and position of this animal are reflected in a similar state of mind for both of us. (Philosophers will argue that the qualia, sensations like brownness, present a problem for agreement because it is something that always remains buried and isolated as experience inside each one of us. But details of the precise quality of an experience are not the issue here. Even the colour-blind will agree, with information received from another source, that daffodils are yellow; people with normal vision may experience yellowness somewhat differently from one another, but that does not get in the way of their agreeing on what colour the flower is.) Just as we can agree reference, so we can agree an action (and perhaps, agreement on action comes first ontogenetically). 'Hold the fork so' or 'You strike the ball with your racquet this way', and you demonstrate the action. I then try to do the same. We both are able to agree when I am not doing it like you, and after appropriate tuition, we will agree when my action is virtually identical to yours. Imitation requires agreement about action, sometimes a strange form of agreement when the imitation is initiated without the help of a teacher, in which one individual matches the inputs from their own behaviour on to the assumed or simulated inputs that were received by the person one is imitating. At other times, and perhaps more usually, the agreement involves a matching by both tutor and pupil. An extension to imitation is agreement about action to attain an end: for example, if you want to open the door then you must key a particular sequence of numbers into the control panel. Reference, action, means–end and cause–effect relationships, no matter how complex the computational requirements, can be agreed upon by any two members of a culture because not only do I know that you have mental states of knowing and wanting as do I, but somehow (and for the moment, it is a complete mystery how) we are able to make a judgement of agreement or disagreement between our mental states. Somehow, and this is the essential bolt-on to the theory of mind module that we need as one of the mechanisms that explains culture, I know, we all know, that our mental states can be brought into an approximate matching relationship with the mental states of others.

In summary, some kind of theory of mind-matching process is one of the crucial cognitive mechanisms that drives culture, that explains what culture is in psychological terms, because agreement is essential to the knowledge that our knowledge is shared. Once we are able to agree on action and reference, that is, on the concrete, then we can begin to enter into agreement on the conceptual and the arbitrary. The assertion that justice is rooted in truth and fairness is no more than that. It is not a 'physical fact'. It is not a law of nature. After all, in some cultures justice is constructed on the basis of revenge or of privilege. It is only so because we agree it so. This is what is at the heart of the social construction that we, in our particular culture, call justice. In exactly the same way, we agree that this thing we call money has value, but that value is built solely on our agreement. Social constructions are complex, arbitrary agreements. They are agreed, matching psychological states.

The American developmental psychologists Alison Gopnik and Andrew Meltzoff put the problem thus: 'How do we ever come to map our experience of ourselves on to our experience of others at all?' The question becomes closer to what is here being called agreement if we rephrase it as 'How do we come to match our experience of ourselves with what we believe is the experience of others?' Most psychologists will agree that imitation of acts by infants and reciprocal play involving facial expressions, eye contact, vocalization and manual gestures, is an essential part of developing 'intersubjectivity' (an odd word that means an interweaving, a sharing, of experience), and it is on intersubjectivity that theory of mind is built. It will be remembered from Chapter 5 that most developmentalists now subscribe to the view that theory of mind is built upon a sequence of cognitive stages which have their origins in innate mental structures. The concept of a theory of mind or mental state attribution is now firmly entrenched as one of the central features of human cognition. It is a relatively short step to move from the attribution of mental states to others to the matching of one's own mental states to those of others. And if theory of mind is a species-specific human trait, then the centrality of theory of mind to culture might be part of the explanation of why only humans possess culture.

The place of extragenetic transmission of information in our equation is easier to understand. If knowledge, beliefs, desires and other features of intentional minds have to be in some form of matching relationship in order for those individual intentional minds to be in a state that defines joint membership of a culture, the vehicle by which this is achieved is in large part the extragenetic transmission of information. (The caution in the phrase 'large part' comes from the likelihood that unintended signalling between people might have effects, though not large effects.) Imitation is undoubtedly important early in infancy for the very beginnings of the process of enculturation. Imitation may continue to play an important role in the acquisition of certain forms of skill. Culture, however, is more than a set of shared actions. It is also a set of shared propositions, beliefs, institutions and goals. The extragenetic transmission of these between individuals occurs overwhelmingly by way of linguistic communication. That, of course, is another reason why culture is confined to just our species.

Quite when language evolved in our ancestors is controversial. Some put it as recently as 100,000 years ago or less, a few put it back beyond two million years from the present, and the majority go for somewhere in the region of 200,000 to 250,000 years ago. It is extremely unlikely to have occurred instantaneously, if one defines instantaneously as either a single miraculous mutation or a period of time less than about 1,000 years, which in the vastness of geological time is indeed instantaneous. It most likely was smeared out over tens of thousands, perhaps a few hundred thousand, years. In 100,000 years there would have been in the region of 5,000 generations. If selection pressures had been strong, this is perhaps enough generations for significant evolutionary change to have occurred even in a trait as complex as language. The main point is that its evolution must have progressed from an initially somewhat simpler form than we know today through time of only guessable quantity to the language of modern humans. Before its appearance culture must have existed in an extremely limited form. It would have been built around and buttressed by the imitation of skilled acts such as tool-making and tool use, methods for activities like foraging, and perhaps group customs such as dominance or precedence based on age, relatedness or prowess of some kind. During what most likely was the relatively long and complex process of language evolution, language must have been increasingly recruited into the existing processes of culture, making culture richer and more complex, with the other processes of culture in turn enriching language.

The evolution of language must have had two specific effects that are of interest to us here. It would have enlarged and facilitated the capacity for matching mental states as language use was incorporated into teaching; and it must have shifted the balance in the content of culture from being focussed almost solely on 'knowing how' to being based increasingly on 'knowing what'. As the facility for language-based communication extended, propositions and beliefs about meaning become possible and narratives expressing the cosmogony and metaphysics of cultures must have appeared which increasingly governed the conduct of the members of a culture. The elaboration and transmission of social constructions became possible only after language had evolved beyond some as yet unknown point.

The final set of psychological processes in our cultural equation has been termed social force in order to signal its function, which is to act as a kind of cement for fixing and maintaining group-level adaptations. A famous demonstration of social force was carried out in the 1930s by the social psychologist Muzafer Sherif, who exploited an optical illusion called the autokinetic effect. This occurs when someone is exposed to a stationary point of light in a darkened room. Asked to fixate their gaze on the light, after a time normal people report that the light moves, and can give an estimate of the amount of movement. Because it is an illusion and they don't know that it is an illusion, when tested separately people report a range of distances through which the light seems to move. But tested in a group and sharing their experiences, the judgement of everyone quickly homes in on some shared standard or norm. Sherif argued that the formation of a common norm is a fundamental feature of social life across a whole range of judgements and beliefs. In the early 1960s, Robert Jacobs and Donald Campbell extended this finding in an intriguing experiment. They put together an experimental group made up of one innocent person and several phoney subjects, let's call them deceivers, who were instructed to give much overstated estimates of the amount of perceived movement of the light. Each person was asked to state the amount of movement seen and the experimenters made sure that the deceivers delivered their false judgements first. The judgement of the innocents was, when compared with controls, markedly skewed towards the overstatements of the deceivers. Then, one by one, more innocents were introduced into the group as deceivers were withdrawn. Eventually the group was made up only of innocents. Yet still the 'cultural tradition' of overstating the supposed distance of movement was maintained. The extraordinary feature of this experiment is that the belief concerned a visual illusion – the light was always completely stationary. Such is the power of social force, even on a belief about something that wasn't real, and even though the people concerned did not know this. Social force of this kind has been given a number of names like conformity, obedience and group cohesiveness by social psychologists who often discuss them as if they originate in different mechanisms. My guess is that they all draw upon a single process that has a single evolutionary origin in maintaining group-level adaptations.

The net result of the action of all three psychological processes, a theory of mind matching mechanism, extragenetic transmission of information and social force, gives us an explanatory handle on that characteristic feature of culture, which is its cohesiveness. Cohesiveness means that key innovators in a social group can be replaced and yet the social norm, which will include belief systems of sufficient complexity that they become social constructions like the money market, remain. Such conservation is possible because accurate and rapid communication of large quantities of information results in matching mental states in all members of a group which, when combined with the power of social force, gives the construction a free-floating character that is independent of any one person. No individual is irreplaceable. In this sense at least, the cultural group is more than its individual members, even though no culture can be other than the combined psychology of those members. Extrasomatic storage strengthens this remarkable characteristic of culture because it increases the fidelity and amount of information that can be stored and transmitted, and such storage truly does stand outside and independent of every member of a culture.

Extrasomatic storage first appears as script about 5,000 to 6,000 years ago. Prior to the invention of writing there were drawings and paintings, and, of course, artifacts like tools. Both could be argued as constituting extrasomatic storage of some kind. However, prior to the appearance of writing culture must have existed for tens or more likely hundreds of thousands of years. It would have taken the form of traditions of crafts where imitation must have had an important role, and narratives. The latter, the oral stories of cultures, were the only repositories of beliefs. The appearance of script (and now films, tapes and disks) changed that. With the invention of these devices, essential aspects of culture are even more disembodied and much larger than the replaceable members of the group.

Extrasomatic storage is everywhere now. In most societies, certainly all developed societies, written script is a dominating feature of daily life for virtually everyone. This has led some to suggest that modern culture may have resulted in a reconfiguring, a reorganization, of human cognition. I very much doubt this. Extrasomatic storage in the form of written language may have been invented thousands of years ago. It remained confined, however, to a tiny elite for most of this time. Widespread literacy is a phenomenon of the last 100 years or so. It is extremely unlikely, therefore, that extrasomatic storage has had much impact at all on the fundamental cognitive processes that allowed culture to emerge, probably very early, in the evolution of *Homo sapiens*. What is likely is that narrative, stories, were the principal means by which beliefs were shared and through which cultures evolved once language had appeared in our ancestors.

Evolutionary theory, cultural change and psychological mechanisms

An essential part of any discussion on the psychological processes and mechanisms underlying human culture concerns the no small matter of how cultures change. It is at this point that evolutionary theory enters the picture in a significant way because, as explained in the opening section of this chapter, the only really well worked through way of thinking of the relationship between biological evolution and human culture is through seeing both as levels in a complex control hierarchy, each level of which is made up of something, of some system, which is transformed in time by identical evolutionary processes embodied in different mechanisms. This is, in fact, a version of what has come to be called universal Darwinism, and universal Darwinism is not itself a new idea. The notion that Darwin's theory of how species are transformed in time could be extended to account for other instances of biological change goes back to within a couple of years after the first publication of *The Origin of Species*. Darwin's young champion, Thomas Henry Huxley, had suggested in the early 1860s that perhaps individual development should be seen as the outcome of an internalized process of variation and selection, as an extension of Darwinian theory. Twenty years on, both Huxley and William James, independently of one another, extended the idea of processes of variation and selection as central to reasoning and creative thought. About ten years later James Mark Baldwin wrote about trial-and-error learning as equivalent to evolution by selection. Proponents of the idea that evolution is a much wider process than Darwin had originally thought include in this century, among quite a few others, Piaget, the philosopher of science Karl Popper, Skinner, H. A. Simon, the immunologist and neuroscientist Gerald Edelman, and the polymathic psychologist Donald Campbell. For most of these theorists, the way in which the brain is transformed in time was the focus of their thinking. Is it possible, they asked, that evolution by selection occurs inside the brain and results in the changed behaviour that follows learning? Then, in the 1950s and 1960s it was discovered that the vertebrate immune system does its job by acting as an internalized Darwin machine, a finding that has been very influential and given added impetus to the idea that evolution by selection is much more widespread than originally thought. It was Dawkins who coined the phrase universal Darwinism. So when, in the 1950s, the idea was put forward that cultural change should be understood as cultural evolution, it was not an outrageous idea. The ground had been long prepared over a period of almost a century with gene–culture, co-evolutionary and dual inheritance theory being the last in a long line of similar notions.

The barest outline of the general notion of cultural change as cultural evolution is as follows. Cultural entities, memes to use Dawkins' word, occur in variant forms. The variation is caused by changes, equivalent to mutations, not directly dictated by selection forces, or caused by changes in memes that occur because of the way they interact with other memes. The forces of selection then result in memes being differentially propagated by copying and transmission processes which move the memes about in space, between people, and conserve them in time. The differential survival of memes that results from such selection and transmission processes leads to changes in meme frequencies in a cultural pool in time. Thus the culture shows descent with modification driven by the same processes as those that drive change in biological systems. However, cultural replicators and vehicles are different things from biological replicators and vehicles, they have different properties, and hence the overall picture of evolution at the cultural level looks rather different to that at the biological level. They are the same only in that cultural replicators, like biological replicators, can copy themselves, and cultural vehicles are what selection acts upon. Dual inheritance and other co-evolutionary theories are based on the assumption that genes and memes act to influence the conservation of one another. This is a complication that will be ignored here. I want to concentrate briefly on just what these memes and their vehicles might be, and what the sources of variation are, because, as Philip Kitcher has pointed out, artifacts and exosomatic storage apart, a theory of culture and cultural change is first and foremost a psychological theory. The mechanisms that embody meme variation, selection and propagation are psychological mechanisms. This must be so because there are no other possible candidates.

So what might memes be? Well, like genes they must be something that contains information which can be transmitted to others and copied. In psychological terms, this means they must be memories, probably of several basic types. However, it is when one compares memes with those archetypal replicators, genes, that a number of serious problems arise. Consider imitation and memory for action which is one of the primary candidates for a memory type of meme. One individual, the tutor, performs an action which is visually observed by another, and then at once, or with some practice, the observer is able to perform an identical action. Now, it is not unreasonable to assume that when the tutor performs the action the state of her neural networks that generate the behaviour is roughly the same each time. ('Roughly', because nervous systems are noisy places, with individual nerve cells being spontaneously active, as well as being active within systematic patterns of neural network function.) In between actions, when the tutor is doing or thinking other things, those neural networks are in a different state. It is the ability to reconstitute near identical neural network states that enables the tutor to perform at will identical actions, and this reconstitution of neural network states can be reasonably construed as a process akin to copying. But even this form of 'systems copying' is a disanalogy with a gene which is a chemical structure that always exists. So the gene is structurally inert and the copying process is well understood in terms of the chemical structure of the complex molecules that code the information held in the gene. The meme as a memory is dynamic and transient and no one has any idea how neural network states are reconstituted to form memories, whether of actions, words, faces or anything else. The inert-versus-dynamic and copy-versus-reconstitute differences appear to be serious disanalogies, and these are not the only ones. In imitation the observer uses visual information which is somehow (and again we don't know how) transformed into a neural network state that generates an action from the observer, which in turn results in an input of information from the muscles and joints of the observer that is matched in some way against an expected input that came from seeing the tutor perform the act. None of this is well understood. Nothing is known about exactly how such cross-modal mapping occurs. But that is not the point. What is the point is that we cannot assume, and it is most unlikely to be the case, that the neural network state of the observer when performing the action, even when it matches closely that of the tutor, is the same as the neural network state of the tutor. The copying-as-reconstitution is internal to, locked inside of, tutor and observer alike. What is literally copied is the behaviour. But the behaviour, surely, is the vehicle on which selection acts. 'No, no,' says the tool-making tutor, 'you're doing it wrong. Strike the stone with the other stone like this, not like that.' The behaviour is the vehicle for the complex of internal information processes that are the memory replicators. Selection is the judgement of tutor and pupil alike that their behaviours match each other. So here is another problem. The distinction between replicators and vehicles is much less easy to maintain when one is thinking about cultural evolution occurring by way of imitation. This may not be a serious disanalogy because, as mentioned earlier in this chapter, sometimes genes are both replicators and vehicles. But our ignorance of the psychological and neural mechanisms involved in imitation makes all judgements as to what is being replicated hazardous, to say the least.

So cultures based purely on imitated action would present serious difficulties of identifying and distinguishing between essential elements in an evolutionary process. They would also be cultures so threadbare in content compared to what we normally understand by the word culture, that we would hardly recognize them as such. And that must have been just the kind of culture that our hominid ancestors of two or three million years ago lived in – a kind of half-way house between the protocultures of modern apes like chimpanzees and modern humans like you and me. Language and the complex cognitive functions that accompany it, and which evolved almost certainly after the ability for skilled imitation, brings a clearer distinction between cultural replicators and vehicles.

Most social scientists would define culture in terms of beliefs and social construction rather than simple 'facts' that can be transmitted linguistically. However, simple facts are a good place to start in thinking about this problem of language entering into culture. Take as an example a parent telling their children that if they, the parents, are not about and somehow the children get into trouble of some kind, then they should go next door to the Smiths who are a good family and fine neighbours. The information that has been transmitted – that the Smiths are good people – is a simple fact, and may be thought of as a meme. Like an imitated act, it is reconstituted in the mind of both parent and child under certain circumstances. And like imitation, there is little likelihood that identical or even similar neural network states underlie the representations of the Smiths as good people in individual children and parents. But unlike imitation, language communication introduces semantics, meaning, and the meaning in the assertion that the Smiths are fine people has indeed been copied from parent to children. This presents another serious puzzle, and has to do with the way in which meaning emerges from incredibly complex neural and psychological states, but whatever these states might be they represent the meaning in those few words about the Smiths. It is the meaning that has been transmitted. So here is a 'fact', simple in meaning, psychologically and neurally complex, and there can be no serious question that somehow such a fact can be transmitted linguistically and its meaning copied in different minds. It is in terms of meaning that we have a replicator. It is worth pointing out a further disanalogy between biological and cultural replicators. In the biological evolution of creatures like ourselves, the replicators first form copies of themselves and it is these copies that are then transmitted via sexual reproduction. In cultural evolution the order is reversed in that transmission may occur first and the copying process appears to follow that transmission process.

What, then, is the vehicle? It must be acting on the fact – the translation of that meaning into an action. In our example, the children find themselves locked out of their house and they go next door to the Smiths. There they get tea, biscuits and sympathy. The behaviour that springs from the fact is the vehicle, and in this example, that selection is positive and the meme 'the Smiths are good people' is conserved and propagated as the children tell their friends.

Facts, however, never exist in isolation except, perhaps, right at the beginning of cognitive life for each person. Facts always aggregate into or become attached to higher-order knowledge structures. Down the years various names have been given to such psychological structures, like schemas, frames, scripts and memory organization packets. Take that Smith family example again. When the parents tell the children that the Smith family are good people, those children have an already developed higher-order knowledge structure of the good family as a close-knit social group of people who are helpful, sympathetic and protective of one another and who do no harm to others. The children simply incorporate the 'fact' that the Smiths are an instance of such a thing into an already existing structure. Such higher-order knowledge structures will be formed in relatively large numbers, though, of course, always in far lesser numbers than the facts that accrete to them. Such structures will be culture-specific. For example, the San people of the Kalahari Desert or the Kwoma of New Guinea do not have (or at least not until recently) higher-order knowledge structures relating to shops or restaurants, while the English or Danes do not have higher-order knowledge structures concerned with the tracks that animals leave or their spirits. One of the most important questions that needs answering is whether there are any culturally non-specific higher-order knowledge structures whose universality derives from innate structuring of the human mind. Such structures might, for instance, be concerned with strangers, sharing resources or dangerous objects. This is an empirical question. The point about higher-order structures like scripts or schemas is that they too are replicators, the copying of them in the minds of young humans being essential to the enculturation of every individual and fundamental to cultural evolution.

Thus we begin to see a rich structure to cultural evolution, which itself is layered. There might be a core of higher-order knowledge structures innately present in all people, and which are directed towards knowledge that is important in any social group. There is also an acquired deep layer which involves the transmission and replication of a relatively limited number of higher-order knowledge structures that are characteristic of a particular culture. The rate of such transmission is roughly the same as that of genetic transmission, usually occurring just once in a lifetime. The surface layer comprises a more rapid, dynamic and shifting set of mechanisms whereby the instances that aggregate around the core-knowledge structures change or are added to, and such change occurs at high rates throughout our lives. We acquire the schema for a restaurant just once. It is an abstraction comprising a place you go to, and in exchange for money you will have food of your choice prepared and brought to you. But whether this or that particular restaurant serves good or bad food, is French or Chinese, has friendly staff, and so on, is the 'small change' of information flow amongst social groups that never ceases. In the case of higher-order knowledge structures the replicator–vehicle distinction is hard to see because part of the process of selection occurs in terms of the coherence of cognitive structures within the mind of the child as higher-order knowledge structures emerge as robust and distinctive features of their minds. The surface changes to these, the added 'facts', have vehicles that are behaviours and it is upon these that selection acts, which then results in the differential conservation of the surface features of knowledge structures.

One of the things we know with empirical certainty about psychological memory is that, unlike genetic memory, it is a labile, active and constructive thing. There is much room here for 'mutation'. New variants will arise as innovations, new ideas or blends of old ideas, and their selection will occur within the context of other memes, as well as the needs of the social group. Some memes are strangely transient and unstable, like fashions in clothes or pop music; others, like religion, are remarkably stable. Multiple parenting seems to occur in the case of some memes but not others, as does blending. So, unlike genes which are characterized by longevity and fidelity of copying, memes may be much more varied in their characteristics. However, much of this is speculative or based on findings that come from mainstream memory studies. There is a whole series of major research programmes on the psychological mechanisms underlying cultural evolution waiting to be done.

The broad picture painted in the previous few paragraphs is no more than an attempt to show what kind of psychological theory we need if we are to take seriously the notion of cultural change as some kind of evolutionary process, and what problems arise as we try to establish what the replicators and vehicles, the units of evolution, are. To it must be added our understanding of skilled motor acts, memory, language, cognitive consistency, theory of mind, and social psychological forces like obedience, status and conformity. In effect, a large part of the field of scientific psychology must be brought to bear if we are to have a proper theory of cultural change. Nothing brings out more clearly just how interdependent human psychology and human culture are than the consideration of how culture changes.

An overview

This chapter has presented the merest thumbnail sketch of the relationships between psychology, culture and evolutionary theory. Although at times it has been highly speculative, I hope that it has given enough background against which one can evaluate the question as to whether an evolutionary perspective really does add to our understanding of human culture. The answer surely must be yes. Intelligent and provocative reconstructions of human evolution, especially psychological evolution, like that of Merlin Donald's *Origins of the Modern Mind*, centre upon the unique supertrait of culture. Culture is what any account of human biology and psychology must ultimately be aimed at. If culture evolved then it did so in step with the evolution of psychological traits like language and mental state attribution, traits that mark us out as a unique kind of animal. In so far as those traits enter into the complex transformation of culture in time, and we choose to interpret such transformation as evolution, then we had better understand as best we can how evolution conventionally understood works, so that we can see where the analogies hold and where disanalogies appear. And if culture is a group-level phenomenon, then we had better look to advances in evolutionary theory that allow us to explain its existence in terms that are acceptable to sober-minded biologists, because we need to keep the biologists on our side. Most important of all, if human culture and human psychology are so intertwined as to be virtually inseparable, then here is a case where the usual form of the question 'How has evolution shaped the human mind?' can be reversed to 'How has the human mind shaped human evolution?'

Suggested Readings

Bock, P. K. (1988) *Rethinking Psychological Anthropology*. New York, Freeman. (Good review of schools of thought relating to psychology and anthropology.)

Boyd, R. and Richerson, P. (1985) *Culture and the Evolutionary Process*. Chicago, University of Chicago Press. (Difficult but classic book on dual-inheritance theory.)

Chomsky, N. (1980) 'Rules and representations.' *The Behavioural and Brain Sciences*, vol. 3, 1–15. (Marvellous account of why human cognitive processes must be constrained.)

Donald, M. (1991) *Origins of the Modern Mind*. Cambridge, Mass., Harvard University Press. (One way of telling the story of how the human mind might have evolved.)

Durham, W. H. (1991) *Coevolution: Genes, Culture and Human Diversity*. Stanford, Stanford University Press. (An anthropologist's view of co-evolutionary theory with lots of anthropological detail.)

Plotkin, H. (1995) *Darwin Machines and the Nature of Knowledge*. London, Penguin. (Accessible account of universal Darwinism.)

Sperber, D. (1996) *Explaining Culture: A Naturalistic Approach.* Oxford, Blackwell. (A psychologist, utterly committed to the modularity of mind thesis, looks at culture through evolutionary eyes.)

Szathmary, E. and Maynard Smith, J. (1995) 'The major evolutionary transitions.' *Nature*, vol. 374, 227–32. (Placing language within the context of other major evolutionary events.)

Tomasello, M., Kruger, A. C. and Ratner, H. H. (1993) 'Cultural learning.' *Behavioural and Brain Sciences*, vol. 16, 495–552. (An appraisal of some of the psychological processes subserving culture.)

Wilson, D. S. and Sober, E. (1994) 'Reintroducing group selection to the human behavioural sciences.' *Behavioural and Brain Sciences*, vol. 17, 585–608. (Excellent summary of the argument in support of group selection as being a force in human evolution.)

7

Promises of a Marriage Made in Heaven?

The philosopher Daniel Dennett in a recent book, *Darwin's Dangerous Idea*, likens Darwinian evolutionary theory to a kind of conceptual acid which is so powerful that it consumes all other explanations of life, mind and culture. It is a vivid image, but not yet an accurate account of what is happening in the human sciences. In the preceding chapters I have tried to show that Dennett's view, if not correct now, may well eventually come to be so in psychology, just as it has come to pass that the theory of evolution has moved centre-stage in so many areas of biology. But in psychology, alas, not yet. It was shown in Chapter 1 that while evolutionary theory has always had a small place in the history of psychological thinking, the more so in the previous century and not much in the first part of this one, it has until relatively recently been lodged somewhere at the back of the collective mind of psychology rather than being its chief driving idea.

Since the 1960s things certainly have begun to change. Chapter 2 argues that the nature–nurture question remains the central causal puzzle that has to be unravelled for every aspect of human psychology and behaviour; and that at the heart of every instance of the nature–nurture problem is an historical, that is evolutionary, cause. Running as a continuous thread through most of this book is a constant message about the need for an evolutionary approach to psychology to understand the individual development of mind, because it is in charting how that development occurs that we come to understand how the forces of nature and nurture come together to cause particular psychological mechanisms to appear as they do. Development is driven by a tight interleaving of historical causes, coming from the genes and placed there by evolutionary processes operating in the past, and the proximate environment of the developing child. Study development and you are unravelling the nature–nurture question as it relates to the psychological mechanism with which you are concerned. The nature–nurture question simply cannot be answered without reference to human evolution, and it is in studying it through development that we make most immediate contact with the forces of evolution in human psychology.

Chapter 3 considered some of the significant changes that occurred in evolutionary thought in the 1960s, and the subsequent attempts, some elegant and potent and others crude and conceptually feeble, to apply them to understanding both animal and human social and sexual behaviour. In Chapters 4 and 5 we saw how 'innatism', which is a strong evolutionary claim, has taken deep hold in the current thinking of those involved in answering the fundamental questions on the structure of the mind and human causal understanding, and how much developmental studies, often in very young children, are contributing to this understanding – in effect, unravelling nature and nurture as discussed in Chapter 2. Then in Chapter 6 the growing movement to see that most unique of all human characteristics, culture, in the light of evolutionary theory was considered. Dobzhansky's dictum discussed in Chapter 1 is indeed beginning to take hold in scientific psychology.

I have not attempted to cover the whole of our subject. That would be too much for one introductory book, and perhaps for one author who is trying to make a single, simple point. This is that psychology needs the theory of evolution just as much as it needs an understanding of how the brain works; and just as understanding how the brain works absolutely requires knowledge of psychology, so understanding human evolution needs an understanding of human psychology and culture. But great tracts of the subject have been left to one side. Motivation and emotion, for instance, have been little mentioned. Darwin himself devoted a whole book and much other writing as well to the expression of emotions, this being a topic that is ripe for picking and placing in an evolutionary basket because emotions are the engines behind our behaviour. It is inconceivable that the mechanisms that fuel what we do are any less a product of our evolutionary history than are the cognitive mechanisms that allow us to use language, understand physical causes and read the minds of others.

Personality also has been given no place at all in previous pages. Yet personality must, like all else, emerge from that complex causal nexus of nature and nurture. Running right across this century has been a dispute among personality theorists that has been, and is, similar in form to the general-purpose versus domain-specific argument among learning theorists and cognitivists. One camp has argued that all human personalities comprise a mix of a limited number, perhaps only three or five, of basic types. This position cries out for an evolutionary analysis because the very phrase 'basic types' is redolent of constraint, and constraint has to originate in genes which are sifted and shuffled by the evolutionary process. The opposite camp asserts that there are as many types of personality as there are individual human histories. This is a *tabula rasa* view of personality. The slate is clean at birth, and then rich individual experience writes any and every possible pattern of personality on to it. The basic-types approach, whatever the number of types might be, is roughly equivalent to the modularity and domain-specific position in cognitive theory. It says that each of us comes into the world with the slate of personality already written upon by our genes, and the final product is the outcome of individual experience filling in the gaps on that already structured slate. That is why one can get such seeming anomalies as the 'social introvert', where the introversion originates from one of the genetically caused basic types, whereas the social comes from life's rich demands.

Is there a plausible evolutionary account of human personality centring on the notion of limited personality types? Perhaps so. It certainly is worth considering that there is a story to be told about selection over the long history of human evolution for specific personality attributes that added to individual fitness both in terms of survival (natural selection) and reproduction (sexual selection), and perhaps also in terms of group solidarity (group selection). With regard to the latter, there is certainly a strong *prima facie* case, as Wilson and Sober point out (see Chapter 6), to believe that we are all possessed of 'Darwinian algorithms', that is, innate tendencies to behave in a particular way, that turn us into 'team players' with remarkably strong identification with the group which we consider ourselves a part of – witness the events at any football ground anywhere in Europe or Latin

America (and doubtless other sports command the same fierce loyalties from their local supporters in other parts of the world). Group selection might have had as strong an effect in moulding human personality types as did individual selection.

Psychopathology can also be given an evolutionary spin. There can, of course, be no doubt that some forms of pathology have proximate causes where things just go wrong, for example in the balance of chemicals (transmitter substances) in parts of the brain or as a consequence of genetic accident leading to improperly structured neural networks. Having said that, it may also be the case that perhaps we are still 'Stone Agers' trying to cope in a world very different from that in which most of human evolution occurred. There are estimates that in the 10,000 years since the invention of agriculture, with all the massive changes that the juggernaut of technological culture has since then imposed, our genes have changed by only a tiny, tiny fraction of 1 per cent – in effect, in the face of enormous cultural change, our biology has not altered at all. So, just as lower back pain, the scourge of large numbers of modern humans, is a consequence of imperfect adaptation of our spines to a bipedal gait, so might some forms of psychopathology be the result of less than perfect adaptation to living under conditions that are vastly different from those that preceded the agricultural revolution. Like other instances of the argument of ancient provenance, as it was dubbed in Chapter 3, there can be no direct evidence to prove this position because we have no time machines. However, support for the general argument that some limited number of psychopathologies are best understood in terms of human evolution does come from the way conditions like phobias manifest themselves. Almost every elementary text notes that if unreasoning and crippling states of fear were to attach to the objects in the modern world most likely to harm us, that is to say, if there were a curious rationality about such unreasoning fears, then those fears would be directed at knives, firearms and motor cars. The overwhelming majority of phobics, however, have their fears centred on objects that are animals, like snakes and insects, and situations such as open, unfamiliar spaces, heights or dark and confined spaces. And it is also the case, as we saw with regard to autism in Chapter 5, that cognitive modules which are human-specific and which must have evolved as a response to human life history strategies, like the theory of mind module, when defective result in specific forms of pathology. For these reasons, then, some light from evolutionary theory can help in understanding aspects of psychopathology.

Then there is consciousness, which to some is the jewel in psychology's crown. Psychology is famous as a subject in which there are few matters, perhaps none, on which there is widespread agreement. The historian of science, the late Thomas Kuhn, wrote an important book in the 1960s, *The Structure of Scientific Revolutions*. In the preface he revealed that some of the ideas came to him during a stay amongst a community of academic psychologists. He had never experienced before, and at first hand, what it is like to live within a science in which there is so little agreement on what is and is not a problem worth pursuing, and what is and is not an empirical finding of note. Consciousness is the extreme example of such disagreement. Banished by the behaviourists, even now there is little consensus as to what consciousness is, how best to think of it, and in some quarters even a sneaking suspicion that the behaviourists were right, that it is not a legitimate part of a scientific psychology. Yet consciousness too has received some attention in terms of evolutionary theory. Dennett's view is that consciousness 'is largely a product of cultural evolution', memes fuelling the virtual machine of our minds – a virtual machine is a device like a computer that is able to run many different kinds of program, a rule-machine with the rules played out on a highly plastic substrate. A somewhat different approach comes from the originator of the social function of intellect hypothesis (see Chapter 5), N. K. Humphrey, who likens consciousness to an 'inner eye'. Consciousness, suggests Humphrey, gives us access of some, perhaps limited, kind to the contents of our minds and allows us to understand something of its workings without the experience being reflected in overt behaviour. As one way of understanding what consciousness is, this is a fairly widespread view among psychologists. In evolutionary terms, it suggests that consciousness might have two related adaptive functions. One, which Popper among others has previously advocated, gives the advantage of being able to manipulate inside our heads possible courses of action and their consequences, and then choosing on the basis of these conscious calculations what is best to do. This kind of internalized, substitute, trial-and-error process must, reasoned Popper, be advantageous over having actually to do the behaviours, be punished or damaged by some of the consequences, and then choosing. In other words, acting as if we are behaviourists in choosing our own course of action is costly and risky. Trying things out in our heads before acting should be a valuable adaptation. Humphrey's main line of argument marries this notion of adaptive, surrogate, internalized action with an extension to the notion of a theory of mind. If we can look into our own minds and think about what we should do (internalized action), and how best to think about it, why then so can we think our way into the minds of others (theory of mind). Consciousness allows us to project the workings of our own minds on to those of others in order to calculate what they are going to do. Consciousness, then, may well have evolved because of its adaptive advantages for us, both as internalized device for testing possible future events, and for projecting on to others the capacity for such internalized testing and predicting the consequences for their behaviour.

Consciousness may be the glamorous high-ground of psychology, but where the bulk of research in psychology continues to be done is in the traditional areas of sensory systems, perception, attention, action, memory and learning. One of the features of all these mainstream areas of psychology is that we can be reasonably certain, given similarity of functional demands, that similar psychological processes are widespread across many animals; and given phylogenetic relatedness, it is likely that some part of the mechanisms underlying these processes is shared in closely related species. Thus can the comparative approach pioneered by nineteenth- and early-twentieth-century biologists be applied to psychology, as advocated in the quotation by Lorenz given in Chapter 2, albeit given a facelift and transformed into a modern 'cladistic' analysis.

Cladistics is an evolutionary taxonomy that reflects real evolutionary history, being constructed largely on the basis of molecular data, rather than just superficial appearance. The results are sometimes startling new insights into evolutionary relatedness. The best-known recent example has been the changes we have had to make to our thinking regarding birds. It was not long ago that birds were thought of as a taxonomic group lying somewhere between reptiles and mammals.

Now it is known with certainty that birds are actually descendants of dinosaurs, and are more closely related to crocodiles than they are to any mammal. This is vital information for comparative behavioural analysis. Bird-song, for example, is a wonderfully complex signalling system that bears some interesting similarities to human language. It is anatomically lateralized, highly constrained within species such that birds can learn only their own species' song and not that of even closely related species, and yet it is utterly dependent upon learning at certain sensitive periods of the birds' lives which gives rise to regional dialects. Well, when we used to think that birds are feathered mammals, such complexity made some kind of sense. Now that we are coming to understand that dinosaurs were anatomically and morphologically a much more diverse and interesting group of animals than previously realized, the complexity of the behaviour of birds makes a different kind of sense – as does the newly discovered complexity of crocodilian behaviour, such as their maternal care. Suddenly, as we come to understand that birds, dinosaurs and crocodiles are a taxonomic unit, a clade because they all derive from a common ancestor that is not ancestral to any other species, then we are not surprised when we find 'advanced' behaviour in the members of the group that previously we had thought of as 'primitive'.

Richard Byrne, the British primatologist and psychologist, provides an excellent example of how to use cladistic analysis to understand the current distribution of a behaviour, and what the phylogenetic history of that behaviour must have been. Thus, to use Byrne's own example, if we have a clade of animals, the individuals of all contemporary species of which use tools, are solitary and can swim; and another clade made up of species all of whom run and use tools; then the deduced common ancestors to both clades must have had each of that set of characters common to contemporary species (solitary, swimming tool-users versus running tool-users). Now, if the molecular evidence tells us that these two clades themselves shared a common ancestor, then that species would have been a user of tools, but we can make no assumptions about either their social behaviour or their mode of locomotion.

Byrne's analysis is illuminating. There are, however, two problems in applying it to psychological processes and mechanisms. The first is that while animal behaviour is often intriguing and field observations are becoming ever richer and more detailed, without appropriate experimentation, reports that such and such a species shows this and that behaviour tell us nothing of the mechanisms underlying the expression of that behaviour. Remember from Chapter 4 the injunction that psychology is *not* a science of behaviour and should never be seen as such, because when it was so thought the subject almost committed intellectual suicide. Psychology is a science of the processes and mechanisms that cause behaviour.

An excellent example of what this means for comparative analysis comes from the tool usage that Byrne used in his example of cladistic behavioural analysis. Early in 1996, Gavin Hunt, a behavioural biologist based in New Zealand, reported some remarkably sophisticated tool use in crows inhabiting a group of Pacific islands. Tool use has been widely reported before in a whole range of animals, including insects. But these crows seem to be different. For one thing, they manufacture tools. By this is meant they manipulate twigs and leaves and alter their form in some way appropriate to their subsequent usage. This has only been seen before in chimpanzees and humans. They also used the tools as hooks and the objects were made to a high degree of standardization. Again, these are characteristics of tool use that, until seen in these New Caledonian crows, were thought to be confined only to chimpanzees and humans. However, what exactly does this mean in terms of the mechanisms underlying the behaviour? Did the crows intend the use of hooks or did they occur through a mix of chance and the nature of the materials used? Did learning play any part in the construction and use of the objects, and if so, what kind of learning? How flexible is the usage? And is there any element of social transmission of the tool-using behaviour? These are just some of the questions that need to be answered before we can form any view at all on psychological mechanisms driving this behaviour, and the data are either only suggestive at best, or completely silent, on these issues. If anyone thinks that asking these kinds of questions is being a kind of scientific killjoy, the fact is that it has been known for years that one of the species of Galapagos finches (see Chapter 1) uses cactus spines as a probe for fishing out insects from underneath bark. No experiments have been done on this species of bird either, but the reports indicate a behaviour so stereotyped and restricted that it is suggestive that no learning or intelligence of any kind is involved in this case. On the other hand, chimpanzees use a wide array of objects as tools for different purposes, their usage is flexible, and there is indeed some evidence of social transmission. So what are we really to make of Hunt's Pacific crows? Are they more like the woodpecker finches of the Galapagos or more like the chimpanzees of Central Africa?

There is a further complication. Even assuming that the crows are like chimpanzees, what is certain is that crow tool use cannot be driven by psychological mechanisms that are homologues to those that are at work in chimpanzees. This is because crows and chimps are only distantly related vertebrates. There are many species sitting between them that show no tool use at all. Crows, in fact, show many remarkable forms of behaviour and so no comparative psychologist is falling out of their chair in surprise that it is a species of crow that may be showing quite advanced tool-using behaviour. But the behaviour, and possibly the underlying mechanisms, have likely evolved quite independently in this group of birds. Equally, no one is arguing about chimpanzees and their use of tools in relation to humans. We share a common ancestral species, probably diverging between six and six and a half million years ago according to recent best estimates. We can conclude that it is likely that the ancestral species was made up of individuals who were either tool-users themselves, or who had the requisite psychological mechanism in place to be so. For example, being able to perceive means–end relationships and then being able to implement the perception in actions employing objects, which then evolved into flexible tool use in modern chimpanzees and human beings. At present there is no evidence, and it would be very hard to find, that the now extinct apes (the australopithecines) that led to early humans used tools. So the latter scenario, that is, that the ancestral species had the psychological mechanisms but may not have used them to drive the specific behaviours of tool use, may be the more realistic.

The second problem in using Byrne's methodology is not with the nature of the analysis but with the poverty of the evidence at present that prevents proper usage of the comparative approach that could otherwise be made with regard to psychological mechanisms. The data, as Cecilia Heyes has repeatedly pointed out, are often compromised by poor experiments when the mechanisms under investigation are cognitive. And when the data are experimentally impeccable, they involve mechanisms such as associative learning which these days are of little interest to most psychologists and primatologists, and in species like rats and pigeons that are phylogenetically remote from humans. Basically, the empirical data is either not good enough yet, or not of the right kind, to support comparative analysis in a way that would be of interest to psychologists or to evolutionists with an interest in our own species. This is not a new complaint. The American comparative psychologist Frank Beach pointed this out nearly half a century ago.

Another thing that this book has not attempted to do is systematically to lay out all possible methodologies that an evolutionary psychologist could use. Part of the reason for not doing this is that some of them hardly pass as methodologies at all. Some are hand-waving and interpretative with little analytical force. Others have recourse to the notion of the environment of evolutionary adaptedness. The problem with the environment of evolutionary adaptedness is that it is a concept that cannot be faulted – all adaptations arose within a particular field of forces made up of selection and historical and structural constraint. But the actual environment is not accessible to us as scientists, unless we think that that environment is still with us here and now. This, of course, as pointed out in Chapter 1, is what makes evolutionary biology a dauntingly difficult science. In order to reach into the past we have to deal with what we have in the present, but in clever ways that allow us to extrapolate backwards in time. Merely invoking an imagined past as something different from the present is simply not science. It is, however, reasonable to assume that some things *are* still the same. A theory of mind is useful now for the same reason that it always was so. It undoubtedly evolved tens of thousands, hundreds of thousands, perhaps millions, of years ago. Its adapative significance as a device for understanding others within one's social group is as potent now as it ever was. We are, and probably always have been, social animals.

For other psychological processes and mechanisms, however, there is much less certainty as to what the environment of evolutionary adaptedness was, or even whether there was just one or many environments. The evolution of the genus *Homo* has occurred over a period of over two million years; it has been about one and a half million years since the appearance of *Homo erectus*, which is the species immediately preceding *Homo sapiens*. This is a long time and covers some 100,000 generations. There were many changes in conditions of climate and habitat in every part of the globe. There is endless, often fascinating, speculation about how these conditions, like temperature, rainfall, vegetation and the presence of competing species, details of which are surprisingly well known, might have affected human evolution, including human psychology. Just recently minuscule evidence has been gathered suggesting that modern humans might have interacted rather more closely than previously thought with Neanderthal people (a species of *Homo* which are now thought to have been an evolutionary dead-end, and who became extinct some 30,000 to 40,000 years ago). But this is mostly the stuff of science fiction. The fact is, we just don't know, and never will know, what kinds of competitive interaction our ancestors had with other species and how it affected our species. Language, for instance, is sometimes invoked as one of the reasons why *Homo sapiens* survived whatever those interactions were and *Homo neanderthalensis* did not. Well, perhaps, but the fact is we do not know when language evolved and why, though there has been endless speculation. The simple fact is we will never know any of this. The environment of evolutionary adaptedness for language was probably not some singular and lasting environment exerting consistent selection pressure over tens of thousands of years. Language must have evolved over a long time, embracing many different kinds of environment. Since we don't have time machines, in the end the speculation can never be supported or refuted. It just isn't science.

This is not to deny that language has evolved, the evidence for which, in my view, is overwhelming. But playing with ideas that can never be tested does evolutionary theory no good in anyone's eyes, not least those of the social scientists who view biologists as a naive and invading horde. As Chapter 4 argues, there are many empirical handles on which to hang the claim that language is a product of evolution, and they are all accessible to psychologists in the human subjects that they study now. In part that is the reason for choosing the psychological topics discussed in earlier chapters. These are the areas of psychology in which the recent rise in nativism has been most marked. And it is no accident that nativist thinking has increased dramatically over the last few decades, especially among developmentalists. It has come from the data. The crucial point about nativism and its commitment to the concept of the innate is that it is a property of our psychology that can be, and indeed is being, empirically tested. If something is innate then it is part caused by genes, and genes have been selected in the past. So historical cause is operating, yes. The precise details of that history are neither available nor necessary, so long as we can detect and study what that historical cause gives rise to, which is constraint on psychological processes and structures operating in the proximate ecology of today. The take-home message is that psychological adaptations, predispositions, somewhat twisted in appearance perhaps because they come from a past that may be different from the present, is what we are after. Projecting backwards into the past can be done in too many ways to be a useful and illuminating exercise.

Because brains and psychological mechanisms don't fossilize, that is the only way we can proceed with a viable evolutionary psychology. That should not, and surely does not, detract from both the importance and fascination of putting evolutionary theory into psychology. Origins are vital. History, remember, is what Darwin taught us to think about. He knew that it would profoundly change the way we see things, especially the way we see ourselves. This is why, to end where we began, Dobzhansky's assertion is correct and applies to all of human science. But the twist in this tale is that the nature and power of our cognitive capacities and our culture have meant that we can no more keep evolution out of psychology than we can keep psychology out of human evolution. It is a complex and awesome light that evolution sheds in psychology because it is a light that reflects back into our evolution.

Suggested Readings

Byrne, R. (1995) *The Thinking Ape*. Oxford, Oxford University Press.
Dennett, D. (1995) *Darwin's Dangerous Idea*. New York, Simon and Schuster.

Index

adaptation, 11–13, 26–7, 59–60, 77, 149, 169–71, 182–6, 198
Aiello, L., 206
altruism, 78–88
ancient provenance thesis, 74–5, 106, 110, 237
Aristotle, 164, 178
Ashby, R., 59
association, laws of, 165
associationism, 164–6
autism, 36, 212–14
Axelrod, R., 116–19

Bacon, F., 38, 179
Baillargeon, R., 190–2
Baldwin, J. M., 252
Baron-Cohen, S., 208–10, 213, 221
Bates, E., 156–7
Bateson, P., 99
Bateson, W., 27
Beach, F., 40, 270
behavioural ecology, 73, 76
behaviourism, 27–33, 44–5, 47, 130, 144
Berkeley, G., 38, 165
birdsong, 267
Boakes, R., 71
Boas, F., 45
Bock, P. K., 259
Boring, E. G., 20, 35
Bowlbey, J., 3
Boyd, R., 238–40, 259

Broadbent, D., 32
Buss, D., 105–9, 119
Byrne, R., 217, 267–9, 272

Campbell, D., 249, 252
causal explanations, 5–19, 32–4
causal understanding, 177–221
cause–effect relations, 177–86
Chomsky, N., 32, 51, 124, 131–8, 141, 146–9, 153–5, 174, 175, 224, 244, 259
cladistics, 266–7
Clark, A., 65
classical conditioning, 195
co-evolution, 159
cognitive constraint, 172–5, 244–5
cognitivism, 32–3, 51, 130ff
comparative study, 54, 61, 215–20, 266–70
connectionism, 65, 168
consciousness, 265–6
constructivism, 150
Cosmides, L., 109, 170
Craig, W., 52
culture, 46–7, 90, 100–101, 174, 222–60

Daly, M., 102–4
Darwin, C., 9–14, 23, 26, 28, 38–43, 51–2, 76–7, 225, 251–2, 262, 271
Dawkins, R., 62, 76, 83, 93–4, 101, 110, 119, 183, 226–7, 231, 252
Deacon, T., 134, 158–9, 175

Dennett, D., 210, 261, 265, 272
deprivation experiment, 52, 55, 57
Descartes, R., 37, 179, 202–3, 210
development, 55–7, 64–6
de Vries, J., 27
Dewey, J., 27
Dickemann, M., 108, 111
Dickenson, A., 198–9
Dobzhansky, T., 1, 5, 15, 19, 262, 272
doctrine of separate determination, 40, 48, 51, 58, 63
Donald, M., 258, 259
dual inheritance theory, 238–40, 252–8
Dunbar, R., 102, 205
Dunlap, K., 44
Durham, W., 232, 234–5, 259

Edelman, G., 252
Einon, D., 108
Elman, J. L., 64–5, 71
Emlen, S., 99
emotion, 262
empiricism, 37, 172
endocannibalism, 235–6
environment of evolutionary adaptedness, 270–1
ethology, 31, 52–8, 73
eugenics, 28, 41, 43–6
evolutionary epistemology, 26
evolutionary Kantianism, 66–8
evolutionary theory, 1–19, 73
extragenetic transmission of information, 222, 245, 247–9
extrasomatic storage, 250–1

Fairbanks, L., 98
Fechner, G. T., 21, 23
Fisher, R. A., 49
Fodor, J., 131, 138, 175, 189
folk psychology, 138–41, 201–2
Freeman, D., 71
Freud, S., 44, 141, 143, 240, 242
Frisch, K. van, 31
Frith, U., 213–14, 221
functionalism, 26–7, 32

Galton, F., 28, 41, 43–4
Game Theory, 61, 73, 76, 82, 87, 111–18
gene selection, 87
gene-culture co-evolutionary theory, 238–40, 252–8
general process versus specific intelligences, 124–76
Gestalt psychology, 48–9
Goodenough, W., 242
Gopnick, A., 210–11, 247
Gould, S. J., 14, 35
Grant, P. R., 35
Greenfield, P., 157
group selection, 77–9, 228–30, 264

Hailman, J. P., 56
Haldane, J. B. S., 83, 85
Hall, G., 145
Hamilton, W. D., 83–7
Hamilton's Rule, 34, 84–7, 96, 102, 110, 240
Harris, R. A., 175
Hauser, M., 98
Hebb, D., 55
Heinroth, O., 52
Helmholtz, H. L. van, 21–2
Heyes, C., 219, 221
hierarchical structure, 226–32, 240, 251
higher-order knowledge structures, 256–7
Hobbes, T., 38
homology, 54, 61
Horzan, J., 119
Hull, C. L., 30, 47, 51
Hume, D., 19, 38, 165, 179–81, 185–8, 196
Humphrey, N. K., 204, 265–6
Hunt, G., 268
Huxley, T. H., 25, 252
Huxley, J., 57

imprinting, 69
incest, 234–5
inclusive fitness, 61, 85–6

individual selection, 77–8, 85
induction, 180
innate, 48, 52, 54, 58–60, 65–7, 132–8,
    154–5, 171–2, 174–5, 187, 214, 262
instincts (see also innate, and
    predispositions), 28–30, 38–42, 44,
    52, 54–7, 124ff
instrumental learning, 198–200
intelligence, 39–46
interactionism, 48–9, 55

Jacobs, R., 249
James, W., 24–6, 29–30, 42, 131, 252
Johnston, T. D., 63–4

Kanner, L., 212
Kant, I., 37, 66–7
Karmiloff-Smith, A., 175
kin selection, 85
Kitcher, P., 90, 119, 253
Kroeber, A., 45–7
Kuhn, T., 265
Kummer, H., 187, 189
kuru, 235–6

lactose tolerance/intolerance, 232–4
language, 124–60, 247–9, 255
Leahey, T., 26, 35
learning as instinct, 58–60
learning theory, 47–8
Lehrman, D. S., 55
Leslie, A., 187–9, 192–3, 209–10, 213
Lévi-Strauss, C., 241, 242
Lewin, K., 48
Locke, J., 19, 38, 165, 172, 174
Lorenz, K., 31, 51–68, 78, 111, 189, 266
Lumsden, C. J., 238

Maynard Smith, J., 112–13
McDougall, W., 44
Mead, M., 45, 241, 242
Meier, R. P., 175
Meltzoff, A., 247
memes, 159, 252–3
Mendeleev, D. I., 7–8, 17

mental state attribution, 200–21
mental states, 200–3
Miller, G., 32
modularity, 138, 160–3, 169–74, 186,
    189, 214
Monod, J., 154
Morgan, C. L., 25, 43
Morgenstern, O., 112
Morris, D., 31
Muller, J., 22

nativism (see also innate, and
    predispositions), 51, 271–2
natural selection, 10, 16, 26–7, 38, 77–8
nature–nurture problem, 36–72, 128,
    134, 214–15, 241, 261–3
Neumann, J. van, 112
Newell, A., 32
Newton, I., 6–8, 14
Nowak, M. A., 119

optimality theory, 61, 76
Oyama, S., 63–5, 72

parent–offspring conflict, 94–9
Pavlov, I. P., 29, 43, 141, 165, 195
Pernau, A. F. van, 52
personality, 263–4
Perusse, D., 111
physical causation, 186–200
Piaget, J., 32, 124, 149–54, 188, 192–3,
    199, 211
Piattelli-Palmirini, M., 153, 176
Pinker, S., 34, 35, 124, 135–6, 176
Plato, 36–7, 172, 174
Plotkin, H., 72, 259
Popper, K., 252, 265–6
Povenelli, D., 218
Poverty of the Stimulus Argument,
    131–4, 138, 166
prediction, 195–8
predispositions (see also innate, and
    instinct), 48, 70–71, 164, 173–4, 187
Premack, D., 186, 194–5, 200, 208, 214,
    216, 221

prisoner's dilemma, 114–18
psychology, the nature of, 19–35
psychopathology, 264–5

rationalism, 37, 172
reductionism, 88–94
replicators, 226–32, 253–8
Rescorla, R., 197
Richards, R. J., 25, 35
Richelle, M., 148
Richerson, P., 238–40
Ridley, M., 35
Rivers, W. H. R., 240, 242
Romanes, G., 25, 43
Rose, S., 120
Rowe, D., 107

Savage-Rumbaugh, S., 126, 176
Schneirla, T. C., 55–6
Searle, J., 210
Selfish Gene Theory, 73–111, 240
sexual selection, 106, 236–7
Shakespeare, W., 36
Shanks, D., 199
shaping versus triggering, 132–3, 136,
    166
Shaw, J. C., 32
Sherif, M., 249
Simon, H. A., 32, 182, 223, 252
Simoons, F. G., 232
Skinner, B. F., 30, 32, 48, 51, 61, 124,
    143–9, 165, 198, 252
social causation, 200–21
social constructions, 223, 245, 247,
    249–50
social force, 245, 249–50
social function of intelligence
    hypothesis, 118, 204–5
social psychology, 49–50
sociobiology, 31, 62–3, 73–120
sociobiology applied to humans,
    100–11
Spalding, D. A., 52
specific intelligences versus general
    process intelligence, 124–76

Spelke, E., 193, 199, 209
Spencer, H., 24, 42
Sperber, D., 154, 221, 260
sterile insects, 76–7
structuralism, 26, 32
structure of mind, 121–76
Szathmary, E., 222, 260

tabula rasa, 37, 42, 160, 164,
    172–4
theory of mind, 206–21, 245–7
Thorndike, E. L., 29, 43, 141, 165
Thorpe, W. H., 53
Tinbergen, N., 31, 52–3, 56–7, 61
Titchner, E., 26
Tolman, E. C., 47, 51
Tomasello, M., 243, 260
Tooby, J., 109, 170
tool use, 268–9
triggering versus shaping, 132–3, 136,
    166
Trivers, R., 94–5

Uexkull, J. van, 52
uncertain futures problem, 194
universal Darwinism, 251–2
universal grammar, 134–6, 141, 153–5,
    159

vehicles, 226–32, 253–8
Vining, D., 110

Waddington, C. H., 65, 194
Watson, J., 27–30, 44, 47, 172
Weber, E. H., 21
Whiten, A., 217
Whitman, C. O., 52
Williams, G. C., 78, 80, 83, 93, 120
Wilson, D. S., 228, 260, 263
Wilson, E. O., 53, 62, 83, 92–3, 101,
    238
Wilson, M., 102–4
Wittgenstein, L., 211
Wundt, W., 21–3, 26
Wynne-Edwards, V. C., 78–80